EDGEWOOD
EDITION

VOLUME VIII

FLORENCE STORER

"Confound the theologies! I'll have no more of them!"

"Confound the theologists! I'll have no more of them!"

THE WORKS OF DONALD G. MITCHELL

DOCTOR JOHNS

BEING A NARRATIVE OF CERTAIN EVENTS IN THE LIFE OF AN ORTHODOX MINISTER OF CONNECTICUT

CHARLES SCRIBNER'S SONS
NEW YORK ❦ ❦ ❦ ❦ 1907

Copyright, 1866, 1883, 1894, by
DONALD G. MITCHELL

Copyright, 1907, by
CHARLES SCRIBNER'S SONS

DEDICATED

TO MY OLD AND CONSTANT FRIEND

WILLIAM HENRY HUNTINGTON

OF THE RUE DE LA BRUYÈRE, PARIS

WHO SAT WITH ME HALF A CENTURY AGO UPON THE BENCHES OF A NEW ENGLAND SCHOOL; AND WHO I HOPE WILL RELISH WHATEVER FRAGRANT WHIFF OF THOSE OLD TIMES AND SCENES MAY COME TO HIM FROM OFF THE PAGES OF THIS NEW ENGLAND STORY

EDGEWOOD
THANKSGIVING DAY, 1883

CONTENTS

		PAGE
I	The Major	3
II	Whither Gone?	9
III	Rachel	13
IV	Ashfield	20
V	Town Worthies	24
VI	Home Established	30
VII	The Owl and Sparrow	37
VIII	An Accomplished Sinner	46
IX	Reuben	58
X	A Cloud	65
XI	Parish Sympathies	71
XII	The Parson's Consolation	77
XIII	Practical Sympathies	81
XIV	A New Mistress	90
XV	Boy Development	99
XVI	A Surprise	107
XVII	Skirmishings	116
XVIII	Expectation	122
XIX	The Arrival	127
XX	Adèle Meets Reuben	135
XXI	Miss Onthank	144

CONTENTS

		PAGE
XXII	RELIGIOUS TEACHING	151
XXIII	REUBEN LEAVES HOME	159
XXIV	REUBEN ESCAPES	171
XXV	REUBEN'S VOYAGE	177
XXVI	A ROSARY	186
XXVII	REUBEN IN NEW YORK	192
XXVIII	ASHFIELD AGAIN	201
XXIX	EVERY-DAY LIFE	209
XXX	NEW PROSPECTS	221
XXXI	A NEW PERSONAGE	227
XXXII	MAVERICK RE-APPEARS	233
XXXIII	IN THE CITY	244
XXXIV	THE NEW REUBEN	253
XXXV	TRAVEL	260
XXXVI	ILLNESS	269
XXXVII	SHORTCOMINGS OF REUBEN	279
XXXVIII	A NEW EXPERIENCE	288
XXXIX	REUBEN MAKES A PROSELYTE	297
XL	DEATH	306
XLI	REUBEN'S STRUGGLE	316
XLII	A REVELATION	326
XLIII	THE SPINSTER'S INDIGNATION	334
XLIV	PHILIP ELDERKIN	346
XLV	THE SPINSTER'S POLICY	354
XLVI	A PHRENZY	366
XLVII	WILL SHE?	377
XLVIII	CAFÉ DE L'ORIENT	389
XLIX	ADÈLE LEAVES THE PARSONAGE	399
L	PHILIP'S CHANCES	407

CONTENTS

		PAGE
LI	Concerning a Colleague	412
LII	News from Maverick	417
LIII	Clear but Dark	423
LIV	Clearer and Darker	431
LV	Confidences	437
LVI	Adèle—Reuben—Maverick	446
LVII	Maverick is Married	453
LVIII	New Complications	460
LIX	A Trust for Phil	467
LX	Father and Child	474
LXI	The Truth at Last	482
LXII	Reuben at Rome	491
LXIII	The Voyage	499
LXIV	A Wreck	508
LXV	The Saved and Lost	521
LXVI	Last Scenes	529
LXVII	The End	539

ILLUSTRATIONS

"CONFOUND THE THEOLOGIES! I'LL HAVE NO MORE OF THEM!" . . . . . . Frontispiece
Facing Page

"OH, NO, NEW PAPA! YOU DON'T THINK I'M DESPERATELY WICKED?" 154

"MA FILLE! MA PAUVRE FILLE!" 316

DOCTOR JOHNS

DOCTOR JOHNS

I

The Major

IN the summer of 1812, when the good people of Connecticut were feeling uncommonly bitter about the declaration of war against England, and were abusing Mr. Madison in the roundest terms, there lived in the town of Canterbury a fiery old gentleman, of near sixty years, and a sterling Democrat, who took up the cudgels bravely for the Administration, and stoutly belabored Governor Roger Griswold for his tardy obedience to the President in calling out the militia, and for what he called his absurd pretensions in regard to State sovereignty. He was a man, too, who meant all that he said, and gave the best proof of it by offering his military services,—first to the Governor, and then to the United States General commanding the Department.

Nor was he wholly unfitted: he was erect,

stanch, well knit together, and had served with immense credit in the local militia, in which he wore the title of Major. It does not appear that his offer was immediately accepted; but the following season he was invested with the command of a company, and was ordered back and forth to various threatened points along the sea-board. His home affairs, meantime, were left in charge of his son, a quiet young man of four-and-twenty, who for three years had been stumbling with a very reluctant spirit through the law-books in the Major's office, and who shared neither his father's ardor of temperament nor his political opinions. Eliza, a daughter of twenty summers, acted as mistress of the house, and stood in place of mother to a black-eyed little girl of thirteen,— the Major's daughter by a second wife, who had died only a few years before.

Notwithstanding the lack of political sympathy, there was yet a strong attachment between father and son. The latter admired exceedingly the energy and full-souled ardor of the old gentleman; and the father, in turn, was proud of the calm, meditative habit of mind which the son had inherited from his mother. "There is metal in the boy to make a judge of," the Major used to say. And when Ben-

THE MAJOR

jamin, shortly after his graduation at one of the lesser New England colleges, had given a hint of his possible study of theology, the Major answered with a "Pooh! pooh!" which disturbed the son—possibly weighed with him—more than the longest opposing argument could have done.

The Major, like all sound Democrats, had always been an ardent admirer of Mr. Jefferson and of the French political school. Benjamin had a wholesome horror of both; not so much from any intimate knowledge of their theories, as by reason of a strong religious instinct, which had been developed under his mother's counsels into a rigid and exacting Puritanism.

The first wife of the Major had left behind her the reputation of "a saint." It was not undeserved: her quiet, constant charities,—her kindliness of look and manner, which were in themselves the best of charities,—a gentle, Christian way she had of dealing with all the vagrant humors of her husband,—and the constancy of her devotion to all duties, whether religious or domestic, gave her better claim to the saintly title than most who wear it. The Major knew this, and was very proud of it. "If," he was accustomed to say, "I am the

DOCTOR JOHNS

most godless man in the parish, my wife is the most godly woman." Yet his godlessness was, after all, rather outside than real; it was a kind of effrontery, provoked into noisy display by the extravagant bigotries of those about him. He did not believe in monopolies of opinion, but in good average dispersion of all sorts of thinking. On one occasion he had horrified his poor wife by bringing home a full set of Voltaire's Works; but having reasoned her—or fancying he had—into a belief in the entire harmlessness of the offending books, he gratified her immensely by placing them out of all sight and reach of the boy Benjamin.

He never interfered with the severe home course of religious instruction entered upon by the mother. On the contrary, he said, "The boy will need it all as an offset to the bedevilments that will overtake him in our profession." The Major had a very considerable country practice, and had been twice a member of the Legislature.

His second wife, a frivolous, indolent person, who had brought him a handsome dowry, and left him the pretty black-eyed Mabel, never held equal position with the first. It was observed, however, with some surprise, that under the sway of the latter he was more

THE MAJOR

punctilious and regular in religious observances than before,—a fact which the shrewd ones explained by his old doctrine of adjusting averages.

Benjamin, Eliza, and Mabel,—each in their way,—waited news from the military campaign of the Major with great anxiety; all the more because he was understood to be a severe disciplinarian; and it had been rumored in the parish that two or three of his company, of rank Federal opinions, had vowed they would sooner shoot the captain than any foreign enemy of the State. The Major, however, heard no guns in either front or rear up to the time of the British attack upon the borough of Stonington, in midsummer of 1814. In the defence here he was very active, in connection with a certain artillery force that had come down the river from Norwich; and although the attack of the British Admiral was a mere feint, yet for a while there was a very lively sprinkling of shot. The people of the little borough were duly frightened, the *Ramilies* seventy-four gun-ship of his Majesty enjoyed an excellent opportunity for long-range practice, and the militia gave an honest airing to their patriotism. The Major was wholly himself. "If the rascals would only attempt a landing!" said he; and as he spoke, a fragment of shell struck his sword-arm at the elbow. The wound was a grievous one, and the surgeon in attendance declared amputation to be necessary. The Major combated the decision for a while, but loss of blood weakened his firmness, and the operation was gone through with very bunglingly. Next morning a country wagon was procured to transport him home. The drive was an exceeding rough one, and the stump fell to bleeding. Most men would have lain by for a day or two, but the Major insisted upon pushing on for Canterbury, where he arrived late at night, very much exhausted.

The country physician declared, on examination next morning, that some readjustment of the amputated limb was necessary, which was submitted to by the Major in a very irritable humor. Friends and enemies of the wounded man were all kind and full of sympathy. Miss Eliza was in a flutter of dreary apprehension that rendered her incapable of doing anything effectively. Benjamin was as tender and as devoted as a woman. The wound healed in due time, but the Major did not rally. The drain upon his vitality had been too great; he fell into a general decline, which within a fortnight gave promise of fatal results. The Major met the truth like a veteran; he arranged his affairs, by the aid of his son, with a great show of method,—closed all in due time; and when he felt his breath growing short, called Benjamin, and like a good officer gave his last orders.

"Mabel," said he, "is provided for; it is but just that her mother's property should be settled on her; I have done so. For yourself and Eliza, you will have need of a close economy. I don't think you 'll do much at law; you once thought of preaching; if you think so now, preach, Benjamin; there 's something in it; at least it 's better than Fed—Federalism."

A fit of coughing seized him here, from which he never fairly rallied. Benjamin took his hand when he grew quiet, and prayed silently, while the Major slipped off the roll militant forever.

II

Whither Gone?

THE funeral was appointed for the second day thereafter. The house was set in order for the occasion. Chairs were brought in from the neighbors. A little table, with a Bible upon it, was placed in the entranceway at the foot of the stairs, that all might hear what the clergyman should say. The body lay in the parlor, with the Major's sword and cocked hat upon the coffin; and the old gentleman's face had never worn an air of so much dignity as it wore now. Death had refined away all trace of his irritable humors, of his passionate, hasty speech. It looked like the face of a good man, — so said nine out of ten who gazed on it that day; yet when the immediate family came up to take their last glimpse, — the two girls being in tears, — in that dreary half-hour after all was arranged, and the flocking-in of the neighbors was waited for, Benjamin, as calm as the dead face below him, was asking himself if the poor gentleman, his father, had not gone away to a place of torment. He feared it; nay, was he not bound to believe it by the whole force of his education? and his heart, in that hour, made only a feeble revolt against the belief. In the very presence of the grim messenger of the Eternal, who had come to seal the books and close the account, what right had human affection to make outcry? Death had wrought the work given him to do, like a

WHITHER GONE?

good servant; had not he, too,—Benjamin,— a duty to fulfil? the purposes of Eternal Justice to recognize, to sanction, to approve? In the exaltation of his religious sentiment it seemed to him, for one crazy moment at least, that he would be justified in taking his place at the little table where prayer was to be said, and in setting forth, as one who knew so intimately the shortcomings of the deceased, all those weaknesses of the flesh and spirit by which the Devil had triumphed, and in warning all those who came to his burial of the judgments of God which would surely fall on them as on him, except they repented and believed.

Happily, however, the officiating clergyman was of a more even temper; and he said what little he had to say in way of "improvement of the occasion" to the text of "Judge not, that ye be not judged."

"We are too apt," said he (and he was now addressing a company that crowded the parlors and flowed over into the yard in front, where the men stood with heads uncovered), "we are too apt to measure a man's position in the eye of God, and to assign him his rank in the future, by his conformity to the external observances of religion,—not remembering, in our complacency, that we see differently from those who look on from beyond the world, and that there are mysterious and secret relations of God with the conscience of every man, which we cannot measure or adjust. Let us hope that our deceased friend profited by such to insure his entrance into the Eternal City, whose streets are of gold, and the Lamb the light thereof."

The listeners said "Amen" to this in their hearts; but the son, still exalted by the fervor of that new purpose which he had formed by the father's death-bed, and riveted more surely as he looked last on his face, asked himself, if the old preacher had not allowed a kindly worldly prudence to blunt the sharpness of the Word.

Sudden contact with Death had refined all his old religious impressions to an intensity that shaped itself into a flaming sword of retribution. All this, however, as yet, lay within his own mind, not beating down his natural affection, or his grief, but struggling for reconcilement with them; no outward expression, even to those who clung to him so nearly, revealed it. The memorial-stone which he placed over his father's grave, and which possibly is standing now within the old church-yard of Canterbury, bore only this:—

> HERE LIES THE BODY OF
> REUBEN JOHNS.
> A GOOD HUSBAND; A KIND FATHER;
> A PATRIOT, WHO DIED FOR HIS COUNTRY,
> 1st SEPT., 1814.

And a little below,—

"Christ died for all."

III

Rachel

IT will be no contravention of the truth of this epitaph, to say that the Major had been always a most miserable manager of his private business affairs; it is even doubtful if the kindest fathers and best husbands are not apt to be. Certain it is, that, when Benjamin came to examine, in connection with a village attorney (for the son had inherited the father's inaccessibility to "profit and loss" statements), such loose accounts as the Major had left, it was found that the poor gentleman had lived up so closely to his income—whether as lawyer or military chieftain—as to leave his little home property subject to the payment of a good many outstanding debts. There appeared, indeed, a great parade of ledgers and day-books and statements of accounts; but it is by no means unusual for those who are careless or ignorant of business system to make a pretty show of the requisite implements, and to confuse themselves in a pleasant way with the intricacy of their own figures.

The Major sinned pretty largely in this way; so that it was plain that, after the sale of all his available effects, including the library with its inhibited Voltaire, there would remain only enough to secure a respectable maintenance for Miss Eliza. To this end, Benjamin determined at once that the residue of the estate should be settled upon her,—reserving only so much as would comfortably maintain him during a three years' course of battling with Theology.

The younger sister, Mabel,—as has already been intimated,—was provided for by an interest in certain distinct and dividend-bearing securities, which—to the honor of the Major—had never been submitted to the alembic of his figures and "accounts current." She was placed at a school where she accomplished herself for three or four years; and put the seal to her accomplishments by marrying very suddenly, and without family consultation,—under which she usually proved restive,—a young fellow, who by aid of her snug fortune succeeded in establishing himself in a thriving business; and as early as the year 1820, Mabel, under her new name of Mrs. Brindlock, was the mistress of one of those fine merchant-palaces at the lower end of Greenwich Street, in New York City, which commanded a view of the elegant Battery, and were the admiration of all country visitors.

Benjamin had needed only his father's hint (for which he was ever grateful), and the solemn scenes of his death and burial, to lead him to an entire renunciation of his law-craft and to an engagement in fervid study for the ministry. This he prosecuted at first with a devout old gentleman who had been a pupil of President Edwards; and this private reading was finished off by a course at Andover. His studies completed, he was licensed to preach; and not long after, without any consideration of what the future of this world might have in store for him, he committed the error which so many grave and serious men are prone to commit,—that is to say, he married hastily, after only two or three months of solemn courtship, a charming girl of nineteen, whose only idea of meeting the difficulties of this life was to love her dear Benjamin with her whole heart, and to keep the parlor dusted.

But unfortunately there was no parlor to dust. The consequence was that the newly married couple were compelled to establish a temporary home upon the second floor of the comfortable house of Mr. Handby, a well-to-do farmer, and the father of the bride. Here the new clergyman devoted himself resolutely to Tillotson, to Edwards, to John Newton, and in the intervals prepared some score or more of sermons,—to all which Mrs. Johns devoutly listening in their fresh state, without ever a wink, entered upon the conscientious duties of a wife. From time to time some old clergyman of the neighborhood would ask the Major's son to assist him in the Sabbath services; and at rarer intervals the Reverend Mr. Johns was invited to some far-away township where the illness or absence of the settled minister might keep the new licentiate for four or five weeks; on which occasions the late Miss Handby was most zealous in preparing a world of comforts for the journey, and invariably followed him up with one or two double letters,

RACHEL

"hoping her dear Benjamin was careful to wear the muffler which his Rachel had knit for him, and not to expose his precious throat,"—or "longing for that quiet home of *their own,* which would not make necessary these *cruel separations,* and where she should have the uninterrupted society of her dear Benjamin."

To all such the conscientious husband dutifully replied, "thankful for his Rachel's expression of interest in such a sinner as himself, and trusting that she would not forget that health or the comforts of this world were but of comparatively small importance, since this was 'not our abiding city.' He trusted, too, that she would not allow the transitory affections of this life, *however dear they might be,* to engross her to the neglect of those which were *far more* important. He permitted himself to hope that Rachel" (he was chary of endearing epithets) "would not murmur against the dispensations of Providence, and would be content with whatever He might provide; and hoping that Mr. Handby and family were in their usual health, remained her Christian friend and devoted husband, Benjamin Johns."

It so happened, that, after this discursive life had lasted for some ten months, a serious

DOCTOR JOHNS

difficulty arose between the clergyman and the parish of the neighboring town of Ashfield. The person who served as the spiritual director of the people was suspected of leaning strongly toward some current heresy of the day; and the suspicion being once set on foot, there was not a sermon the poor man could preach but some quidnunc of the parish snuffed somewhere in it the taint of the false doctrine. The due convocations and committees of inquiry followed sharply after, and the incumbent received his dismissal in due form at the hands of some "brother in the bonds of the Gospel."

A few weeks later, Giles Elderkin, of Ashfield, "Society's Committee," invited, by letter, the Reverend Benjamin Johns to come and "fill their pulpit the following Lord's day"; and added,—"If you conclude to preach for us, I shall be pleased to have you put up at my house over the Sabbath."

"There you are," said Mr. Handby, when the matter was announced in family conclave, —"just the man for them. They like sober, solid preaching in Ashfield."

"I call it real providential," said Mrs. Handby; "fust-rate folks, and 't a'n't a long drive over for Rachel."

Little Mrs. Johns looked upon the grave,

RACHEL

earnest face of her husband with delight and pride, but said nothing.

"I know Squire Elderkin," says Mr. Handby, meditatively,—"a clever man, and a forehanded man,—very. It's a rich parish, son-in-law; they ought to do well by you."

"I don't like," says Mr. Johns, "to look at what may become my spiritual duty in that light."

"I would n't," returned Mr. Handby; "but when you are as old as I am, son-in-law, you'll know that we have to keep a kind of side look upon the good things of this world,—else we should n't be placed in it."

"*He* heareth the young ravens when they cry," said the minister, gravely.

"Just it," says Mr. Handby; "but I don't want your young ravens to be crying."

At which Rachel, with the slightest possible suffusion of color, and a pretty affectation of horror, said,—

"Now, Papa!"

There was an interruption here, and the conclave broke up; but Rachel, stepping briskly to the place she loved so well, beside the minister, said, softly,—

"I hope you'll go, Benjamin; and do, please, preach that beautiful sermon on Revelations."

DOCTOR JOHNS

IV

Ashfield

THIRTY or forty years ago there lay scattered about over Southern New England a great many quiet inland towns, numbering from a thousand to two or three thousand inhabitants, which boasted a little old-fashioned "society" of their own,—which had their important men who were heirs to some snug country property, and their gambrel-roofed houses odorous with traditions of old-time visits by some worthies of the Colonial period, or of the Revolution. The good, prim dames, in starched caps and spectacles, who presided over such houses, were proud of their tidy parlors,—of their old India china,—of their beds of thyme and sage in the garden,—of their big Family Bible with brazen clasps,—and, most times, of their minister.

One Orthodox Congregational Society extended its benignant patronage over all the people of such town; or, if a stray Episcopalian or Seven-Day Baptist were here and there living under the wing of the parish, they were regarded with a serene and stately gravity, as

ASHFIELD

necessary exceptions to the law of Divine Providence,—like scattered instances of red hair or of bow-legs in otherwise well-favored families.

There were no wires stretching over the country to shock the nerves of the good gossips with the thought that their neighbors knew more than they. There were no heathenisms of the cities, no tenpins, no travelling circus, no progressive young men of heretical tendencies. Such towns were as quiet as a sheepfold. Sauntering down their broad central street, along which all the houses were clustered with a somewhat dreary uniformity of aspect, one might of a summer's day hear the rumble of the town mill in some adjoining valley, busy with the town grist; in autumn, the flip-flap of the flails came pulsing on the ear from half a score of wide-open barns that yawned with plenty; and in winter, the clang of axes on the near hills smote sharply upon the frosty stillness, and would be straightway followed by the booming crash of some great tree.

But civilization and the railways have debauched all such quiet, stately, steady towns. There are none of them left. If the iron cordon of travel, by a little divergence, has spared

DOCTOR JOHNS

their quietude, leaving them stranded upon a beach where the tide of active business never flows, all their dignities are gone. The men of foresight and enterprise have drifted away to new centres of influence. The bustling dames in starched caps have gone down childless to their graves, or, disgusted with gossip at second hand, have sought more immediate contact with the world. A German tailor, may be, has hung out his sign over the door of some mouldering mansion, where, in other days, a doughty judge of the county court, with a great raft of children, kept his honors and his family warm. A slatternly "carry-all," with a driver who reeks of bad spirit, keeps up uneasy communication with the outside world, traversing twice or three times a day the league of drive which lies between the post-office and the railway-station. A few iron-pated farmers, and a few gentlemen of Irish extraction who keep tavern and stores, divide among themselves the official honors of the town.

If, on the other hand, the people maintain their old thrift and importance by actual contact with some great thoroughfare of travel, their old quietude is exploded; a mushroom station has sprung up; mushroom villas flank all the hills; the girls wear mushroom hats.

ASHFIELD

A turreted monster of a chapel from some flamboyant tower bellows out its Sunday warning to a new set of church-goers. There is a little coterie of "superior intelligences," who talk of the humanities, and diffuse their airy rationalism over here and there a circle of the progressive town. Even the meeting-house, which was the great congregational centre of the town religion, has lost its venerable air, taken off by some new fancy of variegated painting. The high, square pews are turned into low-backed seats, that flame on a summer Sunday with such gorgeous millinery as would have shocked the grave people of thirty years ago. The deep bass note which once pealed from the belfrey with a solemn and solitary dignity of sound has now lost it all amid the jangle of a half-dozen bells of lighter and airier twang. Even the parson himself will not be that grave man of stately bearing, who met the rarest fun only benignantly, and to whom all the villagers bowed; but some new creature full of the logic of the schools and the latest conventionalisms of manner. The homespun disciples of other days would be brought grievously to the blush, if some deep note of the old bell should suddenly summon them to the presence of so fine a teacher, encompassed with such pretty appliances of upholstery; and, counting their chances better in the strait path they knew on uncarpeted floors and between high pews, they would slink back into their graves content,—all the more content, perhaps, if they should listen to the service of the new teacher, and, in their common-sense way, reckon what chance the dapper talker might have—as compared with the solemn soberness of the old pastor—in opening the ponderous doors for them upon the courts above.

Into this metamorphosed condition the town of Ashfield has possibly fallen in these latter days; but in the good year 1819, when the Reverend Benjamin Johns was invited for the first time to fill its pulpit of an early autumn Sunday, it was still in possession of all its palmy quietude and of its ancient cheery importance. And to that old date we will now transfer ourselves.

V

Town Worthies

EVERY other day the stage-coach comes into Ashfield from the north, on the Hartford turnpike, and rumbles through the main street of the town, seesawing upon its leathern thoroughbraces. Just where the pike forks into the main northern road, and where the scattered farm-houses begin to group more thickly along the way, the country Jehu prepares for a triumphant entry by giving a long, clean cut to the lead-horses, and two or three shortened, sharp blows with his doubled lash to those upon the wheel; then, moistening his lip, he disengages the tin horn from its socket, and, with one more spirited "chirrup" to his team and a petulant flirt of the lines, he gives out, with tremendous explosive efforts, a series of blasts that are heard all down the street. Here and there a blind is coyly opened, and some old dame in ruffled cap peers out, or some stout wench at a backdoor stands gazing with her arms akimbo. The horn rattles back into its socket again; the lines are tightened, and the long lash smacks once more around the reeking flanks of the leaders. Yonder, in his sooty shop, stands the smith, keeping up with his elbow a lazy sway upon his bellows, while he looks admiringly over coach and team, and gives an inquisitive glance at the nigh leader's foot, that he shod only yesterday. A flock of geese, startled from a mud-puddle through which the coach dashes on, rush away with outstretched necks, and wings at their widest, and a great uproar of gabble. Two schoolgirls—home for the nooning—are idling over a gateway, half swinging, half musing, gazing intently. There is a gambrel-roofed mansion, with a balustrade along its upper pitch, and quaint ogees of ancient joinery over the hall-door; and through the cleanly scrubbed parlor-windows is to be seen a prim dame, who turns one spectacled glance upon the passing coach, and then resumes her sewing. There are red houses, with their corners and barge-boards dressed off with white, and on the door-step of one a green tub that flames with a great pink hydrangea. Scattered along the way are huge ashes, sycamores, elms, in somewhat devious line; and from a pendent bough of one of these last a trio of school-boys are seeking to beat down the swaying nest of an oriole with a convergent fire of pebbles.

The coach flounders on,—past an old house with stone chimney (on which an old date stands coarsely cut), and with front-door divided down its middle, with a huge brazen knocker upon its right half,—with two St. Luke's crosses in its lower panels, and two diamond-shaped "lights" above. Hereabout the street widens into what seems a common;

TOWN WORTHIES

and not far below, sitting squarely and authoritatively in the middle of the common, is the red-roofed meeting-house, with tall spire, and in its shadow the humble belfry of the town academy. Opposite these there comes into the main street a highway from the east; and upon one of the corners thus formed stands the Eagle Tavern, its sign creaking appetizingly on a branch of an overhanging sycamore, under which the stage-coach dashes up to the tavern-door, to unlade its passengers for dinner, and to find a fresh relay of horses.

Upon the opposite corner is the country store of Abner Tew, Esq., postmaster during the successive administrations of Mr. Madison and Mr. Monroe. He comes out presently from his shop-door, which is divided horizontally, the upper half being open in all ordinary weathers; and the lower half, as he closes it after him, gives a warning jingle to a little bell within. A square, short, hatchet-faced man is Abner Tew, who walks over with a prompt business-step to receive a leathern pouch from the stage-driver. He returns with it,—a few eager towns-people following upon his steps, —reënters his shop, and delivers the pouch within a glazed door in the corner, where the postmistress *ex officio,* Mrs. Abner Tew, a tall, gaunt woman in black bombazine and spectacles, proceeds to assort the Ashfield mail. By reason of this division of duties, the shop is known familiarly as the shop of "the Tew partners."

Among the waiting expectants who loiter about among the sugar-barrels of the grocery department, there presently appears—with a new tinkle of the little bell—a stout, ruddy man, just past middle age, in broad-brimmed white beaver and sober homespun suit, who is met with a deferential "Good day, Squire," from one and another, as he falls successively into short parley with them: a self-possessed, cheery man, who has strong opinions, and does not fear to express them; Selectman for the last eight years, who has presided in town-meeting time out of mind; member of the Legislature, and once a Senator for the district. This was Giles Elderkin, Esq., the gentleman who, on behalf of the Ecclesiastical Society, had conducted the correspondence with the Reverend Mr. Johns; and he was now waiting his reply. This is presently brought to him by the postmistress, who, catching a glimpse of the Squire through the glazed door, has taken the precaution to adjust her cap-strings and dexterously to flirt one or two of

TOWN WORTHIES

the more apparent creases out of her dingy bombazine. The letter brings acceptance, which the Squire, having made out by private study near to the dusky window, announces to Mrs. Tew,—begging her to inform the people who should happen in from "up the road."

"I hope he 'll suit, Squire," says Mrs. Tew.

"I hope he may,—hope he may, Mrs. Tew; I hear well of him; there 's good blood in him. I knew his father, the Major,—likely man. I hope he may, Mrs. Tew."

And the Squire, having penned a little notice, by favor of one of the Tew partners, proceeds to affix it to the meeting-house door; after which he walks to his own house, with the assured step of a man who is conscious of having accomplished an important duty. It is the very house we just now saw with the ponderous ogees over its front, the balustrade upon its roof, and the dame in spectacles at the window; this latter being the spinster, Miss Meacham, elder sister to the wife of the Squire, and taking upon herself, with active zeal and a neatness that knew no bounds, the office of house-keeper. This was rendered necessary in a manner by the engagement of Mrs. Elderkin with a group of young flax-haired children, and periodic threats of addition to the same.

DOCTOR JOHNS

The hospitalities of the house were fully established, and no state official could visit the town without hearty invitation to the Squire's table. The spinster received the announcement of the minister's coming with a quiet gravity, and betook herself to the needed preparation.

VI

Home Established

MR. JOHNS, meanwhile, when he had left the Handby parlor, where we saw him last, and was fairly upon the stair, had replied to the suggestion of his little wife about the sermon on Revelations with a fugitive kiss, and said, "I will think of it, Rachel."

And he did think of it,—thought of it so well, that he left the beautiful sermon in his drawer, and took with him a couple of strong doctrinal discourses, upon the private hearing of which his charming wife had commented by dropping asleep (poor thing!) in her chair.

But the strong men and women of Ashfield relished them better. There was a sermon for the morning on "Regeneration the work only of grace"; and another for the afternoon, on

HOME ESTABLISHED

the outer leaf of which was written, in the parson's bold hand, "The doctrine of Election compatible with the infinite goodness of God." It is hard to say which of the two was the better, or which commended itself most to the church full of people who listened. Deacon Tourtelot,—a short, wiry man, with reddish whiskers brushed primly forward,—sitting under the very droppings of the pulpit, with painful erectness, and listening grimly throughout, was inclined to the sermon of the morning. Dame Tourtelot, who overtopped her husband by half a head, and from her great scoop hat, trimmed with green, kept her keen eyes fastened intently upon the minister on trial, was enlisted in the same belief, until she heard the Deacon's timid expression of preference, when she pounced upon him, and declared for the Election discourse. It was not her way to allow him to enjoy an opinion of his own getting. Miss Almira, their only child, and now grown into a spare womanhood, that was decorated with another scoop hat akin to the mother's,—from under which hung two yellow festoons of ringlets tied with lively blue ribbons,—was steadfastly observant; though wearing a fagged air before the day was over, and consulting on one or two occasions a little phial of "salts," with a side movement of the head, and an inquiring nostril.

Squire Elderkin, having thrown himself into a comfortable position in the corner of his square pew, is cheerfully attentive; and at one or two of the more marked passages of the sermon bestows a nod of approval, and a glance at Miss Meacham and Mrs. Elderkin, to receive their acknowledgement of the same. The young Elderkins (of whom three are of meeting-house size.) are variously affected; Miss Dora, being turned of six, wears an air of some weariness, and having despatched all the edible matter upon a stalk of caraway, she uses the despoiled brush in keeping the youngest boy, Ned, in a state of uneasy wakefulness. Bob, ranking between the two in point of years, and being mechanically inclined, devotes himself to turning in their sockets the little bobbins which form a balustrade around the top of the pew; but being diverted from this very suddenly by a sharp squeak that calls the attention of his Aunt Joanna, he assumes the penitential air of listener for full five minutes; afterward he relieves himself by constructing a small meeting-house out of the psalm-books and Bible, his Aunt Joanna's spectacle-case serving for a steeple.

HOME ESTABLISHED

There was an air of subdued reverence in the new clergyman, which was not only agreeable to the people in itself, but seemed to very many thoughtful ones to imply a certain respect for them and for the parish.

Deacon Tourtelot, sidling down the aisle after service, out of hearing of his consort, says to Elderkin, "Smart man, Squire."

And the Squire nods acquiescence. "Sound sermonizer,—sound sermonizer, Deacon."

These two opinions were as good as a majority-vote in the town of Ashfield,—all the more since the Squire was a thorough-going Jeffersonian Democrat, and the Deacon a warm Federalist, so far as the poor man could be warm at any thing, who was on the alert every hour of his life to escape the hammer of his wife's reproaches.

So it happened that the parish was called together, and an invitation extended to Brother Johns to continue his ministrations for a month further. Of course the novitiate understood this to be the crucial test; and he accepted it with a composure, and a lack of impertinent effort to please them overmuch, which altogether charmed them. On four successive Saturdays he drove over to Ashfield,—sometimes stopping with one or the other of the two deacons, and at other times with Squire Elderkin,—and on one or two occasions taking his wife by special invitation. Of her, too, the people of Ashfield had but one opinion: that she was of a ductile temper was most easy to be seen; and there was not a strong-minded woman of the parish but anticipated with delight the power and pleasure of moulding her to her wishes. The husband continued to preach agreeably to their notions of orthodoxy, and at the end of the month they gave him a "call," with the promise of four hundred dollars a year, besides sundry odds and ends made up by donation visits and otherwise.

This sum, which was not an inconsiderable one for those days, enabled the clergyman to rent as a parsonage the old house we have seen, with the big brazen knocker, and diamond lights in either half of its green door. It stood under the shade of two huge ashes, at a little remove back from the street, and within easy walk from the central common. A heavy dentilated cornice, from which the paint was peeling away in flaky patches, hung over the windows of the second floor. Within the door was a little entry—(for years and years the pastor's hat and cane used to lie upon a table that stood just within the door); from

HOME ESTABLISHED

the entry a cramped stairway, by three sharp angles, led to the floor above. To the right and left were two parlors. The sun was shining broadly in the south one when the couple first entered the house.

"Good!" said Rachel, with her pleasant, brisk tone,—"this shall be your study, Benjamin; the bookcase here, the table there, a nice warm carpet, we'll paper it with blue, the Major's sword shall be hung over the mantel."

"Tut! tut!" says the clergyman; "a sword, Rachel,—in my study?"

"To be sure! why not?" says Rachel. "And if you like, I will hang my picture, with the doves and the olive-branch, above it; and there shall be a shelf for hyacinths in the window."

Thus she ran on in her pretty housewifely manner, cooing like the doves she talked of, plotting the arrangement of the parlor opposite, of the long dining-room, stretching athwart the house in the rear, and of the kitchen under a roof of its own, still farther back,—he all the while giving grave assent, as if he listened to her contrivance; he was only listening to the music of a sweet voice that somehow charmed his ear, and thanking God in his heart that such music was bestowed upon a sinful world, and praying that he might never listen too fondly.

Behind the house were yard, garden, orchard, and this last drooping away to a meadow. Over all these the pair of light feet pattered beside the master. "Here shall be lilies," she said; "there, a great bunch of mother's peonies; and by the gate, hollyhocks"; —he, by this time, plotting a sermon upon the vanities of the world.

Yet in due time it came to pass that the parsonage was all arranged according to the fancies of its mistress,—even to the Major's sword and the twin doves. Esther, a stout middle-aged dame, and stanch Congregationalist, recommended by the good women of the parish, is installed in the kitchen as maid-of-all-work. As gardener, groom (a sedate pony and square-topped chaise forming part of the establishment), factotum, in short,—there is the frowzy-headed man Larkin, who has his quarters in an airy loft above the kitchen.

The brass knocker is scoured to its brightest. The parish is neighborly. Dame Tourtelot is impressive in her proffers of advice. The Tew partners, Elderkin, Meacham, and all the rest, meet the new housekeepers open-handed. Before mid-winter, the smoke of this new home was piling lazily into the sky above the tree-tops of Ashfield,—a home, as we shall find by and by, of much trial and much cheer. Twenty years after, and the master of it was master of it still,—strong, seemingly, as ever; the brass knocker shining on the door; the sword and the doves in place. But the pattering feet,—the voice that made music,—the tender, wifely plotting,—the cheery sunshine that smote upon her as she talked,—alas for us!—"All is Vanity!"

VII

The Owl and Sparrow

It was not easy in that day to bring together the opinions of a Connecticut parish that had been jostled apart by a parochial quarrel, and where old grievances were festering. Indeed, it is never easy to do this, and unite opinions upon a new-comer, unless he have some rare gift of eloquence, which so dazes the good people that they can no longer remember their petty griefs, or unless he manage with rare tact to pass lightly over the sore points, and to anoint them by a careful hand with such

DOCTOR JOHNS

healing salves as he can concoct out of his pastoral charities. Mr. Johns had neither art nor eloquence, as commonly understood; yet he effected a blending of all interests by the simple, earnest gravity of his character. He ignored all angry disputations; he ignored its results. He came as a shepherd to a deserted sheepfold; he came to preach the Bible doctrines in their literalness. He had no reproofs, save for those who refused the offers of God's mercy,—no commendation, save for those who sought His grace whose favor is everlasting. There were no metaphysical niceties in his discourses, athwart which keen disputants might poise themselves for close and angry conflict; he recognized no necessities but the great ones of repentance and faith; and all the mysteries of the Will he was accustomed to solve by grand utterance of that text which he loved above all others,—however much it may have troubled him in his discussion of Election,— "Whosoever *will*, let him come and drink of the water of life freely."

Inheriting as he did all the religious affinities of his mother, these were compacted and made sensitive by years of silent protest against the proud worldly sufficiency of his father, the Major. Such qualities and experience found

THE OWL AND SPARROW

repose in the unyielding dogmas of the Westminster divines. At thirty the clergyman was as aged as most men at forty-five,—seared by the severity of his opinions, and the unshaken tenacity with which he held them. He was by nature a quiet, almost a timid man; but over the old white desk and crimson cushion, with the choir of singers in his front and the Bible under his hand, he grew into wonderful boldness. He cherished an exalted idea of the dignity of his office,—a dignity which he determined to maintain to the utmost of his power; but in the pulpit only did the full measure of this exaltation come over him. Thence he looked down serenely upon the flock of which he was the appointed guide, and among whom his duty lay. The shepherd leading his sheep was no figure of speech for him; he was commissioned to their care, and was conducting them—old men and maidens, boys and gray-haired women—athwart the dangers of the world, toward the great fold. On one side always the fires of hell were gaping; and on the other were blazing the great candlesticks around the throne.

But when, on some occasion, he had, under the full weight of his office, inveighed against a damning evil, and, as he fondly hoped by the stillness in the old meeting-house, wrought upon sinners effectually, it was disheartening to be met by some hoary member of his flock, whom perhaps he had borne particularly in mind, and to be greeted cheerfully with, "Capital sermon, Mr. Johns! those are the sort that do the business! I like those, parson!" The poor man, humiliated, would bow his thanks. He lacked the art (if it be an art) to press the matter home, when he met one of these parishioners thus. Not that he forgot the dignity of his position for a moment, but he wore it too trenchantly; he could never unbend to the free play of side-talk. Always the weight of his solemn duties pressed sorely on him; always amid pitfalls he was conducting his little flock toward the glories of the Great Court.

It is quite possible that by reason of this grave taciturnity the clergyman won more surely upon the respect of his people. "He is engrossed," said they, "with greater matters; and in all secular affairs he recognizes our superior discernment." Thus his inaptitude in current speech was construed by them into a delicate flattery, and it happened that good Mr. Johns came to win the good-will of all the parish of Ashfield, while he challenged their respect by his uniform gravity. It is even pos-

THE OWL AND SPARROW

sible that a consciousness of a certain stateliness and stiffness of manner became in some measure a source of pride to him, and that he enjoyed, in his subdued way, the disposition of the lads of the town to give him a wide pass, instead of brushing brusquely against him, as if he were some other than the parson.

In those days he wrote to his sister Eliza,—

"We are fairly settled in a pleasant home upon the main street. The meeting-house, which you will remember, is near by; and I have, by the blessing of God, a full attendance every Lord's day. They listen to my poor sermons with commendable earnestness; and I trust they may prove to them 'a savor of life unto life.' We also find the people of the town neighborly and kind. Squire Elderkin has proved particularly so, and is a very energetic man in all matters relating to the parish. I fear greatly, however, that he still lacks the intimate favor of God, and has not humbled himself to entire submission. Yet he is constant in his observance of nearly all the outward forms of devotion and of worship; and we hear of his charities in every house we enter. Strange mystery of Providence, that he should not long since have been broken down by grace, and become in *all* things a devout follower of the Master! His wife is a most excellent person, lowly in her faith, and zealous of good works. The same may also be said of their worthy maiden sister, Miss Joanna Meacham, who is, of a truth, a matron in Israel. Rachel and myself frequently take tea at their house; and she is much interested in the little family of Elderkins, who, I am glad to say, enjoy excellent advantages, and such of them as are of proper age are duly taught in the Shorter Westminster Catechism.

"Deacon Tourtelot, another of our neighbors, is a devout man; and Dame Tourtelot (as she is commonly called) is a woman of quite extraordinary zeal and capacity. Their daughter Almira is untiring in attendance, and aids the services by singing treble. Deacon Simmons, who lives at quite a distance from us, is represented to be a man of large means and earnest in the faith. He has a large farm, and also a distillery, both of which are said to be managed with great foresight and prudence. I trust that the reports which I hear occasionally of his penuriousness are not wholly true, and that in due time his hand will be opened by divine grace to a more effectual showing forth of the deeds of charity. Our home affairs are, I believe, managed prudently,

THE OWL AND SPARROW

—the two servants being most excellent persons, and my little Rachel a very sunbeam in the house."

And the little sunbeam writes to Mrs. Handby at about the same date,—we will say from six to eight months after their entry,—

"Everything goes on *delightfully*, dear mamma. Esther is a good creature, and helps me wonderfully. You would laugh to see me fingering the raw meats at the butcher's cart to choose nice pieces, which I really *can do* now; and it is fortunate I can, for the goodman Benjamin knows *positively nothing* of such things, and I am sure would n't be able to tell mutton from beef.

"The little parlor is nicely furnished; there is an elegant hair sofa, and over the mantel is the portrait of Major Johns; and then the goodman has insisted upon hanging under the looking-glass *my old sampler in crewel,* with a gilt frame around it; on the table is the illustrated 'Pilgrim's Progress' papa gave me, and a volume of 'Calmet's Dictionary' I have taken out of the study,—it is full of *such beautiful pictures,*—and 'Mrs. Hannah More' in full gilt. The big Bible you gave us, the goodman says, is too large for easy handling; so it is kept on a stand in the corner, with the great fly-brush of peacock's feathers hanging over it. I have put charming blue chintz curtains in the spare chamber, and arranging everything there very nicely; so that *before a certain event,* you must be sure to come and take possession.

"Last night we took tea again with the Elderkins, and Mrs. Elderkin was as kind to me as ever, and Miss Meacham is an excellent woman, and the little ones are loves of children; and I wish you could see them. But you will, you know, *quite soon.* Sometimes I fall to crying, when I think of it all; and then the goodman comes and puts his hand on my head, and says, 'Rachel! Rachel, my dear! is this your gratitude for all God's mercies?' And then I jump up, and kiss his grave face, and laugh through my tears. He is a dear good man. This is all very foolish, I suppose; but, mamma, is n't it the way with all women?

"Dame Tourtelot is a great storm of a creature, and she comes down upon us every now and then, and advises me about the housekeeping and the table, and the servants, and Benjamin,—giving me a great many good hints, I suppose; but in such a way, and calling me 'my child,' as makes me feel good for nothing, and as if I were not fit to be mistress

THE OWL AND SPARROW

Miss Almira is a quiet thing, and has a piano. She dresses *very queerly,* and, I have been told, has written poetry for the 'Hartford Courant,' *over two stars*—**. She seems a good creature, though, and comes to see us often. The chaise is a *great* comfort, and our old horse Dobbins is a good, sober horse. Benjamin often takes me with him in his drives to see the parishioners who live out of town. He tells me about the trees and the flowers, and a thousand matters I never heard of. Indeed, he is a good man, and he knows a *world* of things."

The tender-hearted, kind soul makes her way into the best graces of the people of Ashfield; the older ones charmed with that blithe spirit of hers, and all the younger ones mating easily with her simple, outspoken naturalness. She goes freely everywhere; she is not stiffened by any ceremony, nor does she carry any stately notions of the dignity of her office,— some few there may be who wish that she had a keener sense of the importance of her position; she even bursts unannounced into the little glazed corner of the Tew partners, where she prattles away with the sedate Mistress in good, kindly fashion, winning that stiff old lady's heart, and moving her to declare to all customers that the parson's wife has no pride about her, and is "a dear little thing, to be sure!"

On summer evenings, Dobbins is to be seen, two or three times in the week, jogging along before the square-topped chaise, upon some highway that leads into the town, with the parson seated within, with slackened rein, and in thoughtful mood, from which he rouses himself from time to time with a testy twitch and noisy chirrup that urge the poor beast into a faster gait. All the while the little wife sits beside him, as if a twittering sparrow had nestled itself upon the same perch with some grave owl, and sat with him side by side, watching for the big eyes to turn upon her, and chirping some pretty response for every solemn utterance of the wise old bird beside her.

VIII

An Accomplished Sinner

On the return from one of these parochial drives, not long after their establishment at Ashfield, it happened that the good parson and his wife were not a little startled at sight of a

AN ACCOMPLISHED SINNER

stranger lounging familiarly at their door. A little roof jutted out over the entrance to the parsonage, without any apparent support, and flanking the door were two plank seats, with their ends toward the street, cut away into the shape of those "settles" which used to be seen in country taverns and which here seemed to invite a quiet out-of-door gossip. But the grave manner of the parson had never invited to a very familiar use of this loitering-place, even by the most devoted of the parishioners; and the appearance of a stranger of some two-and-thirty years, with something in his manner, as much as in his dress, which told of large familiarity with the world, lounging upon this little porch, had amazed the passers-by, as much as it now did the couple who drove up slowly in the square-topped chaise.

"Who can it be, Benjamin?" says Rachel.

"I really can't say," returns the parson.

"He seems very much at home, my dear,"— as indeed he does, with his feet stretched out upon the bench, and eying curiously the approaching vehicle.

As it draws near, his observation being apparently satisfactory, he walks briskly down to the gate, and greets the parson with,—

"My dear Johns, I 'm delighted to see you!"

DOCTOR JOHNS

At this the parson knew him.

"Maverick, upon my word!" and he offers his hand.

"And this is Mrs. Johns, I suppose," says the stranger, bowing graciously. "Allow me, madam;" and he assists her to alight. "Your husband and myself were old college-friends, partners of the same bench, and I 've used no ceremony, you see, in finding him out."

Rachel, eying him furtively, and with a little rustic courtesy, "is glad to see any of her husband's old friends."

The parson—upon his feet now—shakes the stranger's hand heartily again.

"I am very glad to see you, Maverick; but I thought you were out of the country."

"So I have been, Johns; am home only upon a visit, and hearing by accident that you had become a clergyman—as I always thought you would—and were settled hereabout, I determined to run down and see you before sailing again."

"You must stop with me. Rachel, dear, will you have the spare room made ready for Mr. Maverick?"

"My dear madam, don't give yourself the least trouble; I am an old traveller, and can make myself quite comfortable at the tavern

AN ACCOMPLISHED SINNER

yonder; but if it's altogether convenient, I shall be delighted to pass the night under the roof of my old friend. I shall be off tomorrow noon," continued he, turning to the parson, "and until then I want you to put off your sermons and make me one of your parishioners."

So they all went into the parsonage together.

Frank Maverick, as he had said, had shared the same bench with Johns in college; and between them, unlike as they were in character, there had grown up a strong friendship,—one of those singular intimacies which bind the gravest men to the most cheery and reckless. Maverick was forever running into scrapes and consulting the cool head of Johns to help him out of them. Johns advised with him (giving as serious advice then as he could now), and added from time to time such assistance in his studies as a plodding man can always lend to one of quick brain, who makes no reckoning of time.

Upon a certain occasion Maverick had gone over with Johns to his home, and the Major had taken an immense fancy to the buoyant young fellow, so full of spirits, and so charmingly frank. "If your characters could only be welded together," he used to say to his son, "you would both be the better for it; he a little

DOCTOR JOHNS

of your gravity, and you something of his rollicking carelessness." This bound Johns to his friend more closely than ever. There was, moreover, great honesty and conscientiousness in the lad's composition; he could beat in a tutor's window for the frolic of the thing, and by way of paying off some old grudge for a black mark; but there was a strong spice of humanity at the bottom even of his frolics. It happened one day, that his friend Ben Johns told him that one of the bats which had done terrible execution on the tutor's windows had also played havoc on his table, breaking a bottle of ink, and deluging some half-dozen of the tutor's books; "and do you know," said Johns, "the poor man who has made such a loss is saving up all his pay here for a mother and two or three fatherless children?"

"The Deuce he is!" said Maverick, and his hand went to his pocket, which was always pretty full. "I say, Johns, don't peach on me, but I think I must have thrown that bat (which Johns knew to be hardly possible, for he had only come up at the end of the row), and I want you to get this money to him, to make those books good again. Will you do it, old fellow?"

This was the sort of character to win upon

AN ACCOMPLISHED SINNER

the quiet son of the Major. "If he were only more earnest," he used to say,—"if he could give up his trifling,—if he would only buckle down to serious study, as some of us do, what great things he might accomplish!"

Maverick was altogether his old self this night at the parsonage. Rachel listened admiringly, as he told of his travel and of his foreign experiences. He was the son of a merchant of an Eastern seaport who had been long engaged in the Mediterranean trade, with a branch house at Marseilles; and thither Frank had gone two or three years after leaving college, to fill some subordinate post, and finally to work his way into a partnership, which he now held. Of course he had not lived there those seven or eight years last past without his visit to Paris; and his easy, careless way of describing what he had seen there in Napoleon's day—the fêtes, the processions, the display—was a kind of talk not often heard in a New England village, and which took a strong hold upon the imagination of Rachel.

"And to think," says the parson, "that such a people are wholly infidel!"

"Well, well, I don't know," says Maverick; "I think I have seen a good deal of faith in the Popish churches."

DOCTOR JOHNS

"Faith in images; faith in the Virgin; faith in mummery," says Johns, with a sigh. "'T is always the scarlet woman of Babylon!"

"I know," says Maverick, smiling, "these things are not much to your taste; but we have our Protestant chapels, too."

"Not much better, I fear," says Johns. "They are sadly impregnated with the Genevese Socinianism."

This was about the time that the orthodox Louis Empaytaz was suffering the rebuke of the Swiss church authorities for his "Considerations upon the Divinity of Jesus Christ." Aside from this, all the parson's notions of French religion and of French philosophy were of the most aggravated degree of bitterness. All Frenchmen he had learned to look upon as the children of Satan, and their language as the language of hell. With these sentiments very sincerely entertained, he regarded his poor friend as one living at the very doorposts of Pandemonium. It seemed to him that his easy refinement of manner, in such contrast with the ceremonious stiffness of the New England customs of speech, was but the sliming over of the Serpent's tongue, preparatory to a dreadful swallowing of soul and body; and the careless grace of talk, which so

AN ACCOMPLISHED SINNER

charmed the innocent Rachel, appeared to the exacting Puritan a token of the enslavement of his old friend to sense and the guile of this world.

Nine o'clock was the time for evening prayers at the parsonage, which under no circumstances were ever omitted; and as the little clock in the dining-room chimed the hour, Mr. Johns rose to lead the way from his study, where they had passed the evening.

"It 's our hour for family prayer," says Johns; "will you come with us?"

"Most certainly," says Maverick, rising. "I should be sorry not to have this little scene of New England life to take back with me; it will recall home pleasantly."

The servants were summoned, and the parson read in his wonted way a chapter,—not selected, but designated by the old book-mark, which was carried forward from day to day throughout the sacred volume. In his prayer the parson asked specially for Divine Grace to overshadow all those journeying from their homes,—to protect them,—to keep alive in their hearts the teachings of their youth,—to shield them from the insidious influences of sin and of the world.

Shortly after prayers Rachel retired for the

night. The parson and his old friend talked for an hour or more in the study, but always as men whose thoughts were unlike: Maverick filled and exuberant with the prospects of this life; and the parson, by a settled purpose, which seemed like instinct, making all his observations bear upon futurity.

"The poor man has grown very narrow," thought Maverick.

And yet Johns entered with friendly interest into the schemes of his companion.

"So you count upon spending your life there?" said the parson.

"It is quite probable," said Maverick. "I am doing exceedingly well; the climate, bating some harsh winds in winter, is enjoyable. Why should n't I?"

"It's a question to put to your conscience," says Johns, "not to me. A man can but do his duty, as well there as here perhaps. Do you mean to marry in France, Maverick?"

A shade passed over the face of his friend; but recovering himself, with a little musical laugh, he said,—

"I really can't say: there are very charming women there, Johns."

"I am afraid so, uttered the parson, dryly.

"By the way," said Maverick,—"you will

AN ACCOMPLISHED SINNER

excuse me,—but you will be having a family by and by,"—at which the parson fairly blushed,—"you must let me send over some little gift for your first boy; it sha'n't be one that will harm him, though it comes from our heathen side of the world."

"There's a gift you might bestow, Maverick, that I should value beyond price."

"Pray what is it?"

"Live such a life, my friend, that I could say to any boy of mine, 'Follow the example of that man.'"

"Ah," said Maverick, with his easy, infectious laugh, "that's more than I can promise. To tell the truth, Johns, I don't believe I could by any possibility fall into the prim, stiff ways which make a man commendable hereabout. Even if I were religiously disposed, or should ever think of adopting your profession, I fancy I should take to the gown and liturgy, as giving a little freer movement to my taste. You don't like to think of that, I'll wager."

"You might do worse things," said the parson, sadly.

"I know I might," said Maverick, thoughtfully; "I greatly fear I shall. Yet it's not altogether a bad life I'm looking forward to, Johns; we'll say ten or fifteen more years of business on the other side; marrying sometime in the interval,—certainly not until I have a good revenue; then, possibly, I may come over among you again, establish a pretty home in the neighborhood of one of your towns; look after a girl and a boy or two, who may have come into the family; get the title of Squire; give fairly to the missionary societies; take my place in a good big family-pew; dabble in politics, perhaps, so that people shall dub me 'Honorable'; is n't that a fair show, Johns?"

There was a thief in the candle, which the parson removed with the snuffers.

"As for yourself," continued Maverick, "they 'll give you the title of Doctor after a few years!"—The parson raised his hand, as if to put away the thought.—"I know," continued his friend, "you don't seek worldly honors: but they will drift upon you; they 'll all love you hereabout, in spite of your seriousness (the parson smiled); you 'll have your house full of children; you 'll be putting a wing here and a wing there; and when I come back, twenty years hence, if I live, I shall find you comfortably gray; and your pretty wife in spectacles, knitting mittens for the youngest boy, and the oldest at college, and your girls grown

AN ACCOMPLISHED SINNER

into tall village belles;—but, Johns, don't, I beg, be too strict with them; you can't make a merry young creature the better by insisting upon seriousness; you can't crowd goodness into a body by pounding upon it. What are you thinking of, Johns?"

The parson was sitting with his eyes bent upon a certain figure in the green and red Scotch carpet.

"Thinking, Maverick, that in twenty years' time, if alive, we may be less fit for heaven than we are to-day."

There was a pitying kindliness in the tone of the minister, as he said this, which touched Maverick.

"There's no doubt on your score; Johns, God bless you! But we must paddle our own boats; I dare say you'll come out a long way before me; you always did, you know. Every man to his path."

"There's but *one*," said Johns, solemnly, "that leadeth to eternal rest."

With these words they parted for the night.

Next morning, before the minister was astir, Maverick was strolling about the garden and the village street, and at breakfast appeared with a little bunch of violets he had gathered from Rachel's flower-patch, and laid them by her plate. (It was a graceful attention, that not even the clergyman had ever paid to her.)

At noon Maverick left upon the old swaying stage-coach,—looking out, as he passed, upon the parsonage, with its quaintly panelled door, and its diamond lights, of which he long kept the image in his mind.

"I think Mr. Frank Maverick is a most charming man," said the pretty Mrs. Johns to her husband.

"He is, Rachel, and generous and openhearted,—and yet, in the sight of Heaven, I fear, a miserable sinner."

"But, Benjamin, my dear, we are all sinners."

"All,—all, Rachel, God help us!"

IX

Reuben

In December of the year 1820 came about a certain event of which hint has been already given by the party chiefly concerned; and Mrs. Johns presented her husband with a fine boy, who was in due time christened—Reuben.

Mrs. Handby was present at this eventful

period, occupying the guest-chamber, and delighting in all the little adornments that had been prepared by the loving hands of her daughter; and upon the following Sabbath, Mr. Johns, for the first time since his entrance upon the pastoral duties of Ashfield, ventured to repeat an old sermon. Dame Tourtelot had been present on the momentous occasion, with such a tempest of suggestions in regard to the wrappings and feeding of the new-comer, that the poor mother had quietly begged the good clergyman to decoy her, on her next visit, into his study. This he did, and succeeded in fastening her with a discussion upon the import of the word *baptize,* in which he was in a fair way of being carried by storm, if he had not retreated under cover of his Greek Lexicon.

Mrs. Elderkin had been zealous in neighborly offices, and had brought, in addition to a great basket of needed appliances, a silver porringer, which, with wonderful foresight, had been ordered from a Hartford jeweller in advance. The out-of-door man, Larkin, took a well-meaning pride in this accession to the family,—walking up and down the street with a broad grin upon his face. He also became the bearer, in behalf of the Tew partners, of a certain artful contrivance of tinware for the speedy stewing of pap, which, considering that the donors were childless people, was esteemed a very great mark of respect for the minister.

Would it be strange, if the father felt a new ambition stirring in him, as he listened from his study to that cry of a child in the house? He does feel it, and struggles against it. Shall these human ties supplant the spiritual ones by which we are all coheirs of eternal death or of eternal life?

For all this, however, there is many a walk which would have been taken of old under the orchard trees now transferred to the chamber, where he paces back and forth with the babe in his arms, soothing its outcry, as he thinks out his discourse for the following Sabbath.

In due time Mrs. Handby returns to her home. The little child pushes through its first month of venturesome encounter with the rough world it has entered upon bravely; and the household is restored to its uniform placidity. The affairs of the parish follow their accustomed course. From time to time there are meetings of the "Consociation," or other ministerial assemblages, in the town, when the parsonage is overflowing, and Rachel, with a simple grace, is compelled to do the honors to

REUBEN

a corps of the Congregational brotherhood. As for the parson, he was like a child in all household matters. Over and over he would invite his brethren flocking in from the neighboring villages to pass the night with him, when Rachel would decoy him into a corner, and declare, with a most pitiable look of distress, that not a bed was unoccupied in the house. Whereupon the goodman would quietly take his hat, and trudge away to Squire Elderkin's, or, on rarer occasions, to Deacon Tourtelot's, and ask the favor of lodging with them one of his clerical brethren.

At other times, before some such occasion of clerical entertainment, the little housewife, supported by Esther with broom and a great array of mops, would wait upon the parson in his study and order him away to his walk in the orchard,—an order which the poor man never ventured to resist; but, taking perhaps a pocket volume of Doddridge, or of Cowper,—the only poet he habitually read,—he would sally out with hat and cane,—this latter a gift of an admiring parishioner, which it pleased Rachel he should use, and which she always brought to him at such times, with a winning, mischievous look of half-entreaty and half-command that it was not in his heart to resist, and which on rare occasions (that were subject of self-accusation afterward) provoked him to an answering kiss. At which Rachel:—

"Now go and leave us, please; there's a good man! And mind" (shaking her forefinger at him), "dinner at half past twelve; Larkin will blow the shell."

The parson, as he paced back and forth under the apple-trees, out of sight, and feeling the need of more vigorous exercise than his usual meditative gait afforded, would on occasions brandish his cane and assume a military air and stride (he remembered the Major's only too well), getting in a glow with the unusual movement, and in the heat of it thanking God for all the blessings that had befallen him: a pleasant home; a loving wife; a little boy to bear the name in which, with all his spiritual tendencies, he yet took a very human pride; health,—and he whisked his cane as vigorously as ever the Major had done his cumbrous sword,—the world's comforts; a congregation that met him kindly, that listened kindly. Was he not leading them in the path of salvation, and rejoicing in the leadership?

And then, to himself,—"Be careful, careful, Benjamin Johns, that you take not too great a pride in this work and home of yours. You are but an instrument in greater hands; He doeth with you what seemeth Him best."

As the boy Reuben grows, and gains a firmer footing, he sometimes totters beside the clergyman in these orchard walks, clinging blindly to his hand, and lifting his uncertain feet with great effort over the interrupting tufts of grass, unheeded by the minister, who is pondering some late editorial of the "Boston Recorder." But far oftener the boy is with the mother, burying his face in that dear lap of hers,— lifting the wet face to have tears kissed away and forgotten. And as he thrives and takes the strength of three or four years, he walks beside her under the trees of the village street, clad in such humble finery as the Handby grandparents may have bestowed; and he happens oftenest, on these strolls with Rachel, into the hospitable home of the Elderkins, where there are little ones to romp with the boy. Most noticeable of all, just now, one Philip Elderkin (of whom more will have to be said as this story progresses), only a year the senior of Reuben, but of far stouter frame, who looks admiringly on the minister's child, and as he grows warm in play frights him with some show of threat, which makes the little Reuben run for cover to the arms of Rachel.

Often, too, in the square-topped chaise, the child is seated on a little stool between the parson and his wife, as they drive away upon their visits to the outskirts of the parish,—puzzling them with those strange questions which come from a boy just exploring his way into the world of talk.

"Benjamin," says Rachel, as they were nearing home upon one of these drives, "Reuben is quite a large boy now, you know; have you ever written to your friend, Mr. Maverick? You remember he promised a gift for him."

"Never," said the minister, whose goodness rarely took the shape of letter-writing,—least of all where the task would seem to remind of a promised favor.

"You 've not forgotten it? You 've not forgotten Mr. Maverick?"

"Not forgotten, Rachel,—not forgotten to pray for him."

"I *would* write, Benjamin; it might be something that would be of service to Reuben. *Please* don't forget it, Benjamin."

And the minister promised.

X

A Cloud

IN the autumn of 1824,—the minister of Ashfield being still in good favor with nearly all his parishioners, and his wife Rachel being still greatly beloved,—a rumor ran through the town, one day, that there was serious illness at the parsonage, the Doctor's horse and saddle-bags being observed in waiting at the front gate for two hours together. Following close upon this, the Tew partners reported—having received undoubted information from Larkin, who still kept in his old service—that a daughter was born to the minister, but so feeble that there were grave doubts if the young Rachel could survive. The report was well founded; and after three or four days of desperate struggle with life, the poor child dropped away. Thus death came into the parsonage with so faint and shadowy a tread, it hardly startled one. The babe had been christened in the midst of its short struggle, and in this the father found such comfort as he could; yet reckoning the poor, fluttering little soul as a sinner in Adam, through whom all men fell, he confided it with a great sigh to God.

It would have been well, if his grief had rested there. But two days thereafter there was a rumor on the village street,—flying like the wind, as such rumors do, from house to house,—"The minister's wife is dead!"

"I want to know!" said Mrs. Tew, lifting herself from her task of assorting the mail, and removing her spectacles in nervous haste. "Do tell! It a'n't possible! Miss Johns dead?"

"Yes," says Larkin, "as true as I live, she 's dead;" and his voice broke as he said it —the kind little woman had so won upon him.

Squire Elderkin, like a good Christian, came hurrying to the parsonage to know what this strange report could mean. The study was unoccupied. With the familiarity of an old friend he made his way up the cramped stairs. The chamber-door was flung wide open; there was no reason why the whole parish might not come in. The nurse, sobbing in a corner, was swaying back and forth, her hands folded across her lap. Reuben, clinging to the coverlet, was feeling his way along the bed, if by chance his mother's hand might catch hold upon his; and the minister standing with a chair before him, his eyes turned to heaven

A CLOUD

(the same calm attitude which he took at his evening prayer-meeting), was entreating God to "be over his house, to strengthen him, to pour down his Spirit on him, to bind up the bruised hearts,—to spare,—spare——"

Even the stout Squire Elderkin withdraws outside the door, that he may the better conceal his emotion.

The death happened on a Friday. The Squire, after a few faltering expressions of sympathy, asked regarding the burial. "Should it not be on Sunday?"

"Not on Sunday," said Mr. Johns; "God help me, Squire,—but this is not a work of necessity or mercy. Let it be on Monday."

"On Monday, then," said Elderkin,—"and let me take the arrangement of it all off your thought; and we will provide some one to preach for you on the Sabbath."

"No, Mr. Elderkin, no; I am always myself in the pulpit. I shall find courage there."

And he did. A stranger would not have suspected that the preacher's wife lay dead at home; the same unction and earnestness that had always characterized him; the same unyielding rigidity of doctrine: *"Except ye repent, ye shall all likewise perish."*

Only once—it was in the reading of the last

DOCTOR JOHNS

hymn in the afternoon service—his voice broke, and he sat down half through. But as the song rose under the old roof of the meeting-house, his courage rose with it. He seemed ashamed of the transitory weakness. What right had he to bring private griefs to such a place? What right had the leader to faint, when the army were pressing forward to the triumph God had promised to the faithful? So it was in a kind of ecstasy that he rose, and joined with a firm, loud voice in the final doxology.

One or two of the good old ladies, with a sad misconception of the force that was in him, and of the divine aid which seemed vouchsafed to him during the service, came to him, as he passed out, to give him greeting and a word of condolence. For that time only he passed them by, as if they had been wooden images. His spirit had been strained to its uttermost, and would bear no more. He made his way home with an ungainly, swift gait,—home to the dear bedside,—down upon his knees,—struggling with his weakness,—praying.

At the tea-hour Esther knocked; but in vain. An hour after, his boy came,—came at the old woman's suggestion (who had now the care of him), and knelt by his side.

A CLOUD

"Reuben,—my boy!"

"She 's in heaven, is n't she, father?"

"God only knows, my son. He hath mercy on whom He will have mercy."

Small as he was, the boy flushed at this:—

"I think it 's a bad God, if she is n't in heaven."

"Nay, Reuben, little one, blaspheme not: His ways are not as our ways. Kiss her now, and we will sit down to our supper."

And so they passed out together to their lonely repast. It had been a cheerful meal in days gone, this Sunday's supper. For the dinner, owing to the scruples of the parson, was but a cold lunch always; and in the excited state in which the preacher found himself between services, there was little of speech; even Reuben's prattle, if he ventured upon it, caught a quick "Hist!" from the mamma. But with the return of Esther from the afternoon Bible-class, there was a big fire lighted in the kitchen, and some warm dishes served, such as diffused an appetizing odor through the house. The clergyman, too, wore an air of relief, having preached his two sermons, and showing a capital appetite, like most men who have acquitted themselves of a fatiguing duty. Besides which, the parson guarded that old New

DOCTOR JOHNS

England custom of beginning his Sabbath at sundown on Saturday,—so that, by the time the supper of Sunday was fairly over, Reuben could be counting it no sin, if he should steal a run into the orchard. Nay, it is quite probable that the poor little woman who was dead had always welcomed cheerily the opened door of Sunday evening, and the relaxing gravity, as night fell, of her husband's starched look.

What wonder, if she had loved, even as much as the congregational singing, the music of the birds at the dusk of a summer's day? It is certain that the poor woman had enjoyed immensely those Sabbath-evening strolls through the garden and orchard, hand in hand with Reuben and the minister,—with such keen and exhilarating sense of God's goodness, of trust in Him, of hope, as was not invariably wakened by the sermons of her Benjamin.

On the evening of which we speak, the father and son walked down the orchard alone. The birds sang their merriest as day closed in; and as they turned upon their walk, and the good man saw through the vista of garden and orchard a bright light flitting across an upper window of his house, the mad hope flashed upon him for an instant (such baseless fancies will sometimes possess the calmest minds) that she had waked,—his Rachel,—and was there to meet him. The next moment the light and hope were gone. His fingers gave such a convulsive grip upon the hand of his little boy that Reuben cried out with pain, "Papa, papa, you hurt me!"

The parson bent down and kissed him.

XI

Parish Sympathies

THERE were scores of people in Ashfield who would have been delighted to speak consolation to the bereaved clergyman; but he was not a man to be approached easily with the ordinary phrases of sympathy. He bore himself too sternly under his grief. What, indeed, can be said in the face of affliction, where the manner of the sufferer seems to say, "God has done it, and God does all things well?"

Yet there are those who delight in breaking in upon the serene dignity which this condition of mind implies with a noisy proffer of consolation, and an aggravating rehearsal of the occasion for it; as if such comforters entertained a certain jealousy of the serenity they do not comprehend, and were determined to test its sufficiency. Dame Tourtelot was eminently such a person.

" It 's a dreadful blow to ye, Mr. Johns," said she; "I know it is. Almiry is a'most as much took down by it as you are. 'She was such a lovely woman,' she says; and the poor, dear little boy,—won't you let him come and pass a day or two with us? Almiry is very fond of children."

"Later, later, my good woman," said the parson. "I can't spare the boy now; the house is too empty."

"O Mr. Johns,—the poor lonely thing!" (And she says this, with her hands in black mits, clasped together.) "It 's a bitter blow! As I was a-sayin' to the Deacon, 'Such a lovely young woman, and such a good comfortable home, and she, poor thing, enjoyin' it so much!' I do hope you 'll bear up under it, Mr. Johns."

"By God's help, I will, my good woman."

Dame Tourtelot was disappointed to find the parson wincing so little as he did under her stimulative sympathy. On returning home, she opened her views to the Deacon in this style:—

PARISH SYMPATHIES

"Tourtelot, the parson is not so much broke down by this as we 've been thinkin'; he was as cool, when I spoke to him to-day, as any man I ever see in my life. The truth is, she was a flighty young person, noways equal to the parson. I 've been a-suspectin' it, this long while; she never, in my opinion, took a real hard hold upon him. But, Tourtelot, you should go and see Mr. Johns; and I hope you 'll talk consolingly and Scripterally to him. It 's your duty."

And hereupon she shifted the needles in her knitting, and, smoothing down the big blue stocking-leg over her knee, cast a glance at the Deacon which signified command. Long before, the meek, mild-mannered little man who was her husband had by her active and resolute negotiation been made a deacon of the parish,—for which office he was not indeed ill-fitted, being religiously disposed, strict in his observance of all duties, and well-grounded in the Larger Catechism. He had, moreover, certain secular endowments which were even more marked,—among them, a wonderful instinct at a bargain, which had been polished by Dame Tourtelot's superior address to a wonderful degree of sharpness; and by reason of this the less respectful of the townspeople were

DOCTOR JOHNS

accustomed to say, "The Deacon is very small at home, but great in a trade."

"Squire," he would say, addressing a neighbor on the Common, "what do you s'pose I paid for that brindle ye'rlin' o' mine? Give us a guess."

"Waäl, Deacon, I guess you paid about ten dollars."

"Only eight!" the Deacon would say, with a smile that was fairly luminous,—"and a pootty likely critter I call it for eight dollars."

"Five hogs this year" (in this way the Deacon was used to soliloquize),—"I hope to make 'em three hundred apiece. The price works up about Christmas; Deacon Simmons has sold his'n at five,—distillery-pork; that 's sleezy, wastes in bilin'; folks know it; mine, bein' corn-fed, ought to bring half a cent more,— and say, for Christmas, six; that 'll give a gain of a cent,—on five hogs, at three hundred apiece, will be fifteen dollars. That 'll pay half my pew-rent, and leave somethin' over for Almiry, who 's always wantin' fresh ribbons about New-Year's."

The Deacon cherished a strong dread of formal visits to the parsonage; first, because it involved his Sunday toilet, in which he was never easy, except at conference or in his pew

PARISH SYMPATHIES

at the meeting-house; and next, because he counted it necessary on such occasions to give a Scriptural garnish to his talk, in which attempt he almost always, under the authoritative look of the parson, blundered into difficulty. Yet Tourtelot, in obedience to his wife's suggestion, and primed with a text from Matthew, undertook the visit of condolence,—and, being a really kind-hearted man, bore himself well in it. Over and over the good parson shook his hand in thanks.

"It 'll be all right," says the Deacon. "'Blessed are the mourners,' is the Scripteral language, 'for they shall inherit the earth.'"

"No, not that, Deacon," says the minister, to whom a misquotation was like a wound in the flesh; "the last thing I want is to inherit the earth. *'They shall be comforted,'*—that's the promise, Deacon, and I count on it."

It was mortifying to his visitor to be caught napping on so familiar a text; the parson saw it, and spoke consolingly. But if not strong in texts, the Deacon knew what his strong points were; so, before leaving, he invites a little off-hand discussion of more familiar topics.

"Pootty tight spell o' weather we 've been havin', Parson."

"Rather cool, certainly," says the unsuspecting clergyman.

"Got all your winter's stock o' wood in yit?"

"No, I have n't," says the parson.

"Waäl, Mr. Johns, I 've got a lot of pastur'-hickory cut and corded, that 's well seared over now,—and if you 'd like some of it, I can let you have it *very reasonable indeed.*"

The sympathy of the Elderkins, if less formal, was none the less hearty. Nay, the very religion of the Squire, which the parson had looked upon as somewhat discursive and human,—giving too large a place to good works,—was decisive and to the point in the present emergency.

"It 's God's doing," said he; "we must take the cup He gives us. For the best, is n't it, Parson?"

"I do, Squire. Thank God, I can."

There was good Mrs. Elderkin—who made up by her devotion to the special tenets of the clergyman many of the shortcomings of the Squire—insisted upon sending for the poor boy Reuben, that he might forget his grief in her kindness, and in frolic with the Elderkins through that famous garden, with its huge hedges of box,—such a garden as was certainly not to be matched elsewhere in Ashfield. The same good woman, too, sends down a wagon-load of substantial things from her larder, for the present relief of the stricken household; to which the Squire has added a little round jug of choice Santa Cruz rum,—remembering the long watches of the parson. Those old people nestled under no cover of liver specifics or bitters. Reform has made a grand march indeed; but the Devil, with his square bottles and Scheidam schnapps, has kept a pretty even pace with it.

XII

The Parson's Consolation

THE boy Reuben, in those first weeks after his loss, wandered about as if in a maze, wondering at the great blank that death had made; or, warming himself at some out-door sport, he rushed in with a pleasant forgetfulness,—shouting,—up the stairs,—to the accustomed door, and bursts in upon the cold chamber, so long closed, where the bitter knowledge comes upon him fresh once more. Esther, good soul that she is, has heard his clatter upon the floor, his bound at the old latch, and, fancying what it may mean, has come up in time to soothe him and bear him off with her. The parson, forging some sermon for the next Sabbath, in the room at the foot of the stairs, hears, may be, the stifled sobbing of the boy, as the good Esther half leads and half drags him down, and opens his door upon them.

"What now, Esther? Has Reuben caught a fall?"

"No, sir, no fall; he 's not harmed, sir. It 's only the old room, you know, sir, and he quite forgot himself."

"Poor boy! Will he come with me, Esther?"

"No, Mr. Johns. I 'll find something 'll amuse him; hey, Ruby?"

And the parson goes back to his desk, where he forgets himself in the glow of that great work of his. He has been taught, as never before, that "all flesh is grass." He accepts his loss as a punishment for having thought too much and fondly of the blessings of this life. He has transferred his bed to a little chamber which opens from his study in the rear, and which is at the end of the long dining-room, where every morning and evening the prayers are said, as before. The parishioners see a light burning in the window of his study far into the night.

THE PARSON'S CONSOLATION

For a time his sermons are more emotional than before.

"We ask ourselves," said he, "my brethren, if we shall knowingly meet there—where we trust His grace may give us entrance—those from whom you and I have parted; whether a fond and joyous welcome shall greet us, not alone from Him whom to love is life, but from those dear ones who seem to our poor senses to be resting under the sod yonder. Sometimes I believe that by God's great goodness," (and here he looked, not at his people, but above, and kept his eye fixed there)—"I believe that we shall; that His great love shall so delight in making complete our happiness, even by such little memorials of our earthly affections (which must seem like waifs of thistle-down beside the great harvest of His abounding grace), that all the dear faces of those written in the Golden Book shall beam a welcome, all the more bounteous because reflecting His joy who has died to save."

And the listeners whispered each other as he paused, "He thinks of Rachel."

With his eyes still fixed above, he goes on,—

"Sometimes I think thus; but oftener I ask myself, 'Of what value shall human ties be, or their memories, in His august presence whom to look upon is life? What room shall there be for other affections, what room for other memories, than those of "the Lamb that was slain"?'

"Does this sound harshly, my brethren? Ah, let us beware,—let us beware how we entertain any opinions of that future condition of holiness and of joy promised to the elect, which are dependent upon the gross attachments of earth."

"This man lives above the world," said the people; and if some of them did not give very cordial assent to these latter views, they smothered their dissent by a lofty expression of admiration. It is doubtful, indeed, if they did not make a merit of their placid intellectual admission of such beliefs as most violated the natural sensibilities of the heart. As if mere intellectual adhesion to theological formulas were to pave our way to a knowledge of the Infinite,—as if our sensibilities were to be outraged in the march to heaven,—as if all the emotional nature were to be clipped away by the shears of the doctors, leaving only the metaphysic ghost of a soul to enter the joys of Paradise!

Within eight months after his loss, Mr. Johns thought of Rachel only as a gift that

God had bestowed to try him, and had taken away to work in him a humiliation of the heart. More severely than ever he wrestled with the dogmas of his chosen divines, harnessed them to his purposes as preacher, and wrought on with a zeal that knew no abatement and no rest.

XIII

Practical Sympathies

IN the latter part of the summer of 1826,— a reasonable time having now elapsed since the death of poor Rachel,—the gossips of Ashfield began to discuss the lonely condition of their pastor, in connection with some desirable or feasible amendment of it.

There were some invidious persons in the town who had remarked that Miss Almira Tourtelot had brought quite a new fervor to her devotional exercises in the parish within the last year, as well as a new set of ribbons to her hat; and two maiden ladies opposite, of distinguished pretensions and long experience of life, had observed that the young Reuben, on his passage back and forth from the Elderkins, had sometimes been decoyed within the Tourtelot yard, and presented by the admiring Dame Tourtelot with fresh doughnuts.

Dame Tourtelot had crowned with success all her schemes in life, save one. Almira, her daughter, now verging upon her thirty-second year, had long been upon the anxious-seat as regarded matrimony; and with a sentimental turn that incited much reading of Cowper and Montgomery and (if it must be told) "Thaddeus of Warsaw," the poor girl united a sickly, in-door look, and a peaked countenance, which had not attracted wooers. The wonderful executive capacity of the mother had unfortunately debarred her from any active interest in the household; and though the Tourtelots had actually been at the expense of providing a piano for Almira, (the only one in Ashfield,) —upon which the poor girl thrummed, thinking of "Thaddeus," and, we trust, of better things,—this had not won a roseate hue to her face, or quickened in any perceptible degree the alacrity of her admirers.

Upon a certain night of later October, after Almira has retired, and when the Tourtelots are seated by the little fire, which the autumn chills have rendered necessary, and into the embers of which the Deacon has cautiously

PRACTICAL SYMPATHIES

thrust the leg of one of the fire-dogs, preparatory to a modest mug of flip, (with which, by his wife's permission, he occasionally indulges himself,) the good dame calls out to her husband, who is dozing in his chair,—

"Tourtelot!"

But she is not loud enough.

"TOURTELOT! you 're asleep!"

"No," says the Deacon, rousing himself,—"only thinkin'."

"What are you thinkin' of, Tourtelot?"

"Thinkin'—thinkin'," says the Deacon, rasped by the dame's sharpness into sudden mental effort,—"thinkin', Huldy, if it a'n't about time to butcher: we butchered last year nigh on the twentieth."

"Nonsense!" says the dame; "what about the parson?"

"The parson? Oh! Why, I guess the parson 'll take a side and two hams."

"Nonsense!" says the dame, with a great voice; "you 're asleep, Tourtelot. Is the parson a-goin' to marry, or a'n't he? that 's what I want to know;" and she rethreads her needle.

(She can do it by candle-light at fifty-five, that woman!)

"O,——marry?" replies the Deacon, rousing himself more thoroughly,—"waäl, I don't

DOCTOR JOHNS

see no signs, Huldy. If he *doos* mean to, he's sly about it; don't you think so, Huldy?"

The dame, who is intent upon her sewing again,—she is never without her work, that woman!—does not deign a reply.

The Deacon, after lifting the fire-dog, blowing off the ashes, and holding it to his face to try the heat, says,—

"I guess Almira ha'n't much of a chance."

"What 's the use of your guessin'?" says the dame; "better mind your flip."

Which the Deacon accordingly does, stirring it in a mild manner, until the dame breaks out upon him again explosively:

"Tourtelot, you men of the parish ought to *talk* to the parson; it a'n't right for things to go on this way. That boy Reuben is growin' up wild; he wants a woman in the house to look arter him. Besides, a minister ought to have a wife; it a'n't decent to have the house empty, and only Esther there. Women want to feel they can drop in at the parsonage for a chat, or to take tea. But who 's to serve tea, I want to know? Who 's to mind Reuben in meetin'? He broke the cover off the best hymn-book in the parson's pew last Sunday. Who 's to prevent him a-breakin' all the hymn-books that belong to the parish? You men

PRACTICAL SYMPATHIES

ought to speak to the parson; and, Tourtelot, if the others won't do it, you *must.*"

The Deacon was fairly awake now. He pulled at his whiskers deprecatingly. Yet he clearly foresaw that the emergency was one to be met; the manner of Dame Tourtelot left no room for doubt; and he was casting about for such Scriptural injunctions as might be made available, when the dame interrupted his reflections in more amiable humor,—

"It a'n't Almiry, Samuel, I 'm thinkin' of, but Mr. Johns and the good o' the parish. I really don't know if Almiry would fancy the parson; the girl is a good deal taken up with her pianny and books; but there 's the Hapgoods, opposite; there 's Joanny Meacham"—

"You 'll never make that do, Huldy," said the Deacon, stirring his flip composedly; "they 're nigh on as old as the parson."

"Never you mind, Tourtelot," said the dame, sharply; "only you hint to the parson that they 're good, pious women, all of 'em, and would make proper ministers' wives. Do you think I don't know what a man is, Tourtelot! Humph!" And she threads her needle again.

The Deacon was apt to keep in mind his wife's advices, whatever he might do with Scripture quotations. So when he called at

DOCTOR JOHNS

the parsonage, a few days after,—ostensibly to learn how the minister would like his pork cut,—it happened that little Reuben came bounding in, and that the Deacon gave him a fatherly pat upon the shoulder.

"Likely boy you 've got here, Mr. Johns,— likely boy. But, Parson, don't you think he must feel a kind o' hankerin' arter somebody to be motherly to him? I a'most wonder you don't feel that way yourself, Mr. Johns."

"God comforts the mourners," said the clergyman, seriously.

"No doubt on 't, no doubt on 't, Parson; but the Lord sometimes provides comforts ag'in which we shet our eyes. You won't think hard o' me, Parson, but I 've heerd say about the village that Miss Meacham or one of the Miss Hapgoods would make a pooty good minister's wife."

The parson is suddenly very grave.

"Don't repeat such idle gossip, Deacon. I 'm married to my work. The Gospel is my bride now."

"And a very good un it is, Parson. But don't you rather think, naow, that a godly woman for helpmeet would make the work more effectooal? Miss Meacham is a pattern of a body in the Sunday-school. I guess the

PRACTICAL SYMPATHIES

women o' the parish would rather like to find the doors of the parsonage openin' for 'em ag'in."

"That is to be thought of, certainly," said the minister, musingly.

"You won't think hard o' me, Mr. Johns, for droppin' a word about this matter?" says the Deacon, rising to leave. "And while I think on 't, Parson, I see the sill under the no'theast corner o' the meetin'-house has a little settle to 't. I 've jest been cuttin' a few sticks o' good smart chestnut timber; and if the Committee thinks best, I could haul down one or two on 'em for repairs. It won't cost nigh as much as pine lumber, and it 's every bit as good."

Even Dame Tourtelot would have been satisfied with the politic way of the Deacon, both as regarded the wife and the prospective bargain. The next evening the good woman invited the clergyman—begging him "not to forget the dear little boy"—to tea.

This was by no means the first hint which the minister had had of the tendency of village gossip. The Tew partners, with whom he had fallen upon very easy terms of familiarity,—both by reason of frequent visits at their little shop, and by reason of their steady attendance upon his ministrations,—often dropped hints of the smallness of the good man's grocery account, and insidious hopes that it might be doubled in size at some day not far off.

Squire Elderkin, too, in his bluff, hearty way, had occasionally complimented the clergyman upon the increased attendance latterly of ladies of a certain age, and had drawn his attention particularly to the ardent zeal of a buxom, middle-aged widow, who lived upon the skirts of the town, and was "the owner," he said, "of as pretty a piece of property as lay in the county."

"Have you any knack at farming, Mr. Johns?" continued he, playfully.

"Farming? why?" says the innocent parson, in a maze.

"Because I am of opinion, Mr. Johns, that the widow's little property might be rented by you, under conditions of joint occupancy, on very easy terms."

Such badinage was so warded off by the ponderous gravity which the parson habitually wore, that men like Elderkin loved occasionally to launch a quiet joke at him, for the pleasure of watching the rebound.

When, however, the wide-spread gossip of the town had taken the shape (as in the talk of

PRACTICAL SYMPATHIES

Deacon Tourtelot) of an incentive to duty, the grave clergyman gave to it his undivided and prayerful attention. It was over-true that the boy Reuben was running wild. No lad in Ashfield, of his years, could match him in mischief. There was surely need of womanly direction and remonstrance. It was eminently proper, too, that the parsonage, so long closed, should be opened freely to all his flock; and the truth was so plain, he wondered it could have escaped him so long. Duty required that his home should have an established mistress; and a mistress he forthwith determined it should have.

Within three weeks from the day of the tea-drinking with the Tourtelots, the minister suggested certain changes in the long-deserted chamber which should bring it into more habitable condition. He hinted to his man Larkin that an additional fire might probably be needed in the house during the latter part of winter; and before January had gone out, he had most agreeably surprised the delighted and curious Tew partners with a very large addition to his usual orders,—embracing certain condiments in the way of spices, dried fruits, and cordials, which had for a long time been foreign to the larder of the parsonage.

DOCTOR JOHNS

Such indications, duly commented on, as they were most zealously, could not fail to excite a great buzz of talk and of curiosity throughout the town.

"I knew it," says Mrs. Tew, authoritatively, setting back her spectacles from her postal duties;—"these 'ere grave widowers are allers the first to pop off, and git married."

"Tourtelot!" said the dame, on a January night, when the evidence had come in overwhelmingly,—"Tourtelot! what does it all mean?"

"D'n' know," says the Deacon, stirring his flip,—"d'n' know. It's my opinion the parson has his sly humors about him."

"Do you think it's true, Samuel?"

"Waäl, Huldy,—I *du*."

"Tourtelot! finish your flip, and go to bed: it's past ten."

And the Deacon went.

XIV

A New Mistress

TOWARD the latter end of the winter there arrived at the parsonage the new mistress,—

A NEW MISTRESS

in the person of Miss Eliza Johns, the elder sister of the incumbent, and a spinster of the ripe age of three-and-thirty. For the last twelve years she had maintained a lonely, but matronly, command of the old homestead of the late Major Johns, in the town of Canterbury. She was intensely proud of the memory of her father, and of *his* father before him, — every inch a Johns. No light cause could have provoked her to a sacrifice of the name; and of weightier causes she had been spared the trial. The marriage of her brother had always been more or less a source of mortification to her. The Handbys, though excellent plain people, were of no particular distinction. Rachel had a pretty face, with which Benjamin had grown suddenly demented. That source of mortification and of disturbed intimacy was now buried in the grave. Benjamin had won a reputation for dignity and ability which was immensely gratifying to her. She had assured him of it again and again in her occasional letters. The success of an Election Sermon he had preached at the invitation of Gov. Wolcott had been an event of the greatest interest to her, which she had expressed in an epistle of three pages, with every comma in its place, and full of gratulations. Her commas were *always* in place; so were her stops of all kinds. This precision had enabled her to manage the little property which had been left her in such a way as to maintain always about her establishment an air of well-ordered thrift. She concealed adroitly all the shifts—if there were any—by which she avoided the reproach of seeming poor.

In person she was not unlike her father, the Major,—tall, erect, with a dignified bearing, and so trim a figure, and so elastic a step even at her years, as would have provoked an inquisitive follower to catch sight of the face. This was by no means attractive. Her features were thin, her nose unduly prominent; and both eye and mouth, though well formed, carried about them a kind of hard positiveness that would have challenged respect, perhaps, but no warmer feeling. Two little curls were flattened upon either temple; and her necktie, dress, gloves, hat, were always most neatly arranged, and ordered with the same precision that governed all her action. In the town of Canterbury she was an institution. Her charities and all her religious observances were methodical, and never omitted. Her whole life, indeed, was a discipline. Without any great love for children, she still had her Bible-class; and it was rare that the weather or any

A NEW MISTRESS

other cause forbade attendance upon its duties. Nor was there one of the little ones who listened to that clear, sharp, metallic voice of hers but stood in awe of her; not one that could say she was unkind; not one who had ever bestowed a childish gift upon her,—such little gifts as children love to heap on those who have found the way to their hearts.

Sentiment had never been effusive in her; and it was now limited to quick sparkles, that sometimes flashed into a page of her reading. As regarded the serious question of marriage, implying a home, position, the married dignities, it had rarely disturbed her; and now her imaginative forecast did not grapple it with any vigor or longing. If, indeed, it had been possible that a man of high standing, character, cultivation,—equal, in short, to the Johnses in every way,—should woo her with pertinacity, she might have been disposed to yield a dignified assent; but not unless he could be made to understand and adequately appreciate the immense favor she was conferring. In short, the suitor who could abide and admit her exalted pretensions, and submit to them, would most infallibly be one of a character and temper so far inferior to her own that she would scorn him from the outset. This dilemma, imposed by the rigidity of her smaller dignities, that were never mastered or overshadowed either by her sentiment or her passion, not only involved a life of celibacy, but was a constant justification of it, and made it eminently easy to be borne. There are not a few maiden ladies who are thus lightered over the shoals of a solitary existence by the buoyancy of their own intemperate vanities.

Miss Johns did not accept the invitation of her brother to undertake the charge of his household without due consideration. She by no means left out of view the contingency of his possible future marriage; but she trusted largely to her own influences in making it such a one, if inevitable, as should not be discreditable to the family name. And under such conditions she would retire with serene contentment to her own more private sphere of Canterbury,—or, if circumstances should demand, would accept the position of guest in the house of her brother. Nor did she leave out of view her influence in the training of the boy Reuben. She cherished her own hopes of moulding him to her will, and of making him a pride to the family.

There was of course prodigious excitement in the parsonage upon her arrival. Esther had

A NEW MISTRESS

done her best at all household appliances, whether of kitchen or chamber. The minister received her with his wonted quietude, and a brotherly kiss of salutation. Reuben gazed wonderingly at her, and was thinking dreamily if he should ever love her, while he felt the dreary rustle of her black silk dress swooping round as she stooped to embrace him. "I hope Master Reuben is a good boy," said she; "your Aunt Eliza loves all good boys."

He had nothing to say; but only looked back into that cold gray eye, as she lifted his chin with her gloved hand.

"Benjamin, there's a strong look of the Handbys; but it's your forehead. He's a little man, I hope," and she patted him on the head.

Still Reuben looked — wonderingly — at her shining silk dress, at her hat, at the little curls on either temple, at the guard-chain which hung from her neck with a glittering watch-key upon it, at the bright buckle in her belt, and most of all at the gray eye which seemed to look on him from far away. And with the same stare of wonderment, he followed her up and down throughout the house.

At night, Esther, who has a chamber near him, creeps in to say good-night to the lad, and asks, —

"Do you like her, Ruby, boy? Do you like your Aunt Eliza?"

"I d'n know," says Reuben. "She says she likes good boys; don't you like bad uns, Esther?"

"But you 're not *very* bad," says Esther, whose orthodoxy does not forbid kindly praise.

"Did n't mamma like bad uns, Esther?"

"Dear heart!" and the good creature gives the boy a great hug; it could not have been warmer, if he had been her child.

The household speedily felt the presence of the new-comer. Her precision, her method, her clear, sharp voice,—never raised in anger, never falling to tenderness,—ruled the establishment. Under all the cheeriness of the old management, there had been a sad lack of any economic system, by reason of which the minister was constantly overrunning his little stipend, and making awkward appeals from time to time to the Parish Committee for advances. A small legacy that had befallen the late Mrs. Johns, and which had gone to the purchase of the parsonage, had brought relief at a very perplexing crisis; but against all similar troubles Miss Johns set her face most resolutely. There was a daily examination of butchers' and grocers' accounts, that

A NEW MISTRESS

had been previously unknown to the household. The kitchen was placed under strict regimen, into the observance of which the good Esther slipped, not so much from love of it, as from total inability to cope with the magnetic authority of the new mistress.

"Esther, my good woman, it will be best, I think, to have breakfast a little more promptly,—at half-past six, we will say,—so that prayers may be over and the room free by eight; the minister, you know, must have his morning in his study undisturbed."

"Yes, marm," says Esther; and she would as soon have thought of flying over the house-top in her short gown as of questioning the plan.

Again, the mistress says,—"Larkin, I think it would be well to take up those scattered bunches of lilies, and place them upon either side of the walk in the garden, so that the flowers may be all together."

"Yes, marm," says Larkin.

And much as he had loved the little woman now sleeping in her grave, who had scattered flowers with an errant fancy, he would have thought it preposterous to object to an order so calmly spoken, so evidently intended for execution.

DOCTOR JOHNS

The parishioners were not slow to perceive that new order prevailed at the quiet parsonage. Curiosity, no less than the staid proprieties which governed the action of the chief inhabitants, had brought them early into contact with the new mistress. She received all with dignity and with an exactitude of deportment that charmed the precise ones and that awed the younger folks. The bustling Dame Tourtelot had come among the earliest, and her brief report was,—"Tourtelot, Miss Johns 's as smart as a steel trap."

Nor was the spinster sister without a degree of cultivation which commended her to the more intellectual people of Ashfield. She was a reader of "Rokeby" and of Miss Austen's novels, of Josephus and of Rollin's "Ancient History." The Misses Hapgoods, who were the blue-stockings of the place, were charmed to have such an addition to the cultivated circle of the parish. To make the success of Miss Johns still more decided, she brought with her a certain knowledge of the conventionalisms of the city, by reason of her occasional visits to her sister Mabel, (now Mrs. Brindlock, of Greenwich Street,) which to many excellent women gave larger assurance of her position and dignity than all besides. Before the first year of her advent had gone by, it was quite plain that she was to become one of the prominent directors of the female world of Ashfield. Only in the parsonage itself did her influence find its most serious limitations,—and these in connection with the boy Reuben.

XV

Boy Development

THERE is a deep emotional nature in the lad, which, by the time he has reached his eighth year,—Miss Eliza having now been in the position of mistress of the household a twelvemonth,—works itself off in explosive tempests of feeling, with which the prim spinster has but faint sympathy. No care could be more studious and complete than that with which she looks after the boy's wardrobe and the ordering of his little chamber; nay, his caprices of the table are not wholly overlooked, and she hopes to win upon him by the dishes that are most toothsome; but, however grateful for the moment, his boyish affections can never make their way with any force or passionate flow through the stately proprieties of manner with which the spinster aunt is always hedged about.

He wanders away after school-hours to the home of the Elderkins,—Phil and he being sworn friends, and the good mother of Phil always having ready for him a beaming look of welcome and a tender word or two that somehow always find their way straight to his heart. He loiters with Larkin, too, by the great stableyard of the inn, though it is forbidden ground. He breaks in upon the precise woman's rule of punctuality sadly; many a cold dish he eats sulkily,—she sitting bolt upright in her place at the table, looking down at him with glances which are every one a punishment. Other times he is straying in the orchard at the hour of some home-duty, and the active spinster goes to seek him, and not threateningly, but with an assured step and a firm grip upon the hand of the loiterer, which he knows not whether to count a favor or a punishment, (and she as much at a loss, so inextricably interwoven are her notions of duty and of kindness,) leads him homeward, plying him with stately precepts upon the sin of negligence, and with earnest story of the dreadful fate which is sure to overtake all bad boys who do not obey and keep "by the rules."

BOY DEVELOPMENT

"Who was it they called 'bald-head,' Reuben? Elisha or Elijah?"

He, in no mood for reply, is sulkily beating off the daisies with his feet, as she drags him on; sometimes hanging back, with impotent, yet concealed struggle, which she—not deigning to notice—overcomes with even sharper step, and plies him the more closely with the dire results of badness,—has not finished her talk, indeed, when they reach the door-step and enter. There he, fuming now with that long struggle, fuming the more because he has concealed it, makes one violent discharge with a great frown on his little face, "You 're an ugly old thing, and I don't like you one bit!"

Esther, good soul, within hearing of it, lifts her hands in apparent horror, but inwardly indulges in a wicked chuckle over the boy's spirit.

But the minister has heard him, too, and gravely summons the offender into his study.

"My son, Reuben, this is very wrong."

And the boy breaks into a sob at this stage, which is a great relief.

"My boy, you ought to love your aunt."

"But I can't make myself love her, if I don't," says the boy.

"It is your duty to love her, Reuben; and we can all do our duty."

DOCTOR JOHNS

Even the staid clergyman enjoys the boy's discomfiture under so orthodox a proposition. Miss Johns, however, breaks in here, having overheard the latter part of the talk:—

"No, Benjamin, I wish no love that is given from a sense of duty. Reuben sha'n't be forced into loving his Aunt Eliza."

And there is a subdued tone in her speech which touches the boy. But he is not ready yet for surrender; he watches gravely her retirement, and for an hour shows a certain preoccupation at his play; then his piping voice is heard at the foot of the stairway,—

"Aunt Eliza! Are you there?"

"Yes, Master Reuben!"

Master! It cools somewhat his generous intent; but he is in for it; and he climbs the stair, sidles uneasily into the chamber where she sits at her work, stealing a swift, inquiring look into that gray eye of hers,—

"I say—Aunt Eliza—I 'm sorry I said that —you know what."

And he looks up with a little of the old yearning,—the yearning he used to feel when another sat in that place.

"Ah, that is right, Master Reuben! I hope we shall be friends, now."

Another disturbed look at her,—remember-

BOY DEVELOPMENT

ing the time when he would have leaped into a mother's arms, after such struggle with his self-will, and found gladness. That is gone; no swift embrace, no tender hand toying with his hair, beguiling him from play. And he sidles out again, half shamefaced at a surrender that has wrought so little. Loitering, and playing with the balusters as he descends, the swift, keen voice comes after him,—

"Don't soil the paint, Reuben!"

"I have n't."

And the swift command and as swift retort put him in his old, wicked mood again, and he breaks out into a defiant whistle. (Over and over the spinster has told him it was improper to whistle in-doors.) Yet, with a lingering desire for sympathy, Reuben makes his way into his father's study; and the minister lays down his great folio,—it is Poole's "Annotations,"— and says,—

"Well, Reuben!"

"I told her I was sorry," says the boy; "but I don't believe she likes me much."

"Why, my son?"

"Because she called me Master, and said it was very proper."

"But does n't that show an interest in you?"

"Mamma never called me Master," said Reuben.

The grave minister bites his lip, beckons his boy to him,—"Here, my son!"—passes his arm around him, had almost drawn him to his heart,—

"There, there, Reuben; leave me now; I have my sermon to finish. I hope you won't be disrespectful to your aunt again. Shut the door."

In the summer of 1828 Mr. Johns was called upon to preach a special discourse at the Commencement exercises of the college from which he had received his degree; and so sterlingly orthodox was his sermon, at a crisis when some sister colleges were bolstering up certain new theological tenets which had a strong taint of heresy, that the old gentlemen who held rank as fellows of his college, in a burst of zeal, bestowed upon the worthy man the title of D.D.

The spinster sister, with an ill-concealed pride, was most zealous in the bestowal of it; and before a month had passed, she had forced it into current use throughout the world of Ashfield.

Did a neglectful neighbor speak of the good health of "Mr. Johns," the mistress of the parsonage said,—"Why, yes, the Doctor is working very hard, it is true; but he is quite well; the Doctor is remarkably well."

As for Larkin and Esther, who stumbled dismally over the new title, the spinster plied them urgently.

"Esther, my good woman, make the Doctor's tea very strong to-night."

"Larkin, the Doctor won't ride to-day; and mind, you must cut the wood for the Doctor's fire a little shorter."

To the quiet, staid man himself it was a wholly indifferent matter. In the solitude of his study, however, it recalled a neglected duty, and in so far seemed a blessing. By such paltry threads are the colors woven into our life! It recalled his friend Maverick and his jaunty prediction; and upon that came to him a recollection of the promise which he had made to Rachel, that he would write to Maverick.

So the minister wrote, telling his old friend what grief had stricken his house,—how his boy and he were left alone,—how the church, by favor of Providence, had grown under his preaching,—how his sister had come to be mistress of the parsonage,—how he had wrought the Master's work in fear and trembling; and after this came godly counsel for the exile.

"My friend," he wrote, "God's Word is true; God's laws are just; He will come some day in a chariot of fire. Neither moneys nor high places nor worldly honors nor pleasures can stay or avert the stroke of that sword of divine justice which will 'pierce even to the dividing asunder of the joints and marrow.'"

Whether these words of the minister were met, after their transmission over seas, with a smile of derision,—with an empty gratitude, that said, "Good fellow!" and forgot their burden, we will not say.

The cross-ocean mails were slow in those days; and it was not until nearly four months after the transmission of the Doctor's letter—he having almost forgotten it—that Reuben came one day bounding in from the snow in mid-winter, his cheeks aflame with the keen, frosty air, his eyes dancing with boyish excitement:—

"A letter, papa! a letter!—and Mr. Troop" (it is the new postmaster under the Adams dynasty) "says it came all the way from Europe. It's got a funny postmark."

The minister lays down his book,—takes the letter,—opens it,—reads,—paces up and down his study thoughtfully,—reads again, to the end.

"Reuben, call your Aunt Eliza."

There is matter in the letter that concerns her,—that in its issues will concern the boy,—that may possibly give a new color to the life of the parsonage, and a new direction to our story.

XVI

A Surprise

MISS ELIZA being fairly seated in the Doctor's study, with great eagerness to hear what might be the subject of his communication, the parson, with the letter in his hand, asked if she remembered an old college friend, Maverick, who had once paid them a vacation visit at Canterbury.

"Perfectly," said Miss Eliza, whose memory was both keen and retentive; "and I remember that you have said he once passed a night with you, during the lifetime of poor Rachel, here at Ashfield. You have a letter from him?"

"I have," said the parson; "and it brings a proposal about which I wish your opinion." And the Doctor cast his eye over the letter.

"He expresses deep sympathy at my loss, and alludes very pleasantly to the visit you speak of, all which I will not read; after this he says, 'I little thought, when bantering you in your little study upon your family prospects, that I too was destined to become the father of a child, within a couple of years. Yet it is even so; and the responsibility weighs upon me greatly. I love my Adèle with my whole heart; I am sure you cannot love your boy more, though perhaps more wisely.'"

"And he had never told you of his marriage?" said the spinster.

"Never; it is the only line I have had from him since his visit ten years ago."

The Doctor goes on with the reading:—

"It may be from a recollection of your warnings and your distrust of the French character, or possibly it may be from the prejudices of my New England education, but I can't entertain pleasantly the thought of her growing up under the influences about her here. I am sure it will be enough to win upon your sympathy to say that those influences are Popish and thoroughly French. I feel a strong wish, therefore,—much as I am attached to the dear child,—to give her the advantages of a New England education and training.

A SURPRISE

And with this wish, my thought goes back naturally to the quiet of your little town and of your household; for I cannot doubt that it is the same under the care of your sister as in the old time."

"I am glad he thinks so well of me," said Miss Eliza, but with an irony in her tone that she was sure the good parson would never detect.

The Doctor looks at her thoughtfully a moment, over the edge of the letter, — as if he, too, had his quiet comparisons to make, — then goes on with the letter: —

"This wish may surprise you, since you remember my old battlings with what I counted the rigors of a New England 'bringing-up'; but in this case I should not fear them, provided I could assure myself of your kindly supervision. For my little Adèle, besides inheriting a great flow of spirits (from her father, you will say) and French blood, has been used thus far to a catholic latitude of talk and manner in all about her, which will so far counterbalance the gravities of your region as to leave her, I think, upon a safe middle ground. At any rate, I see enough to persuade me to choose rather the errors that may grow upon her girlhood there than those that would grow upon it here.

DOCTOR JOHNS

"Frankly, now, may I ask you to undertake, with your good sister, for a few years, the responsibility which I have suggested?"

The Doctor looked over the edge of the sheet toward Miss Eliza.

"Read on, Benjamin," said she.

"The matter of expenses, I am happy to say, is one which need not enter into your consideration of the question. My business successes have been such that any estimate which you may make of the moneys required will be at your call at the office of our house in Newburyport.

"I have the utmost faith in you, my dear Johns; and I want you to have faith in the earnestness with which I press this proposal on your notice. You will wonder, perhaps, how the mother of my little Adèle can be a party to such a plan; but I may assure you, that, if your consent be gained, it will meet with no opposition in that quarter. This fact may possibly confirm some of your worst theories in regard to French character; and in this letter, at least, you will not expect me to combat them.

"I have said that she has lived thus far under Popish influences; but her religious character is of course unformed; indeed, she has as yet

A SURPRISE

developed in no *serious* direction whatever; I think you will find a *tabula rasa* to write your tenets upon. But, if she comes to you, do not, I beg of you, grave them too harshly; she is too bird-like to be treated with severity; and I know that under all your gravity, my dear Johns, there is a kindliness of heart which, if you only allowed it utterance, would win greatly upon this little fondling of mine. And I think that her open, laughing face may win upon you.

"Adèle has been taught English, and I have purposely held all my prattle with her in the same tongue, and her familiarity with it is such that you would hardly detect a French accent. I am not particularly anxious that she should maintain her knowledge of French; still, should a good opportunity occur, and a competent teacher be available, it might be well for her to do so. In all such matters I should rely greatly on your judgment.

"Now, my dear Johns,"——

Miss Eliza interrupts by saying, "I think your friend is very familiar, Benjamin."

"Why not? why not, Eliza? We were boys together."

And he continues with the letter:—

"My dear Johns, I want you to consider this

matter fairly; I need not tell you that it is one that lies very near my heart. Should you determine to accept the trust, there is a ship which will be due at this port some four or five months from now, whose master I know well, and with whom I should feel safe to trust my little Adèle for the voyage, providing at the same time a female attendant upon whom I can rely, and who will not leave the little voyager until she is fairly under your wing. In two or three years thereafter, at most, I hope to come to receive her from you; and then, when she shall have made a return visit to Europe, it is quite possible that I may establish myself in my own country again. Should you wish it, I could arrange for the attendant to remain with her; but I confess that I should prefer the contrary. I want to separate her for the time, so far as I can, from *all* the influences to which she has been subject here; and further than this, I have a strong faith in that self-dependence which seems to me to grow out of your old-fashioned New England training."

"That is all," said the Doctor, quietly folding the letter. "What do you think of the proposal, Eliza?"

"I like it, Benjamin."

A SURPRISE

The spinster was a woman of quick decision. Had it been proposed to receive an ordinary pupil in the house for any pecuniary consideration, her pride would have revolted on the instant. But here was a child of an old friend of the Doctor, a little Christian waif, as it were, floating toward them from that unbelieving world of France.

"Surely it will be a worthy and an honorable task for Benjamin" (so thought Miss Eliza) "to redeem this little creature from its graceless fortune; possibly, too, the companionship may soften that wild boy, Reuben. This French girl, Adèle, is rich, well-born; what if, from being inmates of the same house, the two should come by and by to be joined by some tenderer tie?"

The possibility, even, of such a dawn of sentiment under the spinster's watchful tutelage was a delightful subject of reflection to her.

Miss Johns, too, without being imaginative, prefigured in her mind the image of the little French stranger, with foreign air and dress, tripping beside her up the meeting-house aisle, looking into her face confidingly for guidance, attracting the attention of the simple townspeople in such sort that a distinction would be-

DOCTOR JOHNS

long to her *protégée* which would be pleasantly reflected upon herself.

"I think," said she, "that you can hardly decline the proposal of Mr. Maverick, Benjamin."

"And you will take the home care of her?" asked the Doctor.

"Certainly. She would at first, I suppose, attend school with Reuben and the young Elderkins?"

"Probably," returned the Doctor; "but the more special religious training which I fear the poor girl needs must be given at home, Eliza."

"Of course, Benjamin."

It was further agreed between the two that a French attendant would make a very undesirable addition to the household, as well as sadly compromise their efforts to build up the little stranger in full knowledge of the faith.

The Doctor was earnest in his convictions of the duty that lay before him, and his sister's consent to share the charge left him free to act. He felt all the best impulses of his nature challenged by the proposal. Here, at least, was one chance to snatch a brand from the burning, — to lead this poor little misguided wayfarer into those paths which are "paths of pleasantness." No image of French grace or of French modes was prefigured to the mind of the parson; his

A SURPRISE

imagination had different range. He saw a young innocent (so far as any child in his view could be innocent) who prattled in the terrible language of Rousseau and Voltaire, who by the providence of God had been born in a realm where all iniquities flourished, and to whom, by the further and richer providence of God, a means of escape was now offered.

Within that very week the Doctor wrote his reply to Maverick. He assured him that he would most gladly undertake the trust he had proposed,—"hoping, by God's grace, to lead the little one away from the delusions of sense and the abominations of Antichrist, to the fold of the faithful."

"My sister has promised," he continued, "to give home care to the little stranger, and will, I am sure, welcome her with zeal. It will be our purpose to place your daughter at the day-school of a worthy person, Miss Betsey Onthank, who has had large experience, and under whose tuition my boy Reuben has been for some time established. My sister and myself are both of opinion that the presence of any French attendant upon the child would be undesirable.

"I hope that God may have mercy upon the French people,—and that those who dwell

DOCTOR JOHNS

temporarily among them may be watched over and be graciously snatched from the great destruction that awaits the ungodly."

XVII

Skirmishings

MEANTIME Reuben grew into a knowledge of all the town mischief, and into the practice of such as came within the scope of his years. The proposed introduction of the young stranger from abroad to the advantages of the parsonage home did not weigh upon his thought greatly. In his private talk with Esther, he had said, "I hope that French girl'll be a *clever* un; if she a'n't, I'll"———and he doubled up a little fist, and shook it, so that Esther laughed outright.

Not that the boy had any cruelty in him, but he was just now learning from his older companions of the village, who were more steeped in iniquity, that defiant manner by which the Devil in all of us makes his first pose preparatory to the onslaught that is to come.

"Nay, Ruby, boy," said Esther, when she had recovered from her laughter, "you

SKIRMISHINGS

would n't hurt the little un, would ye? Don't ye want a little playfellow, Ruby?"

"I don't play with girls, I don't," said Reuben. "But, I say, Esther, what 'll papa do, if she dances?"

"What makes the boy think she 'll dance?" said Esther.

"Because the Geography says the French people dance; and Phil Elderkin showed me a picture with girls dancing under a tree, and, says he, 'That 's the sort that 's comin' to y'r house.'"

"Well, I don't know," said Esther, "but I guess your Aunt Eliza 'd cure the dancin'."

"She would n't cure me, if I wanted to," said Reuben, who thought it needful to speak in terms of bravado about the spinster, with whom he kept up a series of skirmishing fights from week to week. Over and over, she warned him against the evil associates whom he would find about the village tavern, where he strayed from time to time to be witness to some dog-fight, or to receive a commendatory glance of recognition from one Nat Boody, the tavern-keeper's son, who had run away two years before and made a voyage down the river in a sloop laden with apples and onions to "York." He was a head taller than Reuben, and the latter admired him intensely. Reuben absolutely pined in longing wonderment at the way in which Nat Boody could crack a coach-whip, and with a couple of hickory sticks could "call the roll" upon a pine table equal to a drum-major. Such an air, too, as this Boody had, leaning against the pump-handle by his father's door, and making cuts at an imaginary span of horses! —such a pair of twilled trousers, cut like a man's!—such a jacket, with lapels to the pockets, which he said "the sailors wore on the sloops, and called 'em monkey-jackets!"

The truth is, that it was not altogether from admiration of the accomplished Nat Boody that Reuben was prone to linger about the tavern neighborhood. The spinster had so strongly and constantly impressed it upon him that it was a low and vulgar and wicked place, that the boy, growing vastly inquisitive in these years, was curious to find out what shape the wickedness took; and as he walked by, sometimes at dusk, when thoroughly infused with the last teachings of Miss Eliza, it seemed to him that he might possibly catch a glimpse of the hoofs of some devil (as he had seen devils pictured in an illustrated Milton) capering about the doorway,—and if he had seen them, truth compels us to say that he would have felt a strong inclination to follow them up, at a safe distance, in order to see what kind of creatures might be wearing them. But he was far more apt to see the lounging figure of the shoemaker from down the street, or of Mr. Postmaster Troop, coming thither to have an evening's chat about Vice-President Calhoun, or William Wirt and the Anti-Masons. Or possibly, it might be, he would see the light heels of Suke Boody, the pretty daughter of the tavern-keeper, who had been pronounced by Phil Elderkin, who knew (being a year his senior), the handsomest girl in the town. This might well be; for Suke was just turned fifteen, with pink arms and pink cheeks and blue eyes and a great flock of brown hair: not very startling in her beauty on ordinary days, when she appeared in a pinned-up quilted petticoat, and her curls in papers, sweeping the tavern-steps; but of a Saturday afternoon, in red and white calico, with the curls all streaming,— no wonder Phil Elderkin, who was tall of his age, thought her handsome.

Pondering, as Reuben did, upon the repeated warnings of the spinster against any familiarity with the tavern or tavern people, he came in time to reckon the old creaking sign-board, and the pump in the inn-yard, as the pivotal points of all the town wickedness, just as the meeting-house was the centre of all the town goodness; and since the great world was very wicked, as he knew from overmuch iteration at home, and since communication with that wicked world was kept up mostly by the stage-coach that stopped every noon at the tavern-door, it seemed to him that relays of wickedness must flow into the tavern and town daily upon that old swaying stage-coach, just as relays of goodness might come to the meeting-house on some old lumbering chaise of a neighboring parson, who once a month, perhaps, would "exchange" with the Doctor. And it confirmed in Reuben's mind a good deal that was taught him about natural depravity, when he found himself looking out with very much more eagerness for the rumbling coach, that kept up a daily wicked activity about the tavern, than he did for Parson Hobson, who snuffled in his reading, and who drove an old, thin-tailed sorrel mare, with lopped ears and lank jaws, that made passes at himself and Phil, if they teased her,—as they always did.

So, too, he came to regard, in virtue of misplaced home instruction, the monkey-jacket of Nat Boody, and his fighting-dog "Scamp,"

SKIRMISHINGS

and the pink arms and pink cheeks and brown ringlets of Suke Boody as so many types of human wickedness; and, by parity of reasoning, he came to look upon the two flat curls on either temple of his Aunt Eliza, and her pragmatic way, and upon the yellow ribbons within the scoop-hat of Almira Tourtelot, who sang treble and never went to the tavern, as the types of goodness. What wonder, if he swayed more and more toward the broad and easy path that lay around the tavern-pump ("Scamp" lying there biting at the flies), and toward the bar-room, with its flaming pictures of some past menagerie-show, and big tumblers with lemons atop, rather than to the strait and narrow path in which his Aunt Eliza and Miss Almira would guide him with sharp voices, thin faces, and decoy of dyspeptic doughnuts?

Phil and he sauntering by one day, Phil says,—

"Darst you go in, Reub?"

Phil was under no law of prohibition. And Reuben, glancing around the Common, says,—

"Yes, *I* 'll go."

"Then," says Phil, "we 'll call for a glass of lemonade. Fellows 'most always order somethin', when they go in."

So Phil, swelling with his ten years, and tall of his age, walks to the bar and calls for two tumblers of lemonade, which Old Boody stirs with an appetizing rattle of the toddy-stick,—dropping, meantime, a query or two about the Squire, and a look askance at the parson's boy, who is trying very hard to wear an air as if *he,* too, were ten, and knew the ropes.

"It 's good, a'n't it?" says Phil, putting down his money, of which he always had a good stock.

"Prime!" says Reuben, with a smack of the lips.

And then Suke comes in, hunting over the room for last week's "Courant;" and the boys, with furtive glances at those pink cheeks and brown ringlets, go down the steps.

"A'n't she handsome?" says Phil.

XVIII

Expectation

It was some four or five months after the dispatch of the Doctor's letter to Maverick before the reply came. His friend expressed the ut-

EXPECTATION

most gratitude for the Doctor's prompt and hearty acceptance of his proposal.

"I want," said Maverick in his letter, "that Adèle, while having a thorough womanly education, should grow up with simple tastes. I think I see a little tendency in her to a good many idle coquetries of dress (these you will set down, I know, to her French blood), which I trust your good sister will see the prudence of correcting. My fortune is now such that I may reasonably hope to put luxuries within her reach, if they be desirable; but of this I should prefer that she remain ignorant. I want to see established in her what you would call those moral and religious bases of character that will sustain her under any possible reverses or disappointments.

"And now, my dear Johns, I come to refer to a certain allusion in your letter with some embarrassment. You speak of the weight of a mother's religious influence, and ask what it may have been. Since extreme childhood, Adèle has been almost entirely under the care of her godmother, a quiet old lady, who, though a devotee of the Popish Church, you must allow me to say, is a downright good Christian woman. I am quite sure that she has not pressed upon the conscience of little

Adèle any bigotries of the Church. Why it is that the mother's relations with the child have been so broken you will spare me the pain of explaining.

"Would to God, I think at times, that I had married years ago one nurtured in our old-fashioned faith of New England,—some gentle, pure, loving soul! Shall I confess it, Johns?—the little glimpse of your lost Rachel gave me an idea of the tenderness and depth of devotion and charming womanliness of many of those whom I had counted stiff and repulsive, which I never possessed before.

"Pardon me, my friend, for an allusion which may provoke your grief, and which may seem utterly out of place in the talk of one who is just now confiding to you his daughter.

"When little Adèle comes to me, and sits upon my knee, as I write, I almost lose courage.

"'Adèle,' I say, 'will you leave your father, and go far away over seas to stay perhaps for years?'

"'You talk nonsense, papa,' she says, and leaps into my arms.

"My heart cleaves strangely to her: I do not know wholly why. And yet she must go: it is best.

EXPECTATION

"The vessel of which I spoke will sail in three weeks from the date of my letter for the port of New York. I have made ample provision for her comfort on the passage; and as the date of the ship's arrival in New York is uncertain, I must beg you to arrange with some friend there, if possible, to protect the little stranger, until you are ready to receive her. I enclose my draft for three hundred dollars, which I trust may be sufficient for a year's maintenance, seeing that she goes well provided with clothing: if otherwise, you will please inform me."

Dr. Johns was not a man to puzzle himself with idle conjectures in regard to the private affairs of his friend. With all kind feeling for him,—and Maverick's confidence in the Doctor had insensibly given large growth to it,—the parson dismissed the whole affair with this logical reflection:—

My poor friend has been decoyed into marrying a Frenchwoman. Frenchwomen (like Frenchmen) are all children of Satan. He is now reaping the bitter results.

"As for the poor child," thought the Doctor, and his heart glowed at the thought, "I will plant her little feet upon safe places."

He arranges with Mrs. Brindlock to receive

the child temporarily upon her arrival. Miss Eliza puts even more than her usual vigor and system into her arrangements for the reception of the newcomer. Nothing could be neater than the little chamber, provided with its white curtains, its spotless linen, its dark old mahogany furniture, its Testament and Catechism upon the toilet-table; one or two vases of old china had been brought up and placed upon brackets out of reach of the little hands that might have been tempted by their beauty, and a coquettish porcelain image of a flower-girl had been added to the other simple adornments which the ambitious spinster had lavished upon the chamber.

"There," said she to Esther, as she gave a finishing touch to the disposal of the blue and white hangings about the high-post bedstead, "I wonder if that will be to the taste of the little French lady!"

"I should think it might, marm; it's the beautifullest room I ever see, marm."

Reuben, boy-like, passes in and out with an air of affected indifference, as if the arrangements for the new arrival had no interest for him; and he whistles more defiantly than ever.

THE ARRIVAL

XIX

The Arrival

In early September of 1829, when the orchard behind the parsonage was glowing with its burden of fruit, when the white and crimson hollyhocks were lifting their slanted pagodas of bloom all down the garden, and the buckwheat was whitening with its blossoms broad patches of the hill-sides east and west of Ashfield, news came to the Doctor that his expected guest had arrived safely in New York, and was waiting his presence there at the elegant home of Mrs. Brindlock. And Sister Mabel writes to the Doctor, in the letter which conveys intelligence of the arrival,—"She 's a charming little witch; and if you don't like to take her with you, she may stay here." Mrs. Brindlock had no children.

A visit to New York was an event for the parson. The spinster, eager for his good appearance at the home of her stylish sister, insisted upon a toilet that made the poor man more awkward than ever.

The Brindlocks received the parson with an effervescence of kindness that disturbed him almost as much as the stiff garniture in which he had been invested by the solicitude of Miss Eliza; and when, in addition to his double embarrassment, a little saucy-eyed, brown-faced girl, full of mirthful exuberance, with her dark hair banded in a way that was utterly strange to him, and with coquettish bows of ribbon at her throat, at either armlet of her jaunty frock, and all down either side of her silk pinafore, came toward him with a smiling air, as if she were confident of his caresses, the awkwardness of the poor Doctor was complete.

But, catching sight of a certain frank outlook in the little face which reminded him of his friend Maverick, he felt his heart stirred within him, and in his grave way dropped a kiss upon her forehead, while he took both her hands in his.

"This, then, is little Adaly?"

"Ha! ha!" laughed Adèle, merrily, and, turning round to her new-found friends, says,—"My new papa calls me Adaly!"

The straightforward parson was, indeed, as inaccessible to French words as to French principles. Adèle had somewhat a smack in it of the Gallic Pandemonium. Adaly, to his ear, was a far honester sound.

THE ARRIVAL

And the child seemed to fancy it,—whether for its novelty, or the kindliness that beamed on her from the gravest face she had ever seen, it would be hard to say.

"Call me Adaly, and I will call you New Papa," said she.

And though the parson was not a bargaining man, every impulse of his heart went to confirm this arrangement. It was flattering to his self-love, if not to his principles, to have apparent sanction to his prejudices against French forms of speech; and the "New Papa" on the lips of this young girl touched him to the quick.

From all this it chanced that the best possible understanding was speedily established between the Doctor and his little ward from beyond the seas. For an hour after his arrival, the little creature hung upon his chair, asking questions about her new home, about the schools, about her playmates, patting the great hand of the Doctor with her little fingers, and reminding him sadly of days utterly gone.

Mrs. Brindlock, with her woman's curiosity, seizes an occasion, before they leave, to say privately to the Doctor,—

"Benjamin, the child must have a strange mother to allow this long separation, and the little creature so loving as she is."

"It would be strange enough for any but a Frenchwoman," said he.

"But Adèle is full of talk about her father and her godmother; yet she can tell me scarce anything of her mother. There's a mystery about it, Benjamin."

"There's a mystery in all our lives, Mabel, and will be until the last day shall come."

The parson said this with extreme gravity, and then added,—"He has written me regarding it,—a very unfortunate marriage, I fear. Only this much he has been disposed to communicate; and for myself, I am only concerned to redeem his little girl from gross worldly attachments and to lead her to the truths which take hold upon heaven."

The next day the Doctor set off nomeward upon the magnificent new steamboat *Victory*, which, with two wonderful smoke-pipes, was then plying through the Sound and up the Connecticut River. It was an object of almost as much interest to the parson as to his little companion. A sober costume had now replaced the coquettish one with its furbelows, which Adèle had worn in the city; but there was a bright lining to her little hat that made her brown face more piquant than ever. And as she inclined her head jauntily to this side or that, in

THE ARRIVAL

order to a better listening to the old gentleman's somewhat tedious explanations, or with a saucy smile cut him short in the midst of them, the parson felt his heart warming more and more toward this poor child of heathen France. Nay, he felt almost tempted to lay his lips to the little white ears that peeped forth from the masses of dark hair and seemed fairly to quiver with the eagerness of their listening.

With daylight of next morning came sight of the rambling old towns that lay at the river's mouth,—being little more than patches of gray and white, strewed over an almost treeless country, with some central spire rising above them. Then came great stretches of open pasture, scattered over with huge gray rocks, amid which little flocks of sheep were rambling; or some herd of young cattle, startled by the splashing of the paddles, and the great plumes of smoke, tossed their tails in the air, and galloped away in a fright,—at which Adèle clapped her hands, and broke into a laugh that was as cheery as the new dawn. Next came low, flat meadows of sedge, over which the tide oozed slowly, and where flocks of wild ducks, scared from their feeding-ground, rose by scores, and went flapping off seaward in long, black lines. And from between the hills on either side came glimpses of swamp woodland, in the midst of which some maple, earlier than its green fellows, had taken a tinge of orange, and flamed in the eyes of the little traveller with a gorgeousness she had never seen in the woods of Provence. Then came towns nestling under bluffs and red quarrystones, towns upon wooded plains,—all with a white newness about them; and a brig, with horses on its deck, piled over with bales of hay, comes drifting lazily down with the tide, to catch an offing for the West Indies; and queer-shaped flat-boats, propelled by broad-bladed oars, surge slowly athwart the stream, ferrying over some traveller, or some fish-peddler bound to the "P'int" for "sea-food."

Toward noon the travellers land at a shambling dock that juts into the river, from which point they are to make their way, in such country vehicle as the little village will supply, across to Ashfield. And when they are fairly seated within, the parson, judging that acquaintance has ripened sufficiently to be put to serious uses, says, with more than usual gravity,—

"I trust Adaly, that you are grateful to God for having protected you from all the dangers of the deep."

THE ARRIVAL

"Do you think there was much danger, New Papa?"

"There 's always danger," said the parson, gravely. "The *Victory* might have been blown in pieces last night, and we all been killed, Adaly."

"Oh, terrible!" says Adèle. "And did such a thing ever really happen?"

"Yes, my child."

"Tell me all about it, New Papa, please;" and she put her little hand in his.

"Not now, Adaly,—not now. I want to know if you have been taught about God, in your old home."

"Oh, the good God! To be sure I have, over and over and over;" and she made a little piquant gesture, as if the teaching had been sometimes wearisome.

This gayety of speech on such a theme was painful to the Doctor.

"And have you been taught to pray, Adaly?"

"Oh, yes! Listen now. Shall I tell you one of my prayers, New Papa? *Voyons*, how is it ———"

"Never mind,—never mind, Adaly; not here, not here. We are taught to enter into our closets when we pray."

"Closets?"

"Yes, my child,—to be by ourselves, and to be solemn."

"I don't like solemn people much," said Adèle, in a quiet tone.

"But do you love God, my child?"

"Love Him? To be sure I do;" and after a little pause,—"All good children love Him; and I 'm good, you know, New Papa, don't you?"—and she turned her eyes up toward him with a half-coaxing, half-mischievous look that came near to drive away all his solemnity.

"Ah, Adaly! Adaly! we are all wicked!" said he.

Adèle stared at him in amazement.

"You, too! Yet papa told me you were so good! Ah, you are telling me now a little—what you call—lie! a'n't you, New Papa?"

And she looked at him with such a frank, arch smile,—so like the memory he cherished of the college-boy, Maverick,—that he could argue the matter no further, but only patted her little hand, as it lay upon the cushion of the carriage, as much as to say,—"Poor thing! poor thing!"

Upon this, he fell away into a train of grave reflections on the method which it would be best to pursue in bringing this little benighted wanderer into the fold of the faithful.

And he was still musing thus, when suddenly the spire of Ashfield broke upon the view.

"There it is, Adaly! There is to be your new home!"

"Where? where?" says Adèle, eagerly.

And straightway she is all aglow with excitement. Her swift questions patter on the ears of the old gentleman thick as rain-drops. She looks at the houses, the hills, the trees, the face of every passer-by,—wondering how she shall like them all; fashioning to herself some image of the boy Reuben and of the Aunt Eliza who are to meet her; yet, through all the torrent of her vexed fancies, carrying a great glow of hope, and entering, with all her fresh, girlish enthusiasms unchecked, upon that new phase of life, so widely different from anything she has yet experienced, under the grave atmosphere of a New England parsonage.

XX

Adèle Meets Reuben

MISS JOHNS meets the new-comer with as large a share of kindness as she can force into her manner; but her welcome lacks, somehow, the sympathetic glow to which Adèle has been used; it has not even the spontaneity and heartiness which had belonged to the greeting of that worldly woman, Mrs. Brindlock. And as the wondering little stranger passes up the path, and into the door of the parsonage, with her hand in that of the spinster, she cannot help contrasting the one cold kiss of the tall lady in black with the shower of warm ones which her old godmother had bestowed at parting. Yet in the eye of the Doctor sister Eliza had hardly ever worn a more beaming look, and he was duly grateful for the strong interest which she evidently showed in the child of his poor friend. She had equipped herself indeed in her best silk and with her most elaborate toilet, and had exhausted all her strategy,— whether in respect of dress, of decorations for the chamber, or of the profuse supper which was in course of preparation,—to make a profound and favorable impression upon the heart of the stranger.

The spinster was not a little mortified at her evident want of success, most notably in respect to the elaborate arrangements of the chamber of the young guest, who seemed to regard the dainty hangings of the little bed, and the scattered ornaments, as matters of

ADÈLE MEETS REUBEN

course; but making her way to the window which commanded a view of both garden and orchard, Adèle clapped her hands with glee at sight of the flaming hollyhocks and the trees laden with golden pippins. It was, indeed, a pretty scene: silvery traces of the brook sparkled in the green meadow below the orchard, and the hills beyond were checkered by the fields of buckwheat in broad patches of white bloom, and these again were skirted by masses of luxuriant wood that crowned all the heights. To the eye of Adèle, used only to the bare hill-sides and scanty olive-orchards of Marseilles, the view was marvelously fair.

"*Tiens!* there are chickens and doves," said she, still gazing eagerly out; "oh, I am sure I shall love this new home!"

And thus saying, she tripped back from the window to where Miss Eliza was admiringly intent upon the unpacking and arranging of the little wardrobe of her guest. Adèle in the flush of her joyful expectations from the scene that had burst upon her out of doors, now prattled more freely with the spinster,—tossing out the folds of her dresses, as they successively came to light, with her dainty fingers, and giving some quick, girlish judgment upon each.

"This, godmother gave me, dear, good soul! —and she sewed this bow upon it; is n't it coquette? And there 's the white muslin,—oh, how crushed!—that was for my church-dress, first communion, you know; but papa said, 'Better wait,'—so I never wore it."

Thus woman and child grew into easy acquaintance over the great trunk of Adèle: the latter plunging her little hands among the silken folds of dress after dress with the careless air of one whose every wish had been petted; and the spinster forecasting the pride she would herself take in accompanying this little sprite, in these French robes, to the house of her good friends, the Hapgoods, or in exciting the wonderment of those most excellent people, the Tourtelots.

Meantime Reuben, with a resolute show of boyish indifference, has been straying off with Phil Elderkin, although he has caught a glimpse of the carriage at the door. Later he makes his way into the study, where the Doctor, after giving him kindly reproof for not being at home to welcome them, urges upon him the duty of kindness to the young stranger who has come to make her home with them, and trusts that Providence may overrule her presence there to the improvement and blessing

ADÈLE MEETS REUBEN

of both. It is, in fact, a little lecture which the good, but prosy Doctor pronounces to the boy; from which he slipping away, so soon as a good gap occurs in the discourse, strolls with a jaunty affectation of carelessness into the parlor. His Aunt Eliza is there now, seated at the table, and Adèle standing by the hearth, on which a fire has just been kindled. She gives a quick, eager look at him, under which his assumed carelessness vanishes in an instant.

"This is Adèle, our little French guest, Reuben."

The lad throws a quick, searching glance upon her, but is abashed by the look of half-confidence and half-merriment that he sees twinkling in her eye. The boy's awkwardness seems to infect her, too, for a moment.

"I should think, Reuben, you would welcome Adèle to the parsonage," said the spinster.

And Reuben, glancing again from under his brow, sidles along the table, with far less of ease than he had worn when he came whistling through the hall,—sidles nearer and nearer, till she, with a coy approach that seems to be full of doubt, meets him with a little furtive handshake. Then he, retiring a step, leans with one elbow on the friendly table, eyeing her curiously, and more boldly when he discovers that her look is downcast and that she seems to be warming her feet at the blaze.

Miss Johns has watched narrowly this approach of her two *protégés,* with an interest quite uncommon to her; and now, with a policy that would have honored a more adroit tactician, she slips quietly from the room.

Reuben feels freer at this, knowing that the gray eye is not upon the watch; Adèle too, perhaps; at any rate, she lifts her face with a look that invites Reuben to speech.

"You came in a ship, did n't you?"

"Oh, yes, a big, big ship!"

"I should like to sail in a ship," said Reuben; "did you like it?"

"Not very much," said Adèle, "the deck was so slippery, and the waves were so high, oh, so high!"—and the little maid makes an explanatory gesture with her two hands, the like of which for grace and expressiveness Reuben had certainly never seen in any girl of Ashfield. His eyes twinkled at it.

"Were you afraid?" said he.

"Oh, not much."

"Because, you know," said Reuben, consolingly, "if the ship had sunk, you could have come on shore in the small boats." He saw a merry laugh of wonderment threatening in her

ADELE MEETS REUBEN

face, and continued authoritatively, "Nat Boody has been in a sloop, and he says they always carry small boats to pick up people when the big ships go down."

Adèle laughed outright. "But how would they carry the bread, and the stove, and the water, and the anchor, and all the things? Besides, the great waves would knock a small boat in pieces."

Reuben felt a humiliating sense of being no match for the little stranger on sea topics, so he changed the theme.

"Are you going to Miss Onthank's?"

"*That's* a funny name," said Adèle; "that's the school, is n't it? Yes, I suppose I 'll go there: you go, don't you?"

"Yes," says Reuben, "but I don't think I 'll go very long."

"Why not?" says Adèle.

"I 'm getting too big to go to a girls' school," said Reuben.

'Oh!" and there was a little playful malice in the girl's observation that piqued the boy.

"Do the scholars like her?" continued Adèle.

"Pretty well," said Reuben; "but she hung up a little girl about as big as you, once, upon a nail in a corner of the school-room."

"*Quelle bête!*" exclaimed Adèle.

"That's French, is n't it?"

"Yes, and it means she's a bad woman to do such things."

In this way they prattled on, and grew into a certain familiarity; the boy entertaining an immense respect for her French, and for her knowledge of the sea and ships; but stubbornly determined to maintain the superiority which he thought justly to belong to his superior age and sex.

That evening, after the little people were asleep, the spinster and the Doctor conferred together in regard to Adèle. It was agreed between them that she should enter at once upon her school duties, and that particular inquiry concerning her religious beliefs, or particular instruction on that score,—further than what belonged to the judicious system of Miss Onthank,—should be deferred for the present. At the same time the Doctor enjoined upon his sister the propriety of commencing upon the next Saturday evening the usual instructions in the Shorter Catechism, and of insisting upon punctual attendance upon the family devotions.

The spinster had been so captivated by a certain air of modish elegance in Adèle as to lead her almost to forget the weightier obli-

ADELE MEETS REUBEN

gations of her Christian duty toward her. She conceived that she would find in her a means of recovering some influence over Reuben,— never doubting that the boy would be attracted by her frolicsome humor, and would be eager for her companionship. It was possible, moreover, that there might be some appeal to the boy's jealousies, when he found the favors which he had spurned were lavished upon Adèle. It was therefore in the best of temper and with the airiest of hopes (though not altogether spiritual ones) that Miss Eliza conducted the discussion with the Doctor. In two things only they had differed, and in this each had gained and each lost a point. The Doctor utterly refused to confirm his pronunciation to the rigors which Miss Eliza prescribed; for him Adèle should be always and only Adaly. On the other hand, the parson's exactions in regard to sundry modifications of the little girl's dress miscarried; the spinster insisted upon all the furbelows as they had come from the hands of the French *modiste;* and in this she left the field with flying colors.

The next day Doctor Johns wrote to his friend Maverick, announcing the safe arrival of his child at Ashfield, and spoke in terms which were warm for him, of the interest which both his sister and himself felt in her welfare. "He was pained," he said, "to perceive that she spoke almost with gayety of serious things, and feared greatly that her keen relish for the beauties and delights of this sinful world, and her exuberant enjoyment of mere temporal blessings, would make it hard to wean her from them and to center her desires upon the eternal world."

XXI

Miss Onthank

No such event could take place in Ashfield as the arrival of this young stranger at the parsonage, without exciting a world of talk up and down the street. There were stories that she came of a vile Popish family, and there were those who gravely believed that the poor little creature had made only a hair-breadth escape from the thongs of the Inquisition. There were few even of those who knew that she was the daughter of a wealthy gentleman, now domiciled in France, and an old friend of the Doctor's, who did not look upon her with a tender interest, as one miraculously

MISS ONTHANK

snatched by the hands of the good Doctor from the snares of perdition. The gay trappings of silks and ribbons in which she paced up the aisle of the meeting-house upon her first Sunday, under the patronizing eyes of the stern spinster, were looked upon by the more elderly worshippers—most of all by the mothers of young daughters—as the badges of the Woman of Babylon, and as fit belongings to those accustomed to dwell in the tents of wickedness. Even Dame Tourtelot, in whose pew the face of Miss Almira waxes yellow between two great saffron bows, commiserates the poor heathen child who has been decked like a lamb for the sacrifice. "I wonder Miss Eliza don't pull off them ribbons from the little minx," said she, as she marched home in the "intermission," locked commandingly to the arm of the Deacon.

"Waäl, I s'pose they 're paid for," returns the Deacon.

"What 's that to do with it, Tourtelot?"

"Waäl, Huldy, we do pootty much all we can for Almiry in that line: this 'ere Maverick, I guess, doos the same. What 's the odds, arter all?"

"Odds enough, Tourtelot," as the poor man found before bedtime: he had no flip.

The Elderkins, however, were more considerate. Very early after her arrival, Adèle had found her way to their homestead, under the guidance of Miss Eliza, and by her frank, demonstrative manner had established herself at once in the affections of the whole family. The Squire, indeed, had rallied the parson not a little, in his boisterous, hearty fashion, upon his introduction of such a dangerous young Jesuit into so orthodox a parish.

At all which, so seriously uttered as to take the Doctor fairly aback, good Mrs. Elderkin shook her finger warningly at the head of the Squire, and said, "Now, for shame, Giles!"

Good Mrs. Elderkin was, indeed, the pattern woman of the parish in all charitable deeds; not only outside, (where so many charitable natures find their limits,) but in-doors. With gentle speech and gentle manner, she gave, may be, her occasional closet-counsel to the Squire; but most times her efforts to win him to a more serious habit of thought are covered under the shape of some charming plea for a kindness to herself or the "dear girls," which she knows that he will not have the hardihood to resist.

No wonder that the little half-orphaned creature, Adèle, with her explosive warmth of

MISS ONTHANK

heart, is kindly received among the Elderkins. Phil was some three years her senior, a ruddy-faced, open-hearted fellow, who had been well-nurtured, like his two elder brothers, but in whom a certain waywardness just now appearing was attributed very much, by the closely observing mother, to the influence of that interesting, but mischievous boy, Reuben. Phil was the superior in age, indeed, and in muscle, (as we may find proof,) but in nerve-power the more delicate-featured boy of the parson outranked him.

Rose Elderkin was a year younger than the French stranger, and a marvelously fair type of New England girl-beauty: light brown hair in unwieldy masses; skin wonderfully clear and transparent, and that flushed at a rebuke, or a run down the village street, till her cheeks blazed with scarlet; a lip delicately thin, but blood-red, and exquisitely cut; a great hazel eye, that in her moments of glee, or any occasional excitement, fairly danced and sparkled with a kind of insane merriment, and at other times took on a demure and pensive look, which to future wooers might possibly prove the more dangerous of the two. Adèle thinks her very charming; Reuben is disposed to rank her—whatever Phil may think or say—far above

Suke Boody. And in his reading of the delightful "Children of the Abbey," which he has stolen, (by favor of Phil, who owns the book,) he has thought of Rose when Amanda first appeared; and when the divine Amanda is in tears, he has thought of Rose; and when Amanda smiles, with Mortimer kneeling at her feet, he has still thought of Rose.

These four, Adèle, Phil, Rose, and Reuben, are fellow-attendants at the school of the excellent Miss Betsy Onthank, who is a type of a schoolmistress which is found no longer: grave, stately, with two great moppets of hair on either side her brow, (as in the old engravings of Louis Philippe's good queen Amelia,) very resolute, very learned in the boundaries of all Christian and heathen countries, patient to a fault, with a marvellous capacity for pointing out with her bodkin every letter to some wee thing at its first stage of spelling, and yet keeping an eye upon all the school-room; reading a chapter from the Bible, and saying a prayer each morning upon her bended knees,— the little ones all kneeling in concert,—with an air that would have adorned the most stately prioress of a convent; using her red ferule betimes on little, mischievous, smarting hands, yet not over-severe, and kind beneath all her

MISS ONTHANK

gravity. She regards Adèle with a peculiar tenderness, and hopes to make herself the humble and unworthy instrument of redeeming her from the wicked estate in which she has been reared.

Phil and Reuben, being the oldest boys of the school, resent the indignity of being still subject to woman rule by a concerted series of rebellious outbreaks. Some six or eight months after the arrival of Adèle upon the scene, this rebel attitude culminates in an incident that occasions a change of programme. The rebels on their way to school espy a few clam-shells before some huckster's door, and, putting two or three in their pockets, seize the opportunity when the good lady's eyes are closed in the morning prayer to send two or three scaling about the room, which fall with a clatter among the startled little ones. One, aimed more justly by Reuben, strikes the grave mistress full upon the forehead, and leaves a red cut from which one or two beads of blood trickle down.

Adèle, who has not learned yet that obstinate closing of the eyes which most of the scholars have been taught, and to whom the sight recalls the painted heads of martyrs in an old church at Marseilles, gives a little hysteric scream. But the mistress, with face unchanged and voice uplifted and unmoved, completes her religious duty.

The whole school is horrified, on rising from their knees, at sight of the old lady's bleeding head. The mistress wipes her forehead calmly, and, picking up the shell at her feet, says, "Who threw this?"

There is silence in the room.

"Adèle," she continues, "I heard you scream, child; do you know who threw this?"

Adèle gives a quick, inquiring glance at Reuben, whose face is imperturbable, rallies her courage for a struggle against the will of the mistress, and then bursts into tears.

Reuben cannot stand this.

"*I* threw it, marm," says he, with a great tremor in his voice.

The mistress beckons him to her, and, as he walks thither, motions to a bench near her, and says gravely,—

"Sit by me, Reuben."

There he keeps till school-hours are over, wondering what shape the punishment will take. At last, when all are gone, the mistress leads him into her private closet, and says solemnly,—

"Reuben, this is a crime against God. I

forgive you; I hope He may;" and she bids him kneel beside her, while she prays in a way that makes the tears start to the eyes of the boy.

Then, home,—she walking by his side, and leading him straight into the study of the grave Doctor, to whom she unfolds the story, begging him not to punish the lad, believing that he is penitent. And the meekness and kindliness of the good woman makes a Christian picture for the mind of Reuben, in sad contrast with the prim austerity of Aunt Eliza,—a picture that he never loses,—that keeps him meekly obedient for the rest of the quarter; after which, by the advice of Miss Onthank, both Phil and Reuben are transferred to the boys' academy upon the Common.

XXII

Religious Teaching

MEANTIME, Adèle is making friends in Ashfield and in the parsonage. The irrepressible buoyancy of her character cannot be kept under even by the severity of conduct which belongs to the home of the Doctor. If she yields rigid obedience to all the laws of the household, as she is taught to do, her vivacity sparkles all the more in those short intervals of time when the laws are silent. There is something in this beaming mirth of hers which the Doctor loves, though he struggles against the love. He shuts his door fast, that the snatches of some profane song from her little lips (with him all French songs are profane) may not come in to disturb him; but as her voice rises cheerily, higher and higher, in the summer dusk, he catches himself lending a profane ear; the blitheness, the sweetness, the mellowness of her tones win upon his dreary solitude; there is something softer in them than in the measured vocables of sister Eliza; it brings a souvenir of the girlish Rachel, and his memory floats back upon the strains of the new singer, to the days when that dear voice filled his heart; and he thinks—thanking Adaly for the thought—she is singing with the angels now!

But the spinster, who has no ear for music, in the midst of such a carol, will cry out in sharp tones from her chamber, "Adèle, Adèle, not so loud, child! you will disturb the Doctor!"

Even then Adèle has her resource in the

RELIGIOUS TEACHING

garden and the orchard, where she never tires of wandering up and down,—and never wandering there but some fragment of a song breaks from her lips.

From time to time the Doctor summons her to his study to have serious talk with her. She has, indeed, shared the Saturday-night instruction in the Catechism, in company with Reuben, and being quick at words, no matter how long they may be, she has learned it all; and Reuben and she dash through "what is required" and "what is forbidden" and "the reasons annexed" like a pair of prancing horses, kept diligently in hand by that excellent whip, Miss Johns. But the study has not wrought that gravity in the mind of the child which the good parson had hoped for; he therefore, as we have said, summons her from time to time to his study.

And Adèle comes, always at the first summons, with a tripping step, and with a little coquettish adjustment of her dress and hair, flings herself into the big chair before him,—

"Now, New Papa, here I am!"

"Ah, Adaly! I wish, child, that you could be more serious than you are."

"Serious! ha! ha!"—(she sees a look of pain on the face of the Doctor)—"but I will be,—I am;" and with great effort she throws a most unnatural expression of repose into her face.

"You are a good girl, Adaly; but this is not the seriousness I want to find in you. I want you to feel, my child, that you are walking on the brink of a precipice,—that your heart is desperately wicked."

"Oh, no, New Papa! you don't think I 'm desperately wicked?"—and she says it with a charming eagerness of manner.

"Yes, desperately wicked, Adaly,—leaning to the things of this world, and not fastening your affections on things above, on the realities beyond the grave."

"But all that is so far away, New Papa!"

"Not so far as you think, child; they may come to-day."

Adèle is sobered in earnest now, and tosses her little feet back and forth, in an agony of apprehension.

The Doctor continues,——

"To-day, if ye will hear his voice, harden not your hearts;" and the sentiment and utterance are so like to the usual ones of the pulpit, that Adèle takes courage again.

The little girl has a profound respect for the Doctor; his calmness, his equanimity, his persistent zeal in his work, would alone provoke

"Oh, No, New Papa! You don't think I'm desperately wicked?"

RELIGIOUS TEACHING

it. She sees, furthermore,—what she does not see always in "Aunt Eliza,"—a dignity of character that is proof against all irritating humors; then, too, he has appeared to Adèle a very pattern of justice. She had taken exceptions, indeed, when, on one or two rare occasions, he had reached down the birch rod which lay upon the same hooks with the sword of Major Johns, in the study, and had called in Reuben for extraordinary discipline; but the boy's manifest acquiescence in the affair when his cool moments came next morning, and the melancholy air of kindness with which the Doctor went in to kiss him a good-night, after such regimen, kept alive her faith in the unvarying justice of the parson. Therefore she tried hard to torture her poor little heart into a feeling of its own blackness, (for that it was very black she had the good man's averment,) she listened gravely to all he had to urge, and when he had fairly overburdened her with the enumeration of her wicked, worldly appetites, she could only say, with a burst of emotion,—

"Well, but, New Papa, the good God will forgive me."

"Yes, Adaly, yes,—I trust so, if forgiveness be sought in fear and trembling. But remember, 'When God created man, he entered into a covenant of life with him upon condition of perfect obedience.'"

This brings back to poor Adèle the drudgery of the Saturday's Catechism, associated with the sharp correctives of Aunt Eliza; and she can only offer a pleading kiss to the Doctor, and ask plaintively,—

"May I go now?"

"One moment, Adaly,"—and he makes her kneel beside him, while he prays, fervently, passionately, drawing her frail little figure to himself, even as he prays, as if he would carry her with him in his arms into the celestial presence.

The boy Reuben, too, has had his seasons of this closet struggle; but they are rarer now; the lad has shrewdly learned to adjust himself to all the requirements of such occasions. He has put on a leaden acquiescence in the Doctor's theories, whether with regard to sanctification or redemption, that is most disheartening to the parson. Does any question of the Doctor's, by any catch-word, suggest an answer from the "Shorter Catechism" as applicable, Reuben is ready with it on the instant.

Does the Doctor ask,—

"Do you know, my son, the sinfulness of the estate in which you are living?"

RELIGIOUS TEACHING

"Sinfulness of the estate whereunto man fell?" says Reuben, briskly. "Know it like a book:—'Consists-in-the-guilt-of-*Adam's*-first-sin-the-want-of-original-righteousness-and-the-corruption-of-his-whole-nature-which-is-commonly-called-original-sin-together-with-all-actual-transgressions-which-proceed-from-it.' There's a wasp on your shoulder, father,—there's two of 'em. I'll kill 'em."

No wonder the good Doctor is disheartened.

Adèle has no open quarrels with Miss Johns; she is obedient; she, too, has fallen under the influence of that magnetic voice, and accepts the orders and the commendations conveyed by it as if they were utterances of Fate. Yet, with her childish instincts, she has formed a very fair estimate of the character of Miss Eliza; it is doubtful even if she has not fathomed it in certain directions more correctly and profoundly than the grave Doctor. She sees clearly that the spinster's unvarying solicitude in regard to the dress and appearance of "dear Adèle" is due more to that hard pride of character which she nurses every day of her life than to any tenderness for the little stranger.

"Adèle, my dear, you look charmingly to-day, with that pink bow in your hair. Do you know, I think pink is becoming to you, my child?"

And Adèle listens with a composed smile, not unwilling to be admired.

In the bright belt-buckle, in the big leg-of-mutton sleeves, in the glittering brooch containing coils of the Johns' hair, in the jaunty walk and authoritative air of the spinster, the quick, keen eye of Adèle sees something more than the meek Christian teacher and friend. It is a sin in her to see it, perhaps; but she cannot help it.

Miss Johns has not succeeded in exciting the jealousy of Reuben,—at least, not in the manner she had hoped. He sees, indeed, her exaggerated devotion to the little stranger,—which serves in her presence, at least, to call out all his indifference.

But when they meet down the orchard, away from the lynx eye of Aunt Eliza, there are rare apples far out upon overhanging limbs that he can pluck, by dint of venturous climbing, for her; and as he sees through the boughs her delicate figure tripping through the grass, and lingers to watch it, there comes a thought that *she* must be the Amanda of the story, and not Rose,—and he, perched in the apple-tree, a glowing Mortimer.

XXIII

Reuben Leaves Home

In the year 183–, Mr. Maverick writes to his friend Johns that the disturbed condition of public affairs in France will compel him to postpone his intended visit to America, and may possibly detain him for a long time to come. He further says,—"In order to prevent all possible hazards which may grow out of our revolutionary fervor on this side of the water, I have invested in United States securities, for the benefit of my dear little Adèle, a sum of money which will yield some seven hundred dollars a year. Of this I propose to make you trustee, and desire that you should draw so much of the yearly interest as you may determine to be for her best good, denying her no reasonable requests, and making your household reckoning clear of all possible deficit on her account.

"I am charmed with the improved tone of her letters, and am delighted to see by them that even under your grave regimen she has not lost her old buoyancy of spirits. My dear

Johns, I owe you a debt in this matter which I shall never be able to repay. Kiss the little witch for me; tell her that 'Papa' always thinks of her, as he sits solitary upon the green bench under the arbor."

She, gaining in height now month by month, wins more and more upon the grave Doctor,—wins upon Rose, who loves her as she loves her sisters,—wins upon Phil, whose liking for her is becoming demonstrative to a degree that prompts a little jealousy in the warm-blooded Reuben. Day after day, in summer weather, Rose and Adèle idle together along the embowered paths of the village; the Tew partners greet the pair with smiles; good Mistress Elderkin has always a cordial welcome; the stout Squire stoops to kiss the little Jesuit, who blushes at the tender affront through all the brownness of her cheek, like a rose. Day after day the rumble of the mill breaks on the country quietude; and as autumn comes in, burning with all its forest fires, the farmer's flails beat time together, as they did ten years before.

At the academy, Phil and Reuben plot mischief and they cement their friendship with not a few boyish quarrels.

Thus, Reuben, in the way of the boyish

REUBEN LEAVES HOME

pomologists of those days, has buried at midsummer in the orchard a dozen or more of the finest windfalls from the early apple-trees, that they may mellow, away from the air, into good eating condition; and he has marked the spot in his boyish way with a little pyramid of stones. Strolling down the orchard a few days later, he sees Phil coming away from that locality, with his pockets bulging out ominously, and munching a great apple with extraordinary relish. Perhaps there is a thought that he may design a gift out of the stolen stores for Adèle; at any rate, Reuben flies at him.

"I say, Phil, that's doosed mean now, to be stealing my apples!"

"Who's stole your apples?" says Phil, with a great roar of voice.

"You have," says Reuben; and having now come near enough to find his pyramid of stones all laid low, he says more angrily,—"You're a thief! and you've got 'em in your pocket!"

"Thief!" says Phil, looking threateningly, and throwing away his apple half-eaten; "if you call me a thief, I say you're a——you know what."

"Well, blast you," says Reuben, boiling with rage, "say it! Call me a liar, if you dare!"

DOCTOR JOHNS

"I do dare," says Phil, "if you accuse me of stealing your apples; and I say you 're a liar, and be hanged to you!"

At this, Reuben, though he is the shorter by two or three inches, and no match for his foe at fisticuffs, plants a blow straight in Philip's face. (He said afterward, when all was settled, that he was ten times more mortified to think that he had done such a thing in his father's orchard.)

But Phil closed upon him, and kneading him with his knuckles in the back, and with a trip, threw him heavily, falling prone upon him. Reuben, in a frenzy, and with a torrent of much worse language than he was in the habit of using, was struggling to turn him, when a sharp, loud voice, which they both knew only too well, came down the wind,—"Boys! boys!" and presently the Doctor comes up panting.

"What does this mean? Philip, I 'm ashamed of you!" he continues; and Philip rises.

Reuben, rising, too, the instant after, and with his fury unchecked, dashes at Phil again; when the Doctor seizes him by the collar and drags him aside.

"He struck me," says Phil.

"And he stole my apples and called me a

liar," says Reuben, with the tears starting, though he tries desperately to keep them back, seeing that Phil shows no such evidence of emotion.

"Tut! tut!" says the Doctor,—"you are both too angry for a straight story. Come with me."

And taking each by the hand, he led them through the garden and house, directly into his study. There he opens a closet-door, with the sharp order, "Step in here, Reuben, until I hear Philip's story." This Phil tells straightforwardly,—how he was passing through the orchard with a pocketful of apples, which a neighbor's boy had given, and how Reuben came upon him with swift accusation, and then the fight. "But he hurt me more than I hurt him," says Phil, wiping his nose, which showed a little ooze of blood.

"Good!" says the Doctor,—"I think you tell the truth."

"Thank you," says Phil,—"I know I do, Doctor."

Next Reuben is called out.

"Do you *know* he took the apples?" asks the Doctor.

"Don't know," says Reuben,—"but he was by the place, and the stones thrown down."

DOCTOR JOHNS

"And is that sufficient cause, Reuben, for accusing your friend?"

At which, Reuben, shifting his position uneasily from one foot to the other, says,—

"I believe he did, though."

"Stop, sir!" says the Doctor in a voice that makes Reuben sidle away.

"Here," says Phil, commiserating him in a grand way, and beginning to discharge his pockets on the Doctor's table,. "he may have them, if he wants them."

Reuben stares at them a moment in astonishment, then breaks out with a great tremor in his voice, but roundly enough,—

"By George! they 're not the same apples at all. I 'm sorry I told you that, Phil."

"Don't say 'By George' before me, or anywhere else," says the Doctor, sharply. "It 's but a sneaking oath, sir; yet" (more gently) "I 'm glad of your honesty, Reuben."

At the instigation of the parson they shake hands; after which he leads them both into his closet, beckoning them to kneel on either side of him, as he commends them in his stately way to heaven, trusting that they will live in good fellowship henceforth, and keep His counsel, who was the great Peacemaker, always in their hearts.

REUBEN LEAVES HOME

Next morning, when Reuben goes to reconnoiter the place of his buried treasure, he finds all safe, and taking the better half of the fruit, he marches away with a proud step to the Elderkin house. The basket is for Phil. But Phil is not at home; so he leaves the gift, and a message, with a short story of it all, with the tender Rose, whose eyes dance with girlish admiration at this stammered tale of his, and her fingers tremble when they touch the boy's in the transfer of his little burden.

Reuben walks away prouder yet; is not this sweet-faced girl, after all, Amanda?

There come quarrels, however, with the academy teacher not so easily smoothed over. The Doctor and the master hold long consultations. Reuben, it is to be feared, has bad associates. The boy makes interest, through Nat Boody, with the stage-driver; and one day the old ladies are horrified at seeing the parson's son mounted on the box of the coach beside the driver, and putting his boyish fingers to the test of four-in-hand. Of course he is a truant that day from school, and toiling back footsore and weary, after tea, he can give but a lame account of himself. He brings, another time, a horrid fighting cur, (as Miss Eliza terms it in her disgust,) for which he has bartered away the new muffler that the spinster has knit. He thinks it a splendid bargain. Miss Johns and the Doctor do not.

He is reported by credible witnesses as loitering about the tavern in the summer nights, long after prayers are over at the parsonage, and the lights are out; thus it is discovered, to the great horror of the household, that by connivance with Phil he makes his way over the roof of the kitchen from his chamber-window to join in these night forays. After long consideration, in which Grandfather Handby is brought into consultation, it is decided to place the boy for a while under the charge of the latter for discipline, and with the hope that removal from his town associates may work good. But within a fortnight after the change is made, Grandfather Handby drives across the country in his wagon, with Reuben seated beside him with a comic gravity on his face; and the old gentleman, pleading the infirmities of age, and giving the boy a farewell tap on the cheek, (for he loves him, though he has whipped him almost daily,) restores him to the paternal roof.

At this crisis, Squire Elderkin—who, to tell truth, has a little fear of the wayward propensities of the parson's son in misleading Phil—

REUBEN LEAVES HOME

recommends trial of the discipline of a certain Parson Brummem who fills the parish-pulpit upon Bolton Hill. This dignitary was a tall, lank, leathern-faced man, of incorruptible zeal and stately gravity, who held under his stern dominion a little flock of two hundred souls, and who, eking out a narrow parochial stipend by the week-day office of teaching, had gained large repute for his subjugation of refractory boys.

A feeble little invalid wife cringed beside him along the journey of life; and it would be pitiful to think that she had not long ago entered, in way of remuneration, upon paths of pleasantness beyond the grave.

Parson Brummem received Brother Johns, when he drove with Reuben to the parsonage-door, on that wild waste of Bolton Hill, with all the unction of manner that belonged to him; but it was so grave an unction as to chill poor Reuben to the marrow of his bones. A week's experience only dispersed the chill when the tingle of the parson's big rod wrought a glow in him that was almost madness. Yet Reuben chafed not so much at the whippings—to which he was well used—as at the dreariness of the new home, the melancholy waste of common over which March winds blew all

DOCTOR JOHNS

the year, the pinched faces that met him without other recognition than, "One o' Parson Brummem's b'ys." Nor in-doors was the aspect more inviting: a big red table around which sat six fellow-martyrs with their slates and geographies, a tall desk at which Brummem indited his sermons, and from time to time a little side-door opening timidly, through which came a weary woman's voice, "Ezekiel, dear, one minute!" at which the great man strides thither, and lends his great ear to the family council.

Ah, the long, weary mornings, when the sun, pouring through the curtainless south windows a great blaze upon the oaken floor, lights up for Reuben only the cob-webbed corners, the faded roundabouts of fellow-martyrs, the dismal figures of Daboll, the shining tail-coat of Master Brummem, as he stalks up and down from hour to hour, collecting in this way his scattered thoughts for some new argumentative thrust of the quill into the sixthly or the seventhly of his next week's sermon! And the long and weary afternoons, when the sun with a mocking bounty pours through the dusty and curtainless windows to the west, lighting only again the gray and speckled roundabouts of the fagging boys, the maps of

REUBEN LEAVES HOME

Malte-Brun, and the shining forehead of the Brummem!

There is a dismal, graceless, bald air about town and house and master, which is utterly revolting to the lad, whose childish feet had pattered beside the tender Rachel along the embowered paths of Ashfield. The lack of congeniality affronts his whole nature. In the keenness of his martyrdom, (none the less real because fancied,) the leathern-faced, gaunt Brummem takes the shape of some Giant Despair with bloody maw and mace,—and he, the child of some Christiana, for whose guiding hand he gropes vainly: she has gone before to the Celestial City!

The rod of the master does not cure the chronic state of moody rebellion into which Reuben lapses, with these fancies on him. It drives him at last to an act of desperation. The lesson in Daboll that day was a hard one; but it was not the lesson, or his short-comings in it,—it was not the hand of the master, which had been heavy on him,—but it was a vague, dismal sense of the dreariness of his surroundings, of the starched looks that met him, of the weary monotony, of the lack of sympathy, which goaded him to the final overt act of rebellion,—which made him dash his leathern-

DOCTOR JOHNS

bound arithmetic full into the face of the master, and then sit down, burying his face in his hands.

The stern doctrines of Parson Brummem had taught him, at least, a rigid self-command. He did not strike the lad. But recovering from his amazement, he says, "Very well, very well, Master Reuben, we will sleep upon this"; and then, tapping at the inner door, "Keziah, make ready the little chamber over the hall for Master Johns: he must be by himself to-night: give him a glass of water and a slice of dry bread: nothing else, sir, (turning to Reuben now,) until you come to me to-morrow at nine, in this place, and ask my pardon"; and he motions him to the door.

Reuben staggers out,—staggers up-stairs into the dismal chamber. It looks out only upon a bald waste of common. Shortly after, a slatternly maid brings his prison fare, and, with a little kindly discretion, has added secretly a roll of gingerbread. Reuben thanks her, and says, "You 're a good woman, Keziah; and I say, won't you fetch my cap, there 's a good un; it 's cold here." The maid, with great show of caution, complies; a few minutes after, the parson comes, and looking in warningly, closes and locks the door outside.

XXIV

Reuben Escapes

A WEARY evening follows, in which thoughts of Adèle, of nights at the Elderkins', of Phil, of Rose, flash upon him, and spend their richness, leaving him more madly disconsolate. Then come thoughts of the morning humiliation, of the boys pointing their fingers at him after school.

"No, they sha'n't, by George!"

And with this decision he dropped asleep; with this decision ripened in him, he woke at three in the morning,—waited for the hall clock to strike, that he might be sure of his hour,—tied together the two sheets of Mistress Brummem's bed, opened the window gently, dropped out his improvised cable, slid upon it safely to the ground, and before day had broken or any of the towns-folk were astir, had crossed all the more open portion of the village, and by sunrise had plunged into the wooded swamp-land which lay three miles westward toward the river.

At nine next morning, prayers and break-

DOCTOR JOHNS

fast being dispatched,—during which Parson Brummem had determined to leave Reuben to the sting of his conscience,—the master appears in the school-room with his wristbands turned up, and his ferule in hand, to enforce judgment upon the culprit. It had been a frosty night, and the cool October air had not tempted the boys to any wide movement out of doors, so that no occupant of the parsonage had as yet detected the draggled white banner that hung from the prison-window.

Through Keziah, the parson gave orders for Master Johns to report himself at once in the school-room. The maid returned presently, clattering down the stairs in a great fright,—

"Reuben's gone, sir!"

"Gone?" says the tall master, astounded. He represses a wriggle of healthful satisfaction on the part of his pupils by a significant lift of his ferule, then moves ponderously up the stairs for a personal visit to the chamber of the culprit. The maid had given true report; there was no one there. Never had he been met with such barefaced rebellion. Truants, indeed, there had been in days gone by; but that a pupil under discipline should have tied together Mistress Brummem's linen and left it draggling in this way, in the sight of every

REUBEN ESCAPES

passer-by, was an affront to his authority which he had not deemed possible.

An hour thereafter, and he had assigned the morning's task to the boys (which he had ventured to lengthen by a third, in view—as he said, with a grim humor—of their extremely cheerful spirits); established Mistress Brummem in temporary charge, and was driving his white-faced nag down the road which led toward Ashfield. The frosted pools crackled under the wheels of the old chaise; the heaving horse wheezed as the stern parson gave his loins a thwack with the slackened reins, and urged him down the turnpike which led away through the ill-kept fields, from the rambling, slatternly town. Stone walls that had borne the upheaval of twenty winters reeled beside the way. Broad scars of ocherous earth, from which the turnpike-menders had dug material to patch the wheel-track, showed ooze of yellow mud with honeycombs of ice rimming their edges, and supporting a thin film of sod made up of lichens and the roots of five-fingers. Raw, shapeless stones, and bald, gray rocks, only half unearthed, cumbered the road; while bunches of dwarfed birches, browsed by straying cattle, added to the repulsiveness of the scene. Nor were the enclosed lands scarcely more inviting. Lean shocks of corn that had swayed under the autumn winds stretched at long intervals across fields of thin stubble; a few half-ripened pumpkins, hanging yet to the seared vines,—whose leaves had long since been shrivelled by the frost,—showed their shining green faces on the dank soil. In other fields, overrun with a great shaggy growth of rag-weed, some of the parson's flock—father and blue-nosed boys—were lifting poor crops of "bile-whites" or "merinos." From time to time, a tall house jutted upon the road, with unctuous pig-sty under the lee of the garden-fence and wood-pile sprawling into the highway, where the parson would rein up his nag, and make inquiry after the truant Reuben.

A half-dozen of these stops and inquiries proved wholly vain; yet the sturdy parson urged his poor, heaving nag forward, until he had come to the little gate-house which thrust itself quite across the high road at some six miles' distance from Bolton Church. No stray boy had passed that day. Thereupon the parson turned, and, after retracing his way for two miles or more, struck into a cross-road which led westward. There were the same fruitless inquiries here at the scattered houses, and when he came at length upon the great

REUBEN ESCAPES

river-road along which the boy had passed at the first dawn, there was no one who could tell any thing of him; and by noon the parson reëntered the village, disconsolate and hungry. He was by no means a vindictive man, and could very likely have forgiven Reuben the blow he had struck. He had no conception of the hidden causes which had wrought in the lad such burst of anger. He conceived only that Satan had taken hold of him, and he had strong faith in the efficacy of the rod for driving Satan out.

After dinner he administered a sharp lecture to his pupils, admonishing them of the evils of disobedience, and warning them that "God sometimes left bad boys to their own evil courses, and to run like the herd of swine into which the unclean spirits entered,—of which account might be found in Mark v. 13,—down a steep place, and be choked."

The parson still had hope that Reuben might appear at evening; and he forecast a good turn which he would make, in such event, upon the parable of the Prodigal Son (with the omission, however, of the fatted calf). But the prodigal did not return. Next day there was the same hope, but fainter. Still, the prodigal Reuben did not return. Whereupon the parson thought it his duty to write to Brother Johns, advising him of the escape of Reuben, —"he having stolen away in the night, tying together and much draggling Mrs. Brummem's pair of company sheets, (no other being out of wash,) and myself following after vainly, the best portion of a day, much perturbed in spirit, in my chaise. I duly instructed my parishioners to report him, if found, which has not been the case. I trust that in the paternal home, if he has made his way thither, he may be taught to open his 'ear to discipline,' and 'return from iniquity.' Job xxxvi. 10."

The good parson was a type of not a few retired country ministers in New England forty years ago: a heavy-minded, right-meaning man; utterly inaccessible to any of the graces of life; no bird ever sang in his ear; no flower ever bloomed for his eye; a man to whom life was only a serious spiritual toil, and all human joys a vanity to be spurned; preaching tediously long sermons, and counting the fatigue of the listeners a fitting oblation to spiritual truth; staggering through life with a great burden of theologies on his back, which it was his constant struggle to pack into smaller and smaller compass,—not so much, we fear, for the relief of others as of himself. Let us hope that the burden—like that of Christian in the "Pilgrim's Progress"—slipped away before he entered the Celestial Presence, and left him free to enjoy and admire, more than he found time to do on earth, the beauty of that blessed angel in the higher courts whose name is Charity.

XXV

Reuben's Voyage

Reuben, meantime, pushed boldly down the open road, until broad sunlight warned him to a safer path across the fields. He had been too much of a rambler during those long Saturday afternoons at Ashfield, to have any dread of a tramp through swamp-land or briers. "Who cared for wet feet or a scratch? Who cared for a rough scramble through the bush, or a wade (if it came to that) through ever so big a brook? Who cared for old Brummem and his white-faced nag?" In fact, he had the pleasure of seeing the parson's venerable chaise lumbering along the public road at a safe distance away, an hour before noon; and he half wished he were near enough to

DOCTOR JOHNS

give the jolly old nag a good switching across the flanks. He had begged a bit of warm breakfast in the morning at an outlying house, and at the hour when he caught sight of his pursuer he was lying under the edge of a wood, lunching upon the gingerbread Keziah had provided, and beginning to reckon up soberly what was to be done.

His first impulse had been simply to escape a good flogging and the taunts of the boys. He had shunned the direct Ashfield turnpike, because he knew pursuit—if there were any—would lead off in that direction. From the river road he might diverge into that, if he chose. But if he went home,—what then? The big gray eyes of Aunt Eliza he knew would greet him at the door, looking thunderbolts. Adèle, and may be Rose, would welcome him in kindly way enough,—but very pityingly, when the Doctor should summon him quietly into his low study. For they knew, and he knew, that the big rod would presently come down from its place by the Major's sword,—a rod that never came down, except it had some swift office to perform. And next day, perhaps,—whatever might be the kindly pleadings of Adèle, (thus far he flattered himself,) the old horse Dobbins would be in harness to carry him back to Bolton Hill, where of a surety some new birch was already in pickle for the transgressor. Or, if this mortification were spared, there would be the same weary round of limitations and exactions from which he longed to break away. And as he sits there under the lee of the wood,—seeing presently Brummem's heavy cavalry wheel and retire from pursuit,—the whole scene of his last altercation in the study at Ashfield drifts before him again clear as day.

After it had closed the Doctor, in an agony of spirit, (the boy recalled it perfectly,) had risen and paced back and forth in his study; then, after a little, threw himself upon his knees near to Reuben, and prayed silently, with his hands clasped.

The boy had melted somewhat at this, and still more when the father rose with traces of a tear in his eye.

"Are you not softened now, my son?"

"I always am when I see you going on that way," said Reuben.

"My poor son!"—and he had drawn the boy to him, gazing into the face from which the blue eyes of the lost Rachel looked calmly out, moved beyond himself.

If, indeed, the lost Rachel had been really

DOCTOR JOHNS

there between the two, to interpret the heart of the son to the father!

Is Reuben whimpering as the memory of this last tender episode comes to his memory? What would Phil or the rest of the Ashfield fellows say to a runaway boy sniffling under the edge of the wood? Not he, by George! And he munches at his roll of gingerbread with a new zest,—confirming his vagabond purpose, that just now wavered, with a thought of those tedious Saturday nights and the "reasons annexed," and Aunt Eliza's sharp elbow nudging him upon the hard pew-benches, as she gives a muffled, warning whisper,—"Attend to the sermon, Reuben!"

And so, with glorious visions of Sindbad the Sailor in his mind, and a cheery remembrance of Crusoe when he cut himself adrift from home and family for his wonderful adventures, Reuben pushes gallantly on through the woods in the direction of the river. He knows that somewhere, up or down, a sloop will be found bound for New York. From the heights around Ashfield, he has seen, time and again, their white sails specking some distant field of blue. Once, too, upon a drive with the Doctor, he had seen these marvellous vessels from a nearer point, and had looked wistfully upon their white decks and green companion-ways.

Overhead the jays cried from the bare chestnut-trees; from time to time the whirr of a brood of partridges started him; the red squirrels chattered; still he pushed on, catching a chance dinner at a wayside farm-house, and by night had come within plain sight of the water.

The sloop *Princess* lay at the Glastonbury dock close by, laden with wood and potatoes, and bound for New York the next morning. The kind-hearted skipper, who was also the owner of the vessel, took a sudden fancy to the sore-footed, blue-eyed boy who came aboard to bargain for a passage to the city. The truant was not, indeed, overstocked with ready money, but was willing to pawn what valuables he had about him, and hinted at a rich aunt in the city who would make good what moneys were lacking. The skipper has a shrewd suspicion how the matter stands, and, with a kindly sympathy for the lad, consents to give him passage on condition he drops a line into the mail to tell his friends which way he has gone; and taking a dingy sheet of paper from the locker under his berth, he seats Reuben with pen in hand at the cabin-table, whereupon the boy writes,—

"Dear Father,—I have come away from school. I don't know as you will like it much. I walked all the way from Bolton, and my feet are very sore; I don't think I could walk home. Captain Saul says he will take me by the way of New York. I can go and see Aunt Mabel. I will tell her you are all well.

"How is Adèle and Phil and Rose and the others? I hope you won't be very angry. I don't think Mr. Brummem's is much of a school. I don't learn so much there as I learned at home. I don't think the boys there are good companions. I think they are wicked boys sometimes. Mr. Brummem says they are. And he whips awful hard.

"Yr affect. son,
"Reuben."

And the skipper, taking the letter ashore to post it, adds upon the margin,—

"I opened the Within to see who the boy was; and This is to say, I shall take him Aboard, and shall be off Chatham Red Quarries to-morrow night and next day morning, and, if you signal from the dock, can send him Ashore. Or, if this don't Come in time, my berth is Peck Slip, in York.

"John Saul, Sloop *Princess*."

REUBEN'S VOYAGE

Next day they go drifting down the river. A quiet, smoky October day; the distant hills all softened in the haze; the near shores green with the fresh-springing aftermath. Reuben lounged upon the sunny side of the mainsail, thinking, with respectful pity, of the poor fagged fellows in runabouts who were seated at that hour before the red desks in Parson Brummem's school-room. At length he was enjoying a taste of that outside life of which he had known only from travellers' books, or from such lucky ones as the accomplished Tavern Boody. Henceforth he, too, would have his stories to tell. The very rustle of the water around the prow of the good sloop *Princess* was full of Sindbad echoes. For ten hours the Captain lies off Chatham Quarries, taking on additional freight there; but there is no signal from the passenger dock. The next morning the hawsers were cast off, and the mainsail run up again while the *Princess* surged away into the middle of the current.

"Now, my boy, we're in for a sail!" said Captain Saul.

"I'm glad," said Reuben, who would have been doubly glad, if he had known of his narrow escape at the last landing.

"I suppose you have n't much of a kit?" said the Captain.

The truth is, that a pocket-comb was the extent of Reuben's equipment for the voyage. It came out on further talk with the Captain; and the boy was mortified to make such small show of appliances.

"Well, well," says the Captain, "we must keep this toggery for the city, you know"; and he finds a blue woolen shirt,—for the boy is of good height for his years,—and a foremast hand shortens in a pair of old duck trousers for him, in which Reuben paces up and down the deck, with a mortal dread at first lest the boom may make a dash against the wind and knock him overboard, in quite sailorly fashion. The beef is hard indeed; but a page or two out of "Dampier's Voyages," of which an old copy is in the cabin, makes it seem all right. The shores, too, are changing from hour to hour; a brig drifts within hail of them, which Reuben watches, half envying the fortunate fellows in red shirts and tasselled caps aboard, who are bound to Cuba, and in a fortnight's time can pluck oranges off the trees there, to say nothing of pine-apples and sugar-cane.

Over the Saybrook Bar there is a plunging of the vessel which horrifies him somewhat;

REUBEN'S VOYAGE

but smooth weather follows, with long lines of hills half-faded on the rim of the water, and the country sounds at last all dead. A day or two of this, with only a mild autumnal breeze, and then a sharp wind,—with the foam flying over forecastle and wood-pile, between the winding shores, toward Flushing Bay,—brings sight of great white houses with green turf coming down to the rocks, where the waves play and break among the drifted sea-weed. Captain Saul is fast at his helm, while the big boom creaks and crashes from side to side as he beats up the narrowing channel, rounding Throg's Point, where the light-house and old whitewashed fort stand shining in the sun,— skirting low rocky islands, doubling other points, dashing at half-tide through the roar and whirl of Hell Gate,—Reuben glowing with excitement, and mindful of Kidd and of his buried treasure along these shores. Then came the turreted Bridewell, and at last the spires, the forest of masts, with all that prodigious, crushing, bewildering effect with which the first sight of a great city weighs upon the thought of a country-taught boy.

"Now mind the rogues, Reuben," said Captain Saul, when they were fairly alongside the dock; "and keep by your bunk for a day or two, boy. Don't stray too far from the vessel, —*Princess,* Captain Saul, remember."

XXVI

A Rosary

The Doctor is not a little shocked by the note which he receives from Reuben, and which comes too late for the interception of the boy upon the river. He writes to Mrs. Brindlock, begging the kind offices of her husband in looking after the lad, until such time as he can come down for his recovery. The next day, to complete his mortification, he receives the epistle of Brother Brummem.

The growing vagabondage of the boy distressed him the more by reason of his own responsible connection with the little daughter of his French friend. How should he, who could not guide in even courses the child of his own loins, presume to conduct the little exile from the heathen into paths of piety?

And yet, strange to say, the character of the blithe Adèle, notwithstanding the terrible nature of her early associations, seems to fuse more readily into agreement with the moral atmosphere about her than does that of the recreant boy. If the lithe spirit of the girl bends under the grave teachings of the Doctor, it bends with a charming grace, and rises again smilingly, when sober speech is done, like the floweret she is. And if her mirth is sometimes irrepressible through the long hours of their solemn Sundays, it breaks up like bubbles from the deep quiet bosom of a river, cheating even the grave parson to a smile that seems scarcely sinful.

"Oh, that sermon was so long,—so long to-day, New Papa! I am sure Dame Tourtelot pinched the Deacon, or he would never, never have been awake through it all."

Or, may be, she steals a foot out of doors on a Sunday to the patch of violets, gathering a little bunch, and appeals to the Doctor, who comes with a great frown on his face,—

"New Papa, is it most wicked to carry flowers or fennel to church? Godmother always gave me a flower on holydays."

And the Doctor is cheated of his rebuke; nay, he sometimes wonders, in his self-accusing moments, if the Arch-Enemy himself has not lodged under cover of that smiling face of hers, and is thus winning him to a sinful gayety.

DOCTOR JOHNS

There were snatches, too, of Latin hymns, taught her by the godmother, and only half remembered,—hymns of glorious rhythm, which, as they tripped from her halting tongue, brought a great burden of sacred meanings, and were full of the tenderest associations of her childhood. To these, too, the Doctor was half pained to find himself listening, sometimes at nightfall of a Sunday, with an indulgent ear, and stoutly querying with himself if Satan could fairly lurk in such holy words as

"Dulcis memoria Jesu."

Adèle, with that strong leaning which exists in every womanly nature toward religious faith of some kind, had grown into a respect for even the weightiest of the Christian gravities around her. And if sometimes, as the shrill treble of Miss Almira smote upon her ear, she craved a better music, and remembered the fragrant cloud rising from silver censers as something more grateful than the smoke leaking from the joints of the stovepipe in Ashfield meeting-house, and would have willingly given up Miss Eliza's stately praises of her recitation for one good hug of the godmother,—she yet saw, or thought she saw, the

A ROSARY

same serene trust that belonged to her in the eyes of good Mistress Onthank, in the kind face of Mrs. Elderkin, and in the calm look of the Doctor when he lifted his voice every night at the parsonage in prayer for "all God's people."

Would it be strange, too, if in the heart of a girl taught as she has been, who had never known a mother's tenderness, there should be some hidden leaning toward those traditions of the Romish faith in which a holy mother appeared as one whose favor was to be supplicated? The worship of the Virgin was, indeed, too salient an object of attack among the heresies which the New England teachers combated, not to inspire a salutary caution in Adèle and entire concealment of any respect she might still feel for the Holy Mary. Nor was it so much a respect that shaped itself tangibly among her religious beliefs as a secret craving for that outpouring of maternal love denied her on earth,—a craving which found a certain repose and tender alleviation in entertaining fond regard for the sainted mother of Christ.

When, therefore, on one occasion, Miss Eliza had found among the toilet treasures of Adèle a little lithographic print of the Virgin, with the Christ's head surrounded by a nimbus of glory, and in her chilling way had sneered at it as a heathen vanity, the poor child had burst into tears, and carried the treasure to her bosom to guard it from sacrilegious touch.

The spinster, rendered watchful, perhaps, by this circumstance, had on another day been still more shocked to find in a corner of the escritoire of Adèle a rosary, and with a very grave face had borne it down for the condemnation of the Doctor.

"Adaly, my child, I trust you do not let this bauble bear any part in your devotions?"

And the Doctor made a movement as if he would have thrown it out of the window.

"No, New Papa!" said Adèle, darting toward him, and snatching it from his hand, with a fire in her eye he had never seen there before,—a welling-up for a moment of the hot Provençal blood in her veins; *"de grâce! je vous en prie!"* (in ecstatic moments her tongue ran to her own land and took up the echo of her first speech,)—then growing calm, as she held it, and looked into the pitying, wondering eyes of the poor Doctor, said only, "It was my mother's."

Of course the kind old gentleman never sought to reclaim such a treasure, but in his evening prayer besought God fervently "to overrule all things, our joys, our sorrows, our vain affections, our delight in the vanities of this world, our misplaced longings,—to overrule all to His glory and the good of those that love Him."

The Doctor writes to his friend Maverick at about this date,—

"Your daughter is still in the enjoyment of excellent health, and is progressing with praiseworthy zeal in her studies. I cannot too highly commend her general deportment, by which she has secured the affection and esteem of all in the parish who have formed an acquaintance with her. In respect of her religious duties, she is cheerful and punctual in the performance of them; and I find it hard to believe that they should prove only a 'savor of death unto death.'

"She is fast becoming a tall and graceful girl, and it may soon be advisable to warn her against the vanities that overtake those of her age who are still engrossed with carnal things.

"A little rosary found among her effects has been the occasion of some anxieties to my sister and myself, lest she might still have a leaning toward the mockeries of the Scarlet Woman of Babylon; and I was at first disposed to remove it out of her way. But being advised that it is cherished as a gift of her mother, I have thought it not well to take from her the only memento of so near and, I trust, dear a relative.

"May God have you, my friend, in His holy keeping!"

XXVII

Reuben in New York

REUBEN, taking the advice of Captain Saul, with whom he would cheerfully have gone to China, had the sloop been bound thither, came back to his bunk on the first night after a wandering stroll through the lower part of the city. It is quite possible that he would have done the same, viewing the narrowness of his purse, upon the second night, had he not encountered at noon a gentleman in close conversation with the Captain, whom he immediately recognized—though he had seen him but once before—as Mr. Brindlock. This person met him very kindly, and with a hearty shake of the hand, "hoped he would do his Aunt Mabel the honor of coming to stay with them."

There was an air of irony in this speech which Reuben was quick to perceive: and the knowing look of Captain Saul at once informed him that all the romance of his runaway voyage was at an end. Both Mr. and Mrs. Brindlock received him at their home with the utmost kindness, and were vastly entertained by his story of the dismal life upon Bolton Hill, the pursuit of the parson with his white-faced nag, and the subsequent cruise in the sloop *Princess*. Mrs. Brindlock, a good-natured, self-indulgent woman, was greatly taken with the unaffected country naturalness of the lad, and was agreeably surprised at his very presentable appearance: for Reuben at this date—he may have been thirteen or fourteen—was of good height for his years, with a profusion of light, wavy hair, a thoughtful, blue eye, and a lurking humor about the lip which told of a great faculty for mischief. There was such an absence, moreover, in this city home, of that stiffness with which his Aunt Eliza had such a marvellous capacity for investing everything about her, that the lad found himself strangely at his ease.

"Aunt Mabel," he had said, "I suppose you'll be writing to the old gentleman, and do please take my part. I can't go back to that abominable Brummem; if I do, I shall only run away again, and go farther: do tell him so."

DOCTOR JOHNS

"But why could n't you have stayed at home, pray? Did you quarrel with the little French girl? eh, Reuben?"

The boy flushed.

"Not with Adèle,—never!"

Brindlock, a shrewd, successful merchant, was, on his part, charmed with the adventurous spirit of the boy, and with the Captain's report of the way in which the truant had conducted negotiations for the trip. From all which it came about, that Mrs. Brindlock, in writing to the Doctor to inform him of Reuben's safe arrival, added an urgent request that the boy might be allowed to pass the winter with them in New York; in which event he could either attend school, (there being an excellent one in her neighborhood,) or, if the Doctor preferred, Mr. Brindlock could give him some light employment in the counting-room, and try his capacity for business.

At first thought, this proposition appeared very shocking to the Doctor; but, to his surprise, Miss Eliza was strongly disposed to entertain it.

The Doctor was not fully persuaded by her, and took occasion to consult, as was his wont in practical affairs, his friend Squire Elderkin.

"I rather like the plan," said the Squire,

after some consideration,—"quite like it, Doctor,—quite like it.

"You see, Doctor,"—and he slipped a finger into a button-hole of the good parson's, (the only man in the parish who would have ventured upon such familiarity,)—"I think we 've been a little strict with Reuben,—a little strict. He 's a fine, frank, straightfor'ard lad, but impulsive,—impulsive,. Doctor. Your father, the Major, had a little of it,—quicker blood than you or I, Doctor. We can't wind up every boy like a clock; there 's some that go with weights, and there 's some that go with springs. Then, too, I think, Doctor, there 's a little of the old Major's *fight* in the boy. I think he has broken over a good many of our rules very much because the rules were there, and provoked him to try his strength.

"Now, Doctor, there 's been a good deal of this kind of thing, and our Aunt Eliza puts her foot down rather strongly, which won't be a bugbear to the boy with Mrs. Brindlock; besides which, there 's your old friend, Rev. Dr. Mowry, at the Fulton-Street Church close by"—

"So he is, so he is," said the Doctor; "I had forgotten that."

"And then, to tell the truth, Doctor, between you and I," (and the Squire was working himself into some earnestness,) "I don't believe that all the wickedness in the world is cooped up in the cities. In my opinion, the small towns have a pretty fair sprinkling,— a pretty fair sprinkling, Doctor. And I tell you what it is, Doctor, the Devil" (and he twitched upon the Doctor's coat as if he were in a political argument) "does n't confine himself to large towns. He goes into the rural deestricts, in my opinion, about as regularly as the newspapers."

The result was, that permission was given for the stay of Reuben, on condition that Mr. Brindlock could give him constant occupation, and that he should be regular in his attendance on the Sabbath at the Fulton Street Church. Shortly after, the Doctor goes to the city, provided, by the watchful care of Miss Eliza, with a complete wardrobe for the truant boy, and bearing kind messages from the household. But chiefly it is the Doctor's object to give his poor boy due admonition for his great breach of duty, and to insist upon his writing to the worthy Mr. Brummem a full apology for his conduct. He also engages his friend of the Fulton-Street parish to have an eye upon his son, and to report to him at

REUBEN IN NEW YORK

once any wide departure from the good conduct he promises.

Reuben writes the apology insisted upon to Mr. Brummem in this style:

"My dear Sir,—I am sorry that I threw 'Daboll' in your face as I did, and hope you will forgive the same.
"Yours respectfully."

But after the Doctor's approval of this, the lad cannot help adding a postscript of his own to this effect:—

"P. S. I hope old Whiteface did n't lose a shoe when you drove out on the river road? I saw you; for I was sitting in the edge of the woods, eating Keziah's gingerbread. Please thank her, and give my respects to all the fellows."

Miss Johns considers it her duty to write a line of expostulation to her nephew, which she does, with faultless penmanship, in this strain:—

"We were shocked to hear of your misconduct toward the worthy Mr. Brummem. Your running away was, I think, uncalled for, and the embarkment upon the sloop, under the circumstances, was certainly very reprehensible. I trust that we shall hear only good accounts of you from this period forth, and that you will be duly grateful for your father's distinguished kindness in allowing you to stay in New York. I shall be happy to have you write to me an occasional epistle, and hope to see manifest a considerable improvement in your handwriting. Does Sister Mabel wear her ermine cape this winter? Adèle speaks of you often, and I think misses you very much indeed."

Yet the spinster aunt was not used to flatter Reuben with any such mention as this. "What can she mean," said he, musingly, "by talking such stuff to me?"

Phil Elderkin, too, after a little, writes long letters that are full of the daily boy-life at Ashfield:—how "the chestnutting has been first-rate this year," and he has a bushel of prime ones seasoning in the garret;—how Sam Troop, the stout son of the old postmaster, has had a regular tussle with the master in school, "hot and heavy, over the benches, and all about, and Sam was expelled, and old Crocker got a black eye, and, darn him, he's got it yet";—and how *somebody* (name unknown) tied a smallish tin kettle to old Hob-

REUBEN IN NEW YORK

son's sorrel mare's tail last Saturday night, and the way she went down the street was a caution!"—and how Nat Boody has got a new fighting-dog, and *such* a ratter!—and how Suke, "the divine Suke, is, they say, going to marry the stage-driver. *Sic transit gloria mulie*——something,—for I'll be hanged, if I know the proper case."

And there are some things this boisterous Phil writes in tenderer mood:—how "Rose and Adèle are as thick as ever, and Adèle comes up pretty often to pass an evening,— glad enough, I guess, to get away from Aunt Eliza,—and I see her home, of course. She plays a stiff game of backgammon; she never throws but she makes a point; she beats me."

And from such letters the joyous shouts and merry halloos of the Ashfield boys come back to him again; he hears the rustling of the brook, the rumbling of the mill; he sees the wood standing on the hills, and the girls at the door-yard gates; and he watches again the glancing feet of Rose—who was once Amanda—tripping away under the sycamores; and the city Mortimer bethinks him of another Amanda, of browner hue and in coquettish straw, idling along the same street, with reticule lightly swung upon her finger; and the boy bethinks him of tender things he might have said in the character of Mortimer, but never did say, and of kisses he might have stolen, (in the character of Mortimer,) but never did steal.

And now these sights, voices, vagaries, as month after month passes in his new home, fade,—fade, yet somehow abide. The patter of a thousand feet are on the pavement around him. What wonder, if in the surrounding din, the tranquillity of Ashfield, its scenes, its sounds, should seem a mere dream of the past? What wonder, if the solemn utterances from the old pulpit should be lost in the roar of the new voices? The few months he was to spend in their hearing run into a score, and again into another score. Two or three years hence we shall meet him again,—changed, certainly; but whether for better or for worse the sequel will show.

And Rose?—and Adèle?

Well, well, we must not overleap the quiet current of our story. While the May violets are in bloom, let us enjoy them and be thankful; and when the autumn flowers are come to take their places, let us enjoy those, too, and thank God.

XXVIII

Ashfield Again

"Doctor, we miss Reuby," said the Tew partners. And the good old people said it with feeling,—though, over and over, at winter's dusk, the boy had given a sharp rattle to their shop-door, and the warning bell called them away from their snug fire only to see his light pair of heels whisking around the corner of the Eagle Tavern. The mischief in the lad was, indeed, of such elastic, irrepressible temper, that even the gravest of the parishioners were disposed to regard it with a frown in which a comic pardon was always lurking.

Even the Tourtelots "quite missed the boy;" though over and over the brindle cow of the Deacon was found to have slipped the bars, (a thing the orderly creature was never known to do of her own head,) and was reported at twilight by the sober-faced Reuben as strolling far down upon the Common.

It is but a small bit of canvas we have chosen for the painting in of these figures of ours; and returning to the old town of Ashfield, as we do now, where the central interest must lie, there is little of change to declare, still less of dramatic incident.

The old blear-eyed Boody is not so cheery as we have seen him, although his party has won brilliant success. There is a sad story of domestic grief that has marked a new wrinkle in his forehead and given a droop to his eye, which, had all gone fairly, he might have weathered for ten years more. The glory of the ringleted Suke has indeed gone, as Phil had told; but it has not gone in the way of marriage. God only knows where those pink cheeks are showing their graces just now,—not, surely, in any home of hers,—not in any home at all. But have not the starched, good women of the parish been a little disposed to count the pretty tavern-keeper's daughter as outside the fold—so far as all social influences were concerned—from the beginning?

Certain it is, that Miss Johns indulged in such scathing condemnation of the poor sinner as made Adèle shiver; with the spinster at least, there would be little hope for a Magdalen, or a child of a Magdalen. Nor could such as she fully understand the measured and subdued tone with which the Doctor talked of a lapse from virtue which had so shocked the little community. But the parson lived so

ASHFIELD AGAIN

closely in that spiritual world where all his labor and love centered, that he saw under its ineffable light only two great ranks of people pressing toward the inevitable goal: a lesser rank, which had found favor of God; and a greater, tumultuous one, toward whom his heart yearned, that with wavering and doubt and evil intention pressed on to destruction. What mattered to him the color of the sin, or who was he to judge it? When the secret places of the heart were so full of wickedness, why anathematize above the rest those plague-spots which revealed themselves to mortals? "Fearful above all others," he was wont to say, "will be those sins which, being kept cautiously smouldering through life, will, at the blast of the Archangel's trump, blaze out in inextinguishable fire!"

Though slow to accept theological reforms, the Doctor was not slow to advocate those which promised good influence upon public morals. Thus he had entered with zeal into the Temperance movement; and after 1830, or 1832 at the latest, there was no private locker in the parsonage for any black bottle of choice Santa Cruz. His example had its bearing upon others of the parish; and whether by dint of the Doctor's effective preaching, or whether it were by reason of the dilapidated state of the buildings and the leaky condition of the stills, it is certain that about this time Deacon Simmons, of whom casual mention has been made, abandoned his distillery, and invested such spare capital as he chose to keep afloat, in the business of his son-in-law, Mr. Bowrigg of New York, who had up to this time sold the Deacon's gin upon commission.

Mr. Bowrigg was a thriving merchant, and continued his wholesale traffic with eminent success. In proof of this success, he astonished the good people of Ashfield by building, in the summer of 1833, at the instigation of his wife, an elegant country residence upon the main street of the town; and the following year, the young Bowriggs—two daughters of blooming girl age—brought such a flutter of city ribbons and silks into the main aisle of the meeting-house as had not been seen in many a day. Anne and Sophia Bowrigg, aged respectively thirteen and fifteen, fell naturally into somewhat intimate associations with our little friends, Adèle and Rose; an association that was not much to the taste of the Doctor, who feared that under it Adèle might launch again into those old coquetries of dress against which Maverick had cautioned him,

ASHFIELD AGAIN

and which in their quiet country atmosphere had been subdued into a modest homeliness that was certainly very charming.

Miss Sophia, however, the elder of the two Bowrigg daughters, was a young lady not easily balked of her intent; and conceiving a violent fondness for Adèle, whether by reason of the graces of her character, or by reason of her foreign speech, in which she could stammeringly join, to the great mystification of all others, she soon forced herself into a patronizing intimacy with Adèle, and was a frequent visitor at the parsonage. With a great fund of assurance, a rare and unappeasable glibness of tongue, and that lack of refined delicacy which invariably belongs to such noisy demonstrativeness, Miss Sophia had after only one or two interviews ferreted out from Adèle all that the little stranger herself knew respecting her history.

"And not to know your mother, Adèle! that's so very queer!"

Adèle winces at this, but seems—to so coarse an observer—only preoccupied with her work.

"Is n't it queer?" persists the garrulous creature. "I knew a girl in the city who did not see her mother after she was three,—think of that! But then, you know, she was a bad woman."

The hot Provençal blood mounts to the cheek and brow of Adèle in an instant, and her eye flashes. But it is quite impossible to show anger in view of the stolid face of her companion, with nothing in it but an unthinking, girlish curiosity.

"We will talk of something else, Sophia."

"Oh! then you don't like to speak of it! Dear me! I certainly won't, then."

But it is by no means the first time the sensibilities of Adèle have been touched to the quick. She is approaching that age when they ripen with marvellous rapidity. There is never an evening now at that cheerful home of the Elderkins—lighted up as it is with the beaming smiles of that Christian mother, Mrs. Elderkin—but there sweeps over the mind of the poor girl, at some interval in the games or the chat, a terrible sense of some great loss she has suffered, of which she knows not the limits,—a cruel sense of isolation in which she wanders, and on which comes betimes the recollection of a father's kindly face, that in the growing distance makes her isolation seem even more appalling.

Rose, good soul, detects these humors by a

ASHFIELD AGAIN

keen, girlish instinct, and gliding up to her, passes her arm around her,—

"What is it now, Adèle, dear?"

And she, looking down at her, (for Adèle was the taller by half a head,) says,—

"What a good mother you have, Rose!"

"Only that!"—and Rose laughs gleefully for a moment; when bethinking herself where the secret grief lay, her sweet face is overcast in an instant, and reaching up her two hands, she draws down the face of Adèle to hers, and kisses her on either cheek.

Phil, who is at a game of chess with Grace, pretends not to see this side demonstration; but his next move is to sacrifice his only remaining castle in the most needless manner.

Dame Tourtelot, too, has pressed her womanly prerogative of knowing whatever could be known about the French girl who comes occasionally with Miss Eliza to her tea-drinkings, and who, with a native taste for music, is especially interested in the piano of Miss Almira.

"It must be very tedious," says the Dame, "to be so long away from home and from those that love you. Almiry, now, hardly goes for a week to Cousin Jerushy's at Har'-ford but she is a-frettin' to be back in her old home. Don't you feel it, Adeel?" (The Dame is not to be driven out of her own notions of pronunciation by any French accents.) "But don't be down-hearted, my child; it's God's providence that's brought you away from a Popish country."

The spinster, also, who is mistress of the parsonage, though never giving up her admiring patronage of Adèle, and governing her curiosity with far more tact than belongs to Dame Tourtelot, has yet shown a persistent zeal in pushing her investigations in regard to all that concerned the family history of her little *protégée*. She has lent an eager ear to all the communications which Maverick has addressed to the Doctor; and in moments of what seemed exceptional fondness, when she has toyed with the head-gear of Adèle, has plied the little brain with motherly questions that have somehow widely failed of their intent.

Under all this, Adèle ripens into a certain reserve and individuality of character which might never have belonged to her, had the earlier circumstances of her life been altogether familiar to the circle in which she was placed. The Doctor fastens, perhaps, an undue reliance upon this growing reserve of hers: sure it is that an increasing confidence is establishing itself between them, which it is to be hoped nothing will shake.

And as for Phil, when the Squire teases him with his growing fondness for the little Jesuit of the parsonage, the boy, though past seventeen now, and "with views of his own," (as most young men have at that age,) blushes like a girl.

Rose, seeing it, and her eyes flashing with sisterly pride, says to herself,—

"Oh, I hope it may come true!"

XXIX

Every-Day Life

FROM time to time Maverick had written in reply to the periodical reports of the Doctor, and always with unabating confidence in his discretion and kindness.

"I have remarked what you say" (he had written thus in a letter which had elicited the close attention of Miss Eliza) "in regard to the rosary found among the girlish treasures of Adèle. I am not aware how she can have come by such a trinket from the source named;

but I must beg you to take as little notice as possible of the matter, and please allow her possession of it to remain entirely unmarked."

Heavy losses incident to the political changes of the year 1831 in France had kept him fastened at his post; and with the reviving trade under the peaceful *régime* of Louis Philippe, he had been more actively engaged even than before. Yet there was no interruption to his correspondence with Adèle, and no falling off in its expressions of earnest affection and devotion.

"I fancy you almost a woman grown now, dear Adèle. Those cheeks of yours have, I hope, not lost their roundness or their rosiness. But, however much you may have grown, I am sure that my heart would guide me so truly that I could single you out from a great crowd of the little Puritan people about you. I can fancy you in some simple New England dress, —gliding up the pathway that leads to the door of the old parsonage; I can fancy you dropping a word of greeting to the good Doctor within his study (he must be wearing spectacles now); and at evening I seem to see you kneeling in the long back dining-room, as the parson leads in family prayer. Well, well, don't forget to pray for your old father,

EVERY-DAY LIFE

my child. I shall be all the safer for it, in what the Doctor calls 'this wicked land.' And what of Reuben, whose mischief, you told me, threatened such fearful results? Sobered down, I suppose, long before this, wearing a stout jacket of homespun, driving home the 'keow' at night, and singing in the choir of a Sunday. Don't lose your heart, Adèle, with any of the youngsters about you. I claim the whole of it."

And Adèle writes back:—

"My heart is all yours, papa,—only why do you never come and take it? So many, many years that I have not seen you!

"Yes, I like Ashfield still; it is almost a home to me now, you know. New Papa is very kind, but just as grave and stiff as at the first. I know he loves me, but he never tells me so. But when I sing some song that he loves to hear, I see a little quirk by his temple, and a glistening in his eye, as he thanks me, that tells it plain enough; and most of all when he prays, as he sometimes does after talking to me very gravely, with his arm tight clasped around me, oh, I am sure that he loves me!—and indeed, and indeed, I love him back again!

"It was funny what you said of Reuben;

DOCTOR JOHNS

for you must know that he is living in the city now, and happens upon us here sometimes with a very grand air,—as fine, I dare say, as the people about Marseilles. But I don't think I like him any better; I don't know if I like him as well. Miss Eliza is, of course, very proud of him, as she always was."

As the nicer observing faculties of his child develop,—of which ample traces appear in her letters,—Maverick begs her to detail to him as fully as she can all the little events of her every-day life. Sheet after sheet of this simple, girlish narrative of hers Maverick delights himself with, as he sits upon his balcony, after business hours, looking down upon the harbor of Marseilles.

"After morning prayers, which are very early, you know, Esther places the smoking dishes on the table, and New Papa asks a blessing,—always. Then he says, 'I hope Adaly has not forgotten her text of yesterday.' And I repeat it to him. Such a quantity of texts as I can repeat now! Then Aunt Eliza says, 'I hope, too, that Adèle will make no mistake in her "Paradise Lost" to-day. Are you sure you 've not forgotten that lesson in the parsing, child?' Indeed, papa, I can parse almost any page in the book.

EVERY-DAY LIFE

"'I think,' says New Papa, appealing to Miss Eliza, 'that Larkin may grease the wheels of the chaise this morning, and, if it should be fair, I will make a visit or two at the north end of the town; and I guess Adaly would like to go with me.'

"'Yes, dearly, New Papa,' I say,—which is very true.

"And Miss Eliza says, very gravely, 'I am perfectly willing, Doctor.'

"After breakfast is over, Miss Eliza will sometimes walk with me a short way down the street, and will say to me, 'Hold yourself erect, Adèle; walk trimly.' *She* walks very trimly. Then we pass by the Hapgood house, which is one of the grand houses; and I know the old Miss Hapgoods are looking through the blinds at us, though they never show themselves until they have taken out their curl-papers in the afternoon.

"Dame Tourtelot is n't so shy; and we see her great, gaunt figure in a broad sun-bonnet, stooping down with her trowel, at work among the flower-patches before her door; and Miss Almira is reading at an upper window, in pink muslin. And when the Dame hears us, she lifts herself straight, sets her old flapping bonnet as square as she can, and stares through

DOCTOR JOHNS

her spectacles until she has made us out; then says,-

"'Good mornin', Miss Johns. You 're 'arly this mornin'.'

"'Quite early,' says Miss Eliza. 'Your flowers are looking nicely, Mrs. Tourtelot.'

"'Well, the pi'nys is blowed pretty good. Would n't Adeel like a pi'ny?'

"It 's a great red monster of a flower, papa; but I thank her for it, and put it in my belt. Then the Dame goes on to tell how she has shifted the striped grass, and how the bouncing-Bets are spreading, and where she means to put her Nasturtiums the next year, and brandishes her trowel, as the brigands in the story-books brandish their swords.

"And Miss Eliza says, 'Almiry is at her reading, I see.'

"'Dear me!' says the Dame, glancing up; 'she 's always a-readin'. What with novils and histories, she 's injurin' her health, Miss Johns, as sure as you 're alive.'

"Then, as we set off again,—the Dame calling out some last word, and brandishing her trowel over the fence,—old Squire Elderkin comes swinging up the street with the 'Courant' in his hand; and he lifts his hat, and says, 'Good morning to you, Miss Johns; and how is the little French lady this morning? Bright as ever, I see,' (for he does n't wait to be answered,)—'a peony in her belt, and two roses in her cheeks.' Yet my cheeks are not very red, papa; but it 's his way. . . .

"After school, I go for the drive with the Doctor, which I enjoy very much. I ask him about all the flowers along the way, and he tells me every thing, and I have learned the names of all the birds; and it is much better, I think, than learning at school. And he always says, 'It 's God's infinite love, my child, that has given us all these beautiful things.' When I hear him say it, I believe it, papa.

"Then, very often, he lifts my hand in his, and says, 'Adaly, my dear, God is very good to us. We cannot tell His meaning always, but we may be very sure that He has only a good meaning. You do not know it, Adaly, but there was once a dear one, whom I loved perhaps too well;—she was the mother of my poor Reuben; God only knows how I loved her! But He took her from me.'—Oh, how the hand of New Papa griped on mine, when he said this!—'He took her from me, my child; He has carried her to His home. He is just. Learn to love Him, Adaly.'

"'I do! I do!' I said.

DOCTOR JOHNS

"But then, directly after, he repeated to me some of those dreary things I had been used to hear in the Catechism week after week.

"'*Don't* tell me that, New Papa,' said I, 'it is so old; talk to me as you *were* talking.'

"And then the Doctor looked at me with the keenest eyes I ever saw, and said,—

"'My child, are you right, and are the Doctors wrong?'

"'Is it the Catechism that you call the Doctors?' said I.

"'Yes,' said he.

"'But were they better men than you, New Papa?'

"'All men alike, Adaly, all struggling toward the truth,—all wearying themselves to interpret it in such way that the world may accept it.' And at this he took my hand and said, 'Adaly, trust Him!'

"By this time" (for Adèle's letter is a true transcript of a day) "we have reached the door of some one of his people to whom he is to pay a visit. The blinds are all closed, and nothing seems to be stirring but a gray cat that is prowling about under the lilac bushes. Dobbins is hitched to the post, and the Doctor pounds away at the big knocker. Presently two or three white-headed children come peep-

EVERY-DAY LIFE

ing around the bushes, and rush away to tell who has come. After a little the stout mistress opens the door, and wipes her fingers on her apron, and shakes hands, and bounces into the keeping-room to throw up the window and open the blinds, and dusts off the great rocking chair for the Doctor, and keeps saying all the while that they are 'very back'ard with the spring work, and she really had no time to slick up,' and asks after Miss Eliza and Reuben, and the Tourtelots, and all the people on the street, so fast that I wonder she can keep her breath; and the Doctor looks so calm, and has no time to say anything yet. Then she looks at me, 'Sissy is looking well,' says she, and dashes out to bring in a great plate of gingerbread, which I never like at all, and say, 'No.' But she says, 'It won't hurt ye; it a'n't p'ison, child.' So I find I must eat a little; and while I sit mumbling it, the Doctor and she talk on about a great deal I don't understand, and I am glad when she bounces up again, and says, 'Sis would like to get some posies, p'raps,' and leads me out of doors. 'There's lalocs, child, and flower-de-luce, pick what you want.'

"So I go wandering among the beds along the garden, with the bees humming around

DOCTOR JOHNS

me; and there are great tufts of blue-bell, and spider-wort, and moss-pink; and the white-haired grandchildren come and put their faces to the paling, looking at me through the bars like animals in a cage; and if I beckon to them, they glance at each other, and dash away."

Thus much of Adèle's account. But there are three or four more visits to complete the parson's day. Possibly he comes upon some member of his flock in the field, when he draws up Dobbins to the fence, and his parishioner, spying the old chaise, leaves his team to blow a moment while he strides forward with his long ox-goad in hand, and, seating himself upon a stump within easy earshot, says,—

"Good mornin', Doctor."

And the parson, in his kindly way, "Good morning, Mr. Pettibone. Your family pretty well?"

"Waäl, middlin', Doctor,—only middlin'. Miss Pettibone is a-havin' faintish spells along back; complains o' pain in her side."

"Sorry, sorry," says the good man: and then, "Your team is looking pretty well, Mr. Pettibone."

"Waäl, only tol'able, Doctor. That nigh ox, what with spring work an' grass feed is gittin' kind o' thin in the flesh. Any news abaout, Doctor?"

EVERY-DAY LIFE

"Not that I learn, Mr. Pettibone. We're having fine growing weather for your crops."

"Waäl, only tol'able, Doctor. You see, arter them heavy spring rains, the sun has kind o' baked the graound; the seed don't seem to start well. I don't know as you remember, but in '29, along in the spring, we had jist sich a spell o' wet, an' corn hung back that season amazin'ly."

"Well, Mr. Pettibone, we must hope for the best; it's all in God's hands."

"Waäl, I s'pose it is, Doctor,—I s'pose it is." And he makes a cut at a clover-head with the lash upon his ox-goad; then—as if in recognition of the change of subject—he says,—

"Any more talk on the street abaout repairin' the ruff o' the meetin'-house, Doctor?"

At sundown, all visits being paid, they go jogging into town again,—the Doctor silent by this time, and thinking of his sermon. Dobbins is tied always at the same post,— always the hitch-rain buckled in the third hole from the end.

After tea, perhaps, Phil and Rose come sauntering by, and ask if Adèle will go up "to the house"? Which request, if Miss Eliza meet it with a nod of approval, puts Adèle by their side; Rose, with a beautiful recklessness common to New England girls of that day, wearing her hat drooping half down her neck, and baring her clear forehead to the falling night-dews. Phil, with a pebble in his hand, makes a feint of throwing into a flock of goslings that are waddling disturbedly after a pair of staid old geese, but is arrested by Rose's prompt "Behave, Phil!"

The Squire is reading his paper by the evening lamp, but cannot forbear a greeting to Adèle:—

"Ah, here we are again! and how is Madamòizel?" (this is the Squire's style of French,) —"and has she brought me the peony? Phil would have given his head for it,—eh, Phil?"

Rose is so bright, and glowing, and happy!

Mrs. Elderkin in her rocking-chair, with her gray hair carefully plaited under the white lace cap whose broad strings fall on either shoulder, is a picture of motherly dignity. Her pleasant "Good-evening, Adèle," would alone have paid the warm-hearted exile for her walk.

Then follow games, chat, and an occasional noisy joke from the Squire, until the nine o'clock town-bell gives warning, and Adèle wends homeward under convoy of the gallant Phil.

"Good-night, Adèle!"

"Good-night, Phil!"

Only this at the gate. Then the Doctor's evening prayer; and after it,—in the quiet chamber, where her sweet head lay upon the pillow,—dreams.

XXX

New Prospects

In the autumn of 1836, Maverick wrote to his friend, the Doctor, that in view of the settled condition of business, he intended to visit America some time in the course of the following season.

"Above all," he writes, "I wish to see Adèle as she is, without any note of preparation. You will therefore, I beg, my dear Johns, keep from her scrupulously all knowledge of my present intentions, (which may possibly miscarry, after all,) and let me see, to the very finest touch, whether of a ribbon or of a ringlet, how far you have New-Englandized my dear girl.

"It is quite possible that I may manage for her return with me, (of this plan, too, I beg you to give no hint,) and in view of it I would suggest that any available occasion be seized upon to revive her knowledge of French, which, I fear, in your staid household, she may almost have forgotten. Tell dear Adèle that I am sometimes at Le Pin, where her godmother never fails to inquire after her, and bless the dear child."

Upon this the Doctor and Miss Johns take counsel. Both are not a little disturbed. The grave Doctor finds his heart wrapped about by the winning ways of the little stranger in a manner he could hardly have conceived possible.

The spinster, though she has become unconsciously attached to Adèle, is yet not so much disconcerted by the thought of any violence to her affections,—for all violence of this kind she has schooled herself to regard with cool stoicism,—but the possible interruption of her ambitious schemes with respect to Reuben and Adèle discomposes her. Such a scheme she has never given over for one moment. No plan of hers is ever given over lightly. The growing intercourse with the Elderkins, in view of the evident devotion of Phil, has been, indeed, the source of a little uneasiness; but even this intimacy she has moderated to a certain degree by occasional judicious fears in re-

NEW PROSPECTS

gard to Adèle's exposure to the night air; and has made the most—in her quiet manner—of Phil's exceptional, but somewhat noisy, attentions to that dashing girl, Sophia Bowrigg.

But, like most cool schemers in what concerns the affections, she makes her errors. Her assurance in regard to the improved habits and character of Reuben, and her iteration of the wonderful attachment which the Brindlocks bear to the lad, have a somewhat strained air to the ear of Adèle. And when the spinster says,—folding up his last letter,—"Good fellow! always some tender little message for you, my dear," Adèle thinks—as most girls of her age would be apt to think—that she would like to see the tender message with her own eyes.

But what of the French? Where is there to be found a competent teacher? Not, surely, in Ashfield. Miss Eliza, with grave doubts, however, suggests a winter in New York with the Brindlocks.

Even Adèle, attracted by the novelty of the proposed situation, urged her claim in the cheeriest little manner conceivable.

"Only for the winter, New Papa; please say 'Yes'!"

And the tender hands patted the grave face,

DOCTOR JOHNS

as she seated herself with a childish coquetry upon the elbow of his chair.

"Impossible, quite impossible," says the Doctor. "You are too dear to me, Adaly."

"Oh, now, New Papa, you don't mean that, — not *positively?*" — and the winning fingers tap his cheek again.

But for this time, at least, Adèle is to lose her claim; the Doctor well knows that to suffer such endearments were to yield; so he rises brusquely, —

"I must be just, my child, to the charge your father has imposed upon me. It cannot be."

It will not be counted strange, if a little ill-disguised petulance appeared in the face of Adèle that day and the next.

The winter of 1836–7 was a very severe one throughout New England. Perhaps it was in view of its severity, that, on or about New Year's Day, there came to the parsonage a gift from Reuben for Adèle, in the shape of a fur tippet, very much to the gratification of Miss Eliza and to the pleasant surprise of the Doctor.

Rose and Phil, sitting by the fire next day, Rose says, in a timid voice, with less than her usual sprightliness, —

"Do you know who has sent a beautiful fur tippet to Adèle, Phil?"

NEW PROSPECTS

"No," says Phil, briskly. "Who?"

"Reuben," says Rose,—in a tone as if a blush ran over her face at the utterance.

If there was one, however, Phil could not have seen it; he was looking steadfastly into the fire, and said only,—

"I don't care."

A little after, (nothing having been said, meantime,) he has occasion to rearrange the wood upon the hearth, and does it with such preposterous violence that the timid little voice beside him says,—

"Don't, Phil, be angry with the fire!"

It was a winter, as we have said, for fur tippets and for glowing cheeks; and Adèle had now been long enough under a Northern sky to partake of that exhilaration of spirits which belongs to every true-born New Englander in presence of one of those old-fashioned snow-storms, which, all through the day and through the night, sifts out from the gray sky its fleecy crystals,—covering the frosted highroads, covering the withered grasses, covering the whole summer's wreck in one glorious white burial; and after it, keen frosty mornings, the pleasant jingling of scores of bells, jets of white vapor from the nostrils of the prancing horses, and a quick electric tingle to the blood, that makes every pulse beat a thanksgiving.

In the midst of all this a black shadow fell upon the little town. News came overland (the river being closed), that Mrs. Bowrigg, after an illness of three days, was dead; and the body of the poor woman was to come home for burial.

With the opening of the spring the townspeople were busy with the question, if the Bowriggs would come again to occupy their summer residence, that, with its closed doors and windows, was mournfully silent. But soon the gardeners were set to work; it was understood that a housekeeper had been engaged, and the family were to occupy it as usual. Sophia writes to Adèle, confirming it all, and adding,—"Madame Arles, our new French teacher—delightful accent—only a little time arrived, has proposed to make us a visit; which papa hearing, and wishing us to keep up our studies, has given her an invitation to pass the summer with us. She says she will. I am so glad! We had told her very much of you, and I know she will be delighted to have you as a scholar."

At this Adèle feels a thrill of satisfaction, and looks longingly forward to the time when she shall hear again from native lips the language of her childhood.

"*Ma fille! ma fille!*"

The voices of her early home seem to ring again in her ear. She basks once more in the delicious flow of the sunshine, and the perfume of the orange-blossoms regales her.

———"*Ma fille!*"

Is it the echo of your voice, good old godmother, that comes rocking over the great reach of the sea, and so touches the heart of the exile?

XXXI

A New Personage

MADAME ARLES was a mild and quiet little woman, with a singular absence of that vivacity which most people are disposed to attribute to all of French blood. Her age—so far as one could judge from outward indications—might have been anywhere from twenty-eight to forty. There were no wrinkles in that smooth, calm forehead of hers; and if there were lines of gray amid her hair, this indication of age was so contradicted by the youthfulness of her eye, that a keen observer would have been disposed to attribute it rather to some weight of past grief that had left its silvery imprint than to the mere burden of her years.

If past griefs have belonged to her, however, they have become long since a part of her character; they are in no way obtrusive. There was, indeed, a singular cast in one of her eyes, which in moments of excitement—such few as came over her—impressed the observer very strangely; as if, while she looked straight upon you and calmly with one eye, the other were bent upon some scene far remote and out of range, some past episode it might be of her own life, by over-dwelling upon which she had brought her organs of sight into this tortured condition. Nine out of ten observers, however, would never have remarked the peculiarity we have mentioned, and would only have commented upon Madame Arles—if they had commented at all—as a quiet person, in whom youth and age seemed just now to struggle for the mastery, and in whom no trace of French birth and rearing was apparent, save her speech, and a certain wonderful aptitude in the arrangement of her dress. The poor lady, moreover, who showed traces of a vanished beauty, was not strong, and for this

A NEW PERSONAGE

reason, perhaps, had readily accepted the relief afforded by this summer vacation with two of her city pupils. A violent palpitation of the heart, after sudden or undue exertion or excitement, shook the poor woman's frail hold upon life. Possibly from this cause—as is the case with many who are compelled to listen to those premonitory raps of the grim visitor at the very seat of life—Madame Arles was a person of strong religious proclivities.

Adèle, accompanied by her friend Rose,— who, notwithstanding the quiet remonstrances of the Doctor, had won her mother's permission for such equipment in French as she could gain from a summer's teaching,—went with early greeting to the Bowriggs. The curiosity of Adèle was intense to listen to the music of her native speech once more; and when Madame Arles slipped quietly into the room, Adèle darted toward her with warm, girlish impulse, and the poor woman, excited beyond bounds by this heartiness of greeting, and murmuring some tender words of endearment, had presently folded her to her bosom.

Adèle, blushing as much with pleasure as with a half-feeling of mortification at the wild show of feeling she had made, was stammering her apology, when she was arrested by a sudden change in the aspect of her new friend.

"My dear Madame, you are suffering?"

"A little, my child!"

It was too true, as the quick glance of her old pupils saw in an instant. Her lips were pinched and blue; that strange double look in her eyes,—one fastened upon Adèle, and the other upon vacancy; her hands clasped over her heart as if to stay its mad throbbings. While Sophia supported and conducted the sufferer to her own chamber, the younger sister explained to Adèle that such spasmodic attacks were of frequent occurrence.

Nothing more was needed to enlist Adèle's sympathies to the full. She carried home the story of it to the Doctor, and detailed it in such an impassioned way, and with such interpretation of the kind lady's reception of herself, that the Doctor was touched, and abated no small measure of the prejudice he had been disposed to entertain against the Frenchwoman.

But her heresies in the matter of religion remained,—it being no secret that Madame Arles was thoroughly Popish; and these disturbed the good Doctor the more, as he perceived the growing and tender intimacy which was establishing itself, week by week, between

A NEW PERSONAGE

Adèle and her new teacher. Indeed, he has not sanctioned this without his own private conversation with Madame, in which he has set forth his responsibility respecting Adèle and the wishes of her father, and insisted upon entire reserve of Madame's religious opinions in her intercourse with his *protégée*. All which the poor lady had promised with a ready zeal that surprised the minister.

"It is that I know too little, Doctor; I could wish she might be better than I. May God make her so!"

"I do not judge you, Madame; it is not ours to judge; but I would keep Adaly securely, if God permit, in the faith which we reverence here, and which I much fear she could never learn in her own land or her own language."

"May be, may be, my good Doctor; her faith shall not be overset by me; I promise it."

Adèle, with her quick ear and eye, has no difficulty in discovering the ground of the Doctor's uneasiness and of Miss Eliza's frequent questionings in regard to her intercourse with the new teacher.

"I am sure they think you very bad," she said to Madame Arles, one day, in a spirit of mischief.

"Bad! bad! Adèle, why? how?"—and that

DOCTOR JOHNS

strange tortuous look came to her eye, with a quick flush to her cheeks.

"Ah, now, dear Madame, don't be disturbed; 't is only your religion they think so bad, and fear you will mislead me. *Tenez!* this little rosary" (and she displays it to the eye of the wondering Madame Arles) "they would have taken from me."

Madame pressed the beads reverently to her lips.

"And you did demand it, my child?"

"Not for any faith I had in it; but it was my mother's."

The good woman kissed Adèle.

"It must be that you long to see her, my child!"

A shade of sorrow and doubt ran over the face of the girl. This did not escape the notice of Madame Arles, who, with a dejected and distracted air, replaced the rosary in her hands.

"Mon ange!" (in this winsome way she was accustomed at times to address Adèle) "we cannot talk of these things. I have promised so much to the Doctor; it is better so; he is a good man."

Adèle sat toying for a moment with the rosary upon her fingers, looking down; then, seeing that woe-begone expression that had fastened upon the face of her companion, she sprang up, kissed her forehead, and, restoring thus—as she knew she could do—a cheeriness to her manner, resumed her lesson.

XXXII

Maverick Re-appears

IN the summer of 1837, Maverick determined to sail for America, and to make good his promise of a visit to the Doctor and Adèle.

He shows no more appearance of age than when we saw him years before, placing his little offering of flowers upon the breakfast-table of poor Rachel,—an excellent, well-preserved man,—dressed always in that close conformity to the existing mode which of itself gives a young air,—regulating all his table indulgences with the same precision with which he governs his business,—using all the appliances of flesh-brushes and salt-baths to baffle any insidious ailment,—a strong, hale, cheery man, who would have ranked by a score (judging from his exterior) younger than the Doctor.

Shall we look for a moment at the French

home which Maverick is leaving? A compact country-house of yellow stone upon a niche of the hills that overlook the blue Bay of Lyons; a green arbor over the walk leading to the door; clumps of pittosporum and of jessamine, with two or three straggling fig-trees, within the inclosure; a billiard-room and *salle-à-manger* in the basement, and on the first floor a *salon,* opening by its long, heavily draped windows, upon a balcony shielded with striped awning. Here on many an evening, when the night-wind comes in from the sea, Maverick lounges sipping at his *demi-tasse,* whiffing at a fragrant Havana, (imported to order,) and chatting with some friend he has driven out from the stifling streets of Marseilles about the business chances of the morrow. A tall, agile Alsatian woman, with a gilt crucifix about her neck, and a great deal of the peasant beauty still in her face, glides into the *salon* from time to time, acting apparently in the capacity of mistress of the establishment,— respectfully courteous to Maverick and his friend, yet showing something more than the usual familiarity of a dependent housekeeper.

The friend who sits with him enjoying the night breeze and those rare Havanas is an

MAVERICK RE-APPEARS

open-faced, middle-aged companion of the city, with whom Maverick has sometimes gone to a *bourgeois* home near to Montauban, where a wrinkle-faced old Frenchman in velvet skull-cap—the father of his friend—has received him with profound obeisance, brought out for him his best *cru* of St. Peray, and bored him with long stories of the times of 1798, in which he was a participant. Yet the home-scenes there, with the wrinkled old father and the stately mamma for partners at whist or Boston, have been grateful to Maverick, as reminders of other home-scenes long passed out of reach; and he has opened his heart to this son of the house.

'Monsieur Papiol," (it is the Alsatian woman who is addressing the friend of Maverick,) "ask, then, why it is Monsieur Frank is going to America."

"Ah, Lucille, do you not know, then, there is a certain Puritan belle he goes to look after?"

"Pah!" says the Alsatian. "Monsieur is not so young!"

Maverick puffs at his cigar thoughtfully,— a thoughtfulness that does not encourage the Alsatian to other speech,—and in a moment more she is gone.

"Seriously, Maverick," says Papiol, when they are alone again, "what will you do with this Puritan daughter of yours?"

"Keep her from ways of wickedness," said Maverick, without losing his thoughtfulness.

"Excellent!" said the friend, laughing; "but you will hardly bring her to this home of yours, then?"

"Hardly to this country of yours, Pierre."

"Nonsense, Maverick! You will be too proud of her, *mon ami*. I'm sure of that. You'll never keep her cribbed yonder. We shall see you escorting her some day up and down the Prado, and all the fine young fellows hereabout paying court to the *belle Américaine*. My faith! I shall be wishing myself twenty years younger!"

Maverick is still very thoughtful.

"What is it, my good fellow? Is it—that the family question gives annoyance among your friends yonder?"

"On the contrary," says Maverick,—and reaching a file of letters in his cabinet, he lays before his companion that fragment of the Doctor's epistle which had spoken of the rosary, and of his discovery that it had been the gift of the mother, "so near, and he trusted dear a relative."

MAVERICK RE-APPEARS

"Mais, comme il est innocent, your good old friend there!"

"I wish to God, Pierre, I were as innocent as he," said Maverick, and tossed his cigar over the edge of the balcony.

Upon his arrival at New York, Maverick did not communicate directly with the Doctor, enjoying the thought, very likely, of surprising his old friend by his visit, very much as he had surprised him many years before. He takes boat to a convenient point upon the shore of the Sound, and thence chooses to approach the town that holds what is most dear to him by an old, lumbering stage-coach, which still plies across the hills, as twenty years before, through the parish of Ashfield. The same patches of tasselled corn, (it is August,) the same outlying bushy pastures, the same reeling walls of mossy cobble-stones meet his eye that he remembered on his previous visit. But he looks upon all wayside views carelessly,—as one seeing, and yet not seeing them.

His daughter Adèle, she who parted from him a toy-child eight years gone, whom a new ribbon would amuse in that day, must have changed. That she has not lost her love of him, those letters have told; that she has not lost her girlish buoyancy, he knows. She must be tall now, and womanly in stature, he thinks. She promised to be graceful. That he will love her, he feels; but will he be proud of her? A fine figure, a sweet, womanly voice, an arch look, a winning smile, a pretty coquetry of glance,—will he find these? Will she be clever? Will there be traces, ripened in these last years, of the mother,—offensive traces possibly?

But Maverick is what the world calls a philosopher; he hums, unconsciously, a snatch of a French song, by which he rouses the attention of the spectacled old lady, (the only other occupant of the coach,) with whom he has already made some conversational ventures, and who has just finished a lunch which she has drawn from her capacious work-bag. Reviving now under the influence of Maverick's chance fragment of song, and dusting the crumbs from her lap, she says,—

"We don't have very good singin' now in the Glostenbury meetin'."

"Ah!" says Maverick.

"No; Squire Peter's darters have been gittin' married, and the young girls ha'n't come on yit."

"You attend the Glostenbury Church, then,

MAVERICK RE-APPEARS

madam?" says Maverick, who enjoys the provincialisms of her speech, like a whiff of the lilac perfume which he once loved.

"In gineral, sir; but we come down odd spells to hear Dr. Johns, who preaches at the Ashfield meetin'-house. *He's* a real smart man."

"Ah! And this Dr. Johns has a family, I think?"

"Waäl, the Doctor lost his wife, you see, quite airly; and Miss Johns—that's his sister—has bin a-keepin' house for him ever sence. I'm not acquainted with her, but I've heerd she's a very smart woman. And there's a French girl that came to live with 'em, goin' on now seven or eight year, who was a reg'lar Roman Catholic; but I kind o' guess the old folks has tamed her down afore now."

"Ah! I should think that a Roman Catholic would have but a poor chance in a New England village."

"Not much of a chance anywhere, I guess," said the old lady, wiping her spectacles, "if folks only preached the Gospil."

Even now the coach is creaking along through the outskirts of Ashfield; and presently the driver's horn wakes the echoes of the hills, while the horses plunge forward at a doubled pace. The eyes of Maverick are intent upon every house, every open window, every moving figure.

"It 's a most a beautiful town," said the old lady.

"Charming, charming, madam!"—and even as he spoke, Maverick's eye fastens upon two figures before them with a strange yearning in his gaze,—two figures of almost equal height; a little, coquettish play of ribbons about the head of one, which on the other are absent; a girlish, elastic step to one, that does not belong to the other.

Is there something in the gait, something in the poise of the head, to which the memory of Maverick so cleaves? It is, indeed, Adèle, taking her noon-day walk with Madame Arles; a lithe figure and a buoyant step, holding themselves tenderly in check for the slower pace of the companion. Maverick's gaze keeps fast upon them,—fast upon them, until the old coach is fairly abreast,—fast upon them; until by a glance back he has caught full sight of the faces.

"Mon Dieu!" he exclaims, and throws himself back in the coach.

"Häow?" says the old lady.

"Mon Dieu, it is she!" continues Maverick,

MAVERICK RE-APPEARS

speaking under intense excitement to himself, as if unconscious of any other presence.

"Häow?" urged the old lady, more persistently.

"Damn it, nothing, madam!"

And the old lady drew the strings of her bag closely, and looked full out of the opposite window.

Within a half-hour the stage-coach arrived at the Eagle Tavern. Maverick demanded a chamber, and asked to see the landlord. The stout, blear-eyed Boody presently made his appearance.

"How can I reach New York soonest, my friend?"

Mr. Boody consulted his watch.

"Well, by fast driving you might catch the night-boat on the river."

"Can you get me there in time?"

"Well, sir," reflecting a moment, "I guess I can."

"Very good. Have your carriage ready as soon as possible."

And within an hour, Maverick, dejected, and with an anxious air, was on his return to the city.

Three days after, the Doctor summons Adèle into his study.

"Adaly, here is a letter from your father, which I wish you to read."

The girl takes it eagerly, and at the first line exclaims,—

"He is in New York! Why does n't he come here?"

"My Dear Johns," (so his letter runs,) "I had counted on surprising you completely by dropping in upon you at your parsonage, in Ashfield; but circumstances have prevented. Can I ask so large a favor of you as to bring my dear Adèle to meet me here? I fancy her now so accomplished a young lady, that there will be needed some ceremony of presentation at your hands; besides which, I want a long talk with you. We are both many years older since we have met; you have had your trials, and I have escaped with only a few rubs. Let us talk them over. Slip away quietly, if you can; beyond Adèle and your good sister, can't you conceal your errand to the city? Your country villagers are so prone to gossip, that I would wish to clasp my little Adèle before your towns-folk shall have talked the matter over. Pray ask your good sister to prepare the wardrobe of Adèle for a month or two of absence, since I mean she shall be my attendant on a little

MAVERICK RE-APPEARS

jaunt through the country. I long to greet her; and your grave face, my dear Johns, is always a welcome sight."

Adèle is in a fever of excitement. In her happy glee she would have gone out to tell all the village what pleasure was before her. Even the caution she receives from the Doctor cannot control her spirits absolutely.

"I suppose you will see Reuben in the city," Rose had said, in a chance way.

"Oh, I hope so!" said Adèle.

And of Reuben neither of them said anything more.

Then with what a great storm of embraces Adèle parted from Rose! A parting only for a month, perhaps; both knew that. But the friendship of young girls can build a week into a monstrous void.

Phil, who is a sturdy and somewhat timid lover, without knowing it, affects an air of composure, and says,—

"I hope you 'll have a good time, Adèle; and I suppose you 'll forget us all here in Ashfield."

"No, you don't suppose any such thing, Mister Philip," says Adèle, roundly, and with a frank, full look at him that makes the color come to his face; and he laughs, but not easily.

"Well, good-by, Adèle."

She takes his hand, eagerly.

"Good-by, Phil; you 're a dear, good fellow; and you 've been very kind to me."

XXXIII

In the City

It is at Jennings's old City Hotel, far down Broadway, that Maverick has taken rooms and awaits the arrival of Adèle. That glimpse of her upon the street of Ashfield (ay, he knew it must be she!) has added pride to the instinctive love of the parent. The elastic step, the graceful figure, the beaming, sunny face,— they all haunt him; they put him in a fever of expectation. He reads over again the few last letters of hers under a new light; up and down along the page, that lithe, tall figure is always coming forward, and the words of endearment are coupled with that sunny face.

He even prepares his toilet to meet her, as a lover might do to meet his affianced. And the meeting, when it comes, only deepens the pride.

IN THE CITY

Graceful? Yes! That bound toward him,—can any thing be fuller of grace? Natural? The look and the speech of Adèle are to Maverick a new revelation of Nature. Loving? That clinging kiss of hers was worth his voyage over the sea.

And she, too, is so beautifully proud of her father! She has loved the Doctor for his serenity, his large justice, notwithstanding his stiffness and his awkward gravity; but she regards with new eyes the manly grace of her father, his easy self-possession, his pliability of talk, his tender attention to her comfort, his wistful gaze at her, so full of a yearning affection, which, if the Doctor had ever felt, he had counted it a duty to conceal. Nay, the daughter, with a womanly eye, took pride in the aptitude and becomingness of his dress,—so different from what she had been used to see in the clumsy toilet of the Doctor, or of the good-natured Squire Elderkin. Henceforth she will have a new standard of comparison, to which her lovers, if they ever declare themselves, must submit.

"And so you have stolen a march upon them all, Adèle? I suppose they have n't a hint of the person you were to meet?"

"All,—at least nearly all, dear papa; there

was only good Madame Arles, to whom I could not help saying that I was coming to see you."

A shade passed over the face of Maverick, which it required all his self-possession to conceal from the quick eye of his daughter.

"And who, pray, is this Madame Arles, Adèle?"

"Oh, a good creature! She has taught me French; no proper teaching, to be sure; but in my talk with her, all the old idioms have come back to me; at least, I hope so."

And she rattles on in French speech, explaining how it was,—how they walked together in those sunny noontides at Ashfield; and taking a girlish pride in the easy adaptation of her language to forms which her father must know so well, she rounds off a little torrent of swift narrative with a piquant, coquettish look, and says,—

"N'est ce pas, que j'y suis, mon père?"

"Parfaitement, ma chère," says the father, and drops an admiring kiss upon the glowing cheeks of Adèle.

But the shade of anxiety has not passed from the face of Maverick.

"This Madame Arles, Adèle,—has she been long in the country?"

IN THE CITY

"I don't know, papa; yet it must be some time; she speaks English passably well."

"And she has told you, I suppose, very much about the people among whom you were born, Adèle?"

"Not much, papa,—and never anything about herself or her history; yet I have been so curious!"

"Don't be too curious, *petite;* you might learn only of badness."

"Not badness, I am very, very sure, papa!"

Adèle is sitting on the arm of his chair, fondling those sparse locks of his, sprinkled with gray. It is a wholly new sensation for him; charming, doubtless; but even under the caresses of this daughter, of whom he has reason to be proud, anxious thoughts crowd upon him.

The Doctor is met very warmly by Maverick, and feels something like a revival of the glow of his youthful days as he takes his hand; and yet they are wider apart by far than when they met in the lifetime of Rachel. Both feel it; they have travelled divergent roads, these last twenty years. The Doctor is satisfied by the bearing and talk of Maverick (whatever kindness may lie in it) that his worldliness is more engrossing and decided than ever. And Maverick, on his part, scrutinizing carelessly, but unerringly, that embarrassed country manner of the parson's, that stark linen in which he is arrayed by the foresight of the spinster sister, and the constraint of his speech, is sure that his old friend more than ever bounds his thought by the duties of his sacred office.

The Doctor is, moreover, sadly out of place in that little parlor of the hotel, looking out upon Broadway; there is no adaptiveness in his nature: he comes out from the little world of his study, where Tillotson and Poole and Newton have been his companions, athwart the roar of the city street, and it sounds in his ear like an echo of the murmurs of Pandemonium. Under these circumstances he scarce dares to expostulate so boldly as he would wish with Maverick upon the worldliness of his career; it would seem like bearding the lion in his own den. Nor, indeed, does Maverick provoke such expostulation; he is so considerate of the Doctor's feelings, so grateful for his attentions to Adèle, so religiously disposed (it must be said) in all that concerns the daughter's education and future, and waives the Doctor's personal advices with so kind and easy a grace, that the poor parson despairs of reach-

IN THE CITY

ing him with the point of the sword of Divine truth.

"My good friend," says Maverick, "you have been a father to my child,—a better one than I have made,—I wish I could repay you."

The Doctor bows stiffly; he has lost the familiarity which at their last interview had lingered from their boyish days at college.

"I suppose that under your teaching," continues Maverick, "she is so fixed in the New England faith of our fathers, that she might be trusted now even to my bad guidance."

"I have tried to do my duty, Maverick. I could have wished to see more of self-abasement in her, and a clearer acceptance of the doctrine we are called upon to teach."

"But she has been constant to the duties you have enjoined, has n't she, Doctor?"

"Entirely so,—entirely; but, my friend, our poor worldly efforts at duty do not always call down the gift of Grace."

"By Jove, Doctor, but that seems hard doctrine."

"Hard to carnal minds, Maverick; but the evidences"—

"Nay, nay," said Maverick, interrupting him; "you know I 'm not strong in theology; I don't want to be put *hors de combat* by you.

DOCTOR JOHNS

But about that little affair of the rosary,—no harm came of it, I hope?"

"None, I believe," said the Doctor; "but I must not conceal from you, Maverick, that a late teacher of hers, to whom, unfortunately, she seems very much attached, is strongly wedded to the Romish Church."

"That would seem a very awkward risk to take, Doctor," said Maverick, with more of seriousness than he had yet shown.

"A risk, certainly; but I took the precaution of warning Madame Arles, who is the party in question, against any conversation with Adaly upon religious subjects."

"And you ventured to trust her? Upon my word, Johns, you give me a lesson in faith. I should have been more severe than you. I would n't have admitted such intercourse; and, my good friend, if I should ask permission to reinstate Adèle in your household for a time, promise me, please, that all intercourse with Madame Arles shall be cut off. I know Frenchwomen better than you, my friend."

"No doubt—no doubt!"

And the Doctor assured him that he would do as he desired, and would be glad to have the father's authority for the interruption of

IN THE CITY

an intercourse which had almost the proportions of a tender friendship.

Maverick was thoughtful for a moment.

"Well, yes, Doctor, be gentle—I know you are always—with the dear girl; but if there be any demur on her part, pray give her to understand that what you will ask in this respect has my express sanction. If I know myself, Johns, there is no object I have so near at heart as the happiness of my child; not alone now; but in her future, I hope to God (I speak reverently, Doctor) that she may have immunity from suffering of whatever kind. I wish wealth could buy it; but it can't. Mind the promise, Johns; keep her away from this Frenchwoman."

The Brindlocks, of course, with whom the Doctor was quartered during his stay, took an early occasion to show civilities to Mr. Maverick and his daughter; and Mrs. Brindlock kindly offered her services to Adèle in negotiating such additions to her wardrobe as the proud father insisted upon her making; and in the necessary excursions up and down the city, Reuben, by the pleasant devices of Mrs. Brindlock, was an almost constant out-of-door attendant.

He was no longer the shy boy Adèle had at

first encountered. Nay, grown bold by his city experiences, he was disposed to assume a somewhat patronizing air toward the bright-eyed country-girl who was just now equipping herself for somewhat larger contact with the world. Adèle did not openly resent the proffered patronage, but, on the contrary, accepted it with an excess of grateful expressions, whose piquant irony, for two whole days, Reuben, with his blunter perceptions, never suspected. What boy of eighteen is a match for a girl of sixteen? Patronize, indeed! But suspicion came at last, and full knowledge broke upon him under a musical little laugh of Adèle's, (half smothered in her kerchief) when the gallant young man had blundered into some idle compliment.

But if the laugh of Adèle cured Reuben of his patronage, it did not cure him of thought about her. It kindled a new train, indeed, of whose drift he was himself unconscious.

He is not altogether the same lad we saw upon the deck of the *Princess,* under Captain Saul. He would hardly sail for China now in a tasselled cap. He never will,—this much we can say, at least, without anticipating the burden of our story.

XXXIV

The New Reuben

REUBEN has in many respects vastly improved under his city education. It would be wrong to say that the good Doctor did not take a very human pride in his increased alertness of mind, in his vivacity, in his self-possession,— nay, even in that very air of world-acquaintance which now covered entirely the old homely manner of the country lad. He thought within himself, what a glad smile of triumph would have been kindled upon the face of the lost Rachel, could she but have seen this tall youth with his kindly attentions and his graceful speech. May be she did see it all.

But the Doctor underneath all his pride carried a great deal of anxious doubt; and as he walked beside his boy upon the thronged street, elated in some strange way by the touch of that strong arm of the youth, whose blood was his own,—so dearly his own,—he pondered gravely with himself, if the mocking delusions of the Evil One were not the occasion of his pride? Was not Satan setting himself artfully to the work of quieting all sense of responsibility in regard to the lad's future, by thus kindling in his old heart anew the vanities of the flesh and the pride of life?

"I say, father, I want to put you through now. It 'll do you a great deal of good to see some of the wonders here in the city."

"The very voice,—the very voice of Rachel!" says the Doctor to himself, quickening his laggard step to keep pace with Reuben.

"There are such lots of things to show you, father! Look in this store, now. You can step in, if you like. It 's the largest carpet-store in the United States,—three stories packed full. There 's the head man of the firm,—the stout man in a white choker; with half a million, they say: he 's a deacon in Mowry's Church."

"I hope, Reuben, that he makes a worthy use of his wealth."

"Oh, he gives thunderingly to the missionary societies," said Reuben, with a glibness that grated on the father's ear.

"You see that building yonder? That 's Gothic. They 've got the finest bowling-alleys in the world there."

"I hope, my son, you never go to such places?"

THE NEW REUBEN

"Bowl? Oh, yes, I bowl sometimes: the physicians recommend it; good exercise for the chest. Besides, it 's kept by a fine man, and he 's got one of the prettiest little trotting horses you ever saw in your life."

"Why, my son, you don't mean to tell me that you have acquaintance with the keeper of this bowling-alley?"

"Oh, yes, father,—we fellows all know him; and his cigars are tip-top."

"You don't mean to say that you smoke, Reuben?" said the old gentleman, gravely.

"Not much, father: but then, everybody smokes now and then. Mowry—Dr. Mowry smokes, you know."

"Is it possible? Well, well!"

"You see that fine building over there?" said Reuben, as they passed on.

"Yes, my son."

"That 's the theatre,—the Old Park."

The Doctor ran his eye over it, and its effigy of Shakspeare upon the niche in the wall, as Gabriel might have looked upon the armor of Beelzebub.

"I hope, Reuben, you never enter those doors?"

"Well, father, since Kean and Mathews are gone, there 's really nothing worth seeing."

"Kean! Mathews!" said the Doctor, stopping in his walk and confronting Reuben with a stern bow,—"is it possible, my son, that I hear you talking in this familiar way of play-actors? You don't tell me that you have been a participant in such orgies of Satan?"

"Why, father!" said Reuben, a little startled by the Doctor's earnestness, "the truth is, Aunt Mabel goes occasionally, like 'most all the ladies; but we go, you know, to see the moral pieces, generally."

"Moral pieces!" said the Doctor with a withering scowl. "Reuben! those who go thither take hold on the door-posts of hell!"

"That's the Tract Society building yonder," said Reuben, wishing to divert the Doctor, if possible, from the special objects of his reflections.

"Rachel's voice!—always Rachel's voice!"—said the Doctor to himself.

"Would you like to go in, father?"

"No, my son, we have no time; and yet"—meditating, and thrusting his hand in his pocket—"there is a tract or two I would like to buy for you, Reuben."

"Go in, then," says Reuben. "Let me tell them who you are, father, and you can get them at wholesale prices. It's the merest song."

THE NEW REUBEN

"No, my son, no," said the Doctor, disheartened by the blithe air of Reuben. "I fear it would be wasted effort. Yet I trust that you do not wholly neglect the opportunities for religious instruction on the Sabbath?"

"Oh, no," says Reuben, gayly. "I see Dr. Mowry off and on, pretty often. He's a clever old gentleman,—Dr. Mowry."

Clever old gentleman!

The Doctor walked on, oppressed with grief,—silent, but with lips moving in prayer,—beseeching God to take away the stony heart from this poor child of his, and to give him a heart of flesh.

The city Doctor was a ponderously good man, preaching for the most part ponderous sermons, and possessed of a most imposing friendliness of manner. When Reuben had presented to him the credentials from his father, (which he could hardly have done save for the urgency of the Brindlocks,) the ponderous Doctor had patted him upon the shoulder, and said,—

"My young friend, your father is a most worthy man,—most worthy. I should be delighted to see you following in his steps. I shall be most glad to be of service to you. Our meetings for Bible instruction are on Wednesdays, at seven: the young men upon the left the young ladies on the right."

The memory of old teachings did, for a year or more, make any divergence from the severe path of boyhood seem to Reuben a sin.

The first visit to the theatre was like a bold push into the very domain of Satan. Even the ticket-seller at the door seemed to him on that eventful night an understrapper of Beelzebub, who looked out at him with the goggle eyes of a demon. That such a man could have a family, or family affections, or friendships, or any sense of duty or honor, was to him a thing incomprehensible; and when he passed the wicket for the first time into the vestibule of the old Park Theatre, the very usher in the corridor had to his eye a look like the Giant Dagon, and he conceived of him as mumbling, in his leisure moments, the flesh from human bones. And when at last the curtain rose, and the damp air came out upon him from behind the scenes as he sat in the pit, and the play began with some wonderful creature in tight bodice and painted cheeks, sailing across the stage, it seemed to him that the flames of Divine wrath might presently be bursting out over the house, or a great judgment of God break down the roof and destroy them all.

THE NEW REUBEN

But it did not; and he took courage. If in his moments of reflection—these being not yet wholly crowded out from his life—there came a shadowy hope of better things, of some moral poise that should be in keeping with the tenderer recollections of his boyhood,—all this can never be, (he bethinks himself, in view of his old teaching,) except on the heel of some terrible conviction of sin; and the conviction will hardly come without some deeper and more damning weight of it than he feels as yet.

The minister's son had no love for gross vices; there were human instincts in him (if it may be said) that rebelled against his more deliberate sinnings. But the father, as we have seen, could not reach down to any religious convictions of the son; and Reuben keeps him at bay with a banter, and an exaggerated attention to the personal comforts of the old gentleman, that utterly baffled him.

So it was with a profound sigh that the father bade his son adieu after this city visit.

"Good-by, father! Love to them all in Ashfield."

So like Rachel's voice! So like Rachel's! And the heart of the old man yearned toward him and ached bitterly for him. *"O my son Absalom! my son!"*

XXXV

Travel

MAVERICK hurried his departure from the city; and Adèle, writing to Rose to announce the programme of her journey, says only this much of Reuben:—"We have of course seen R—, who was very attentive and kind. He has grown tall,—taller, I should think, than Phil; and he is quite well-looking, and gentlemanly. I think he has a very good opinion of himself."

The summer's travel offered a season of rare enjoyment to Adèle. The lively sentiment of girlhood was not yet wholly gone, and the thoughtfulness of womanhood was just beginning to tone, without controlling, her sensibilities. The delicate attentions of Maverick were more like those of a lover than of a father. Through his ever-watchful eyes, Adèle looked upon the beauties of Nature with a new halo on them. How the water sparkled to her vision! How the days came and went like golden dreams!

Ah, happy youth-time! The Hudson, Lake George, Saratoga, the Mountains, the Beach,

TRAVEL

—to us old stagers, who have breasted the tide of so many years, and flung off long ago all the iridescent sparkles of our sentiment, these are only names of summer thronging-places. Upon the river we watch the growth of the crops, or ask our neighbors about the cost of our friend Faro's new country-seat; we lounge upon the piazzas of the hotels, reading price-lists, or (if not too old) an editorial; we complain of the windy currents upon the lake, and find our chiefest pleasure in a trout boiled plain, with a dressing of champagne sauce; we linger at Fabyan's on a sunny porch, talking politics with a rheumatic old gentleman in his overcoat, while the youngest go ambling through the fir woods and up the mountains with shouts and laughter. Yet it was not always thus. There were times in the lives of us old travellers—let us say from sixteen to twenty—when the great river was a glorious legend trailing its storied length through the Highlands; when in every opening valley there lay purple shadows whereon we painted castles: when the corridors and shaded walks of the "United States" were like a fairy land, with flitting skirts and waving plumes, and some delicately gloved hand beating its reveille upon the heart; and when every floating film of the mist along the sea, whether at Newport or Nahant, tenderly entreated the fancy.

But we forget ourselves, and we forget Adèle. In her wild exuberance of joy Maverick shares with a spirit that he had believed to be dead in him utterly. And if he finds it necessary to check from time to time the noisy effervescence of her pleasure, as he certainly does at first, he does it in the most tender and considerate way; and Adèle learns, what many of her warm-hearted sisters never do learn, that a well-bred control over our enthusiasms in no way diminishes the exquisiteness of their savor.

Maverick should be something over fifty now, and his keenness of observation in respect to feminine charms is not perhaps so great as it once was; but even he cannot fail to see, with a pride that he makes no great effort to conceal, the admiring looks that follow the lithe, graceful figure of Adèle, wherever their journey may lead them. Nor, indeed, were there any more comely toilets for a young girl to be met with anywhere than those which had been provided for the young traveller under the advices of Mrs. Brindlock.

It may be true—what his friend Papiol had

TRAVEL

predicted—that Maverick will be too proud of his child to keep her in a secluded corner of New England.

Yet weeks had run by, and Maverick had never once broached the question of a return. The truth was, that the new experience was so charming and so engrossing for him, the sweet, intelligent face ever at his side was so full of eager wonder, and he so delightfully intent upon providing new sources of pleasure, and calling out again and again the gushes of her girlish enthusiasm, that he shrunk instinctively from a decision in which must be involved so largely her future happiness.

At last it was Adèle herself who suggested the inquiry,—

"Is it true, dear papa, what the Doctor tells me, that you may possibly take me back to France with you?"

"What say you, Adèle? Would you like to go?"

"Dearly!"

"But," said Maverick, "your friends here,—can you so easily cast them away?"

"No, no, no!" said Adèle,—"not cast them away! Could n't I come again some day? Besides, there is your home, papa; I should love any home of yours, and love your friends."

"For instance, Adèle, there is my book-keeper, a lean Savoyard, who wears a red wig and spectacles,—and Lucille, a great, gaunt woman, with a golden crucifix about her neck, who keeps my little parlor in order,—and Papiol, a fat Frenchman, with a bristly mustache and iron-gray hair, who, I dare say, would want to kiss the pet of his dear friend,—and Jeannette, who washes the dishes for us, and wears great wooden sabots"—

"Nonsense, papa! I am sure you have other friends; and then there's the good Godmother."

"Ah, yes,—she indeed," said Maverick; "what a precious hug she would give you, Adèle!"

"And then—and then—should I see mamma?"

The pleasant humor died out of the face of Maverick on the instant; and then, in a slow, measured tone,—

"Impossible, Adèle,—impossible! Come here, darling!" and as he fondled her in a wild, passionate way, "I will love you for both, Adèle; she was not worthy of you, child."

Adèle, too, is overcome with a sudden seriousness.

TRAVEL

"Is she living, papa?" And she gives him an appealing look that must be answered.

And Maverick seems somehow appalled by that innocent, confiding expression of hers.

"May be, may be, my darling; she was living not long since; yet it can never matter to you or me more. You will trust me in this, Adèle?" And he kisses her tenderly.

And she, returning the caress, but bursting into tears as she does so, says,—

"I will, I do, papa."

"There, there, darling!"—as he folds her to him; "no more tears,—no more tears, *chérie!*"

But even while he says it, he is nervously struggling with his own emotion.

Meantime Adèle is not without her little mementos of the life at Ashfield, which come in the shape of thick double letters from that good girl Rose,—her dear, dear friend, who has been advised by the little traveller to what towns she should direct these tender missives; and Adèle is no sooner arrived at these postal stations than she sends for the budget which she knows must be waiting for her. And of course she has her own little pen in a certain travelling-escritoire the good papa has given her; and she plies her white fingers with it often and often of an evening, after the day's sight-seeing is over, to tell Rose in return what a charming journey she is having, and how kind papa is, and what a world of strange things she is seeing; and there are descriptions of sunsets and sunrises, and of lakes and of mountains, on those close-written sheets of hers, which Rose, in her enthusiasm, declares to be equal to many descriptions in print.

Poor Rose feels that she has only very humdrum stories to tell in return for these; but she ekes out her letters pretty well, after all, and what they lack in novelty is made up in affection.

"There is really nothing new to tell," she writes, "except it be that our old friend, Miss Almira Tourtelot, astonished us all with a new bonnet last Sunday, and with new saffron ribbons; and she has come out, too, in the new tight sleeves, in which she looks drolly enough. Phil is very uneasy, now that his schooling is done, and talks of going to the West Indies about some business in which papa is concerned. I hope he will go, if he does n't stay too long. He is such a dear, good fellow! Madam Arles asks after you, when I see her, which is not very often now; for since the Doctor has come back from New York, he has had a new talk with mamma, and has quite won her over to *his*

TRAVEL

view of the matter. So good-by to French for the present! Heigho! But I don't know that I 'm sorry, now that you are not here, dear Ady.

"Another queer thing I had almost forgotten to tell you. The poor Boody girl,—you must remember her? Well, she has come back on a sudden; and they say her father will not receive her in his house,—there are *terrible stories* about it!—and now she is living with an old woman far out upon the river-road,— only a little garret-chamber for herself and *the child she brought back with her.* Of course *nobody* goes near her, or looks at her, if she comes on the street. But—the queerest thing! —when Madame Arles heard of it and of her story, what does she do but *walk far out to visit her,* and talked with her in her broken English for an hour, they say. Papa says she (Madame A.) must be a very bad woman or a very good woman. But—good or bad— she goes away presently; rumor says to France."

And again, at a later date, Rose writes,—

"The Bowriggs are all off for the winter, and the house closed. Reuben has been here on a flying visit to the parsonage; and how proud Miss Eliza was of *her nephew!* He came over to see Phil, I suppose; but Phil had gone two weeks before. Mamma thinks he is *fine-looking*. I fancy he will never live in the country again. When shall I see you again, *dear,* DEAR Ady? I have so *much* to talk to you about!"

A month thereafter Maverick and his daughter find their way to Ashfield. Of course Miss Johns has made magnificent preparations to receive them. She surpassed herself in her toilet on the day of their arrival, and fairly astonished Maverick with the warmth of her welcome to his child. Yet he could not help observing that Adèle met it more coolly than was her wont, and that her tenderest words were reserved for the good Doctor. And how proud she was to walk with her father upon the village street, glancing timidly up at the windows from which she knew those stiff old Miss Hapgoods must be peeping out! How proud to sit beside him in the parson's pew, feeling that the eyes of half the congregation were fastened on the tall gentleman beside her!

Important business letters command Maverick's early presence abroad; and, after conference with the Doctor, he decides to leave Adèle once more under the roof of the parsonage.

"Under God, I will do for her what I can," said the Doctor.

"I know it, I know it, my good friend," says Maverick. "Teach her self-reliance; she may need it some day. And mind what I have said of this French woman, should she appear again. Adèle seems to have a *tendresse* that way. Those Frenchwomen are very insidious, Johns."

"You know their ways better than I," said the Doctor.

A little afterward Maverick was humming a snatch from an opera under the trees of the orchard; and Adèle went bounding toward him, to take the last walk with him for so long,—so long!

XXXVI

Illness

AUTUMN and winter passed by, and the summer of 1838 opened upon the old quiet life of Ashfield. The stiff Miss Johns, busy with her household duties, or with her stately visitings. The Doctor's hat and cane in their usual place upon the little table within the door, and of a Sunday his voice is lifted up under the old meeting-house roof in earnest expostulation. The birds pipe their old songs, and the orchard has shown once more its wondrous glory of bloom. But all these things have lost their novelty for Adèle. Would it be strange, if the tranquil life of the little town had lost something of its early charm? That swift French blood of hers has been stirred by contact with the outside world. She has, perhaps, not been wholly insensible to those admiring glances which so quickened the pride of the father.

The young girl is, moreover, greatly disturbed at the thought of separation from her father continued and indefinite. It is all the worse that she does not clearly perceive the necessity for it. Is she not of an age now to contribute to the cheer of whatever home he may have beyond the sea? Why, pray, has he given her such uninviting pictures of his companions there? Or is it that her religious education is not yet thoroughly complete, and that she still holds out against a full and public avowal of all the doctrines which the Doctor urges upon her acceptance? And the thought of this makes his kindly severities appear more irksome than ever.

ILLNESS

Another cause of grief to Adèle is the extreme disfavor in which she finds that Madame Arles (who has now re-appeared in Ashfield) is regarded by the towns-people. Her sympathies had run toward the unfortunate woman in some inexplicable way, and held there even now, so strongly that contemptuous mention of her stung like a reproach to herself.

"I never liked her countenance, Adèle," said the spinster, in her solemn manner; "and I am rejoiced that you will not be under her influence the present summer."

"And I 'm sorry," said Adèle, petulantly.

"It is gratifying to me," continued Miss Eliza, without notice of Adèle's interruption, "that Mr. Maverick has confirmed my own impressions, and urged the Doctor against permitting so unwise association."

"When? how?" said Adèle, sharply. "Papa has never seen her."

"But he has seen other Frenchwomen, Adèle, and he fears their influence."

Adèle looked keenly at the spinster for a moment, as if to fathom the depth of this reply, then burst into tears.

"Oh, why, why did n't he take me with him?" But this she says under breath, and to herself, as she rushes into the Doctor's study to question him.

"Is it true, New Papa, that papa thought badly of Madame Arles?"

"Not personally, my child, since he had never seen her. But, Adaly, your father, though I fear he is far away from the true path, wishes you to find it, my child. He has faith in the religion we teach so imperfectly; he wishes you to be exposed to no influences that will forbid your full acceptance of it."

"But Madame Arles never talked of religion to me;" and Adèle taps impatiently upon the floor.

"That may be true, Adaly,—it may be true; but we cannot be thrown into habits of intimacy with those reared in iniquity without fear of contracting stain. I could wish, my child, that you would so far subdue your rebellious heart, and put on the complete armor of righteousness, as to be able to resist all attacks."

"And it was for this papa left me here?" And Adèle says it with a smile of mockery that alarms the good Doctor.

"I trust, Adaly, that he had that hope."

The little foot taps more and more impatiently as he goes on to set forth (as he had so

ILLNESS

often done) the heinousness of her offences and the weight of her just condemnation. Yet the antagonism did not incline her to open doubt; but after she had said her evening prayer that night, (taught her by the parson,) she drew out her little rosary and kissed reverently the crucifix. It is so much easier at this juncture for her tried and distracted spirit to bolster its faith upon such material symbol than to find repose in any merely intellectual conviction of truth.

Adèle's intimacy with Rose and with her family retained all its old tenderness, but that good fellow Phil was gone. Adèle missed his kindly attentions more than she would have believed. The Bowriggs have come again to Ashfield, but their clamorous friendship is more than ever distasteful to Adèle. Over and over she makes a feint of illness to escape the noisy hilarity. Nor, indeed, is it wholly a feint. Whether it were that her state of moral perturbation and unrest reacted upon the physical system, or that there were other disturbing causes, certain it was that the roses were fading from her cheeks, and that her step was losing day by day something of its old buoyancy. It is even thought best to summon the village doctor to the family council. He is a

DOCTOR JOHNS

gossiping, kindly old gentleman, who spends an easy life, free from much mental strain, in trying to make his daily experiences tally with the little fund of medical science which he accumulated thirty years before.

The serene old gentleman feels the pulse, with his head reflectively on one side,—tells his little jokelet about Sir Astley Cooper, or some other worthy of the profession,—shakes his fat sides with a cheery laugh,—"And now, my dear," he says, "let us look at the tongue. Ah, I see, I see,—the stomach lacks tone."

"And there's dreadful lassitude, sometimes, Doctor," speaks up Miss Eliza.

"Ah, I see,—a little exhaustion after a long walk,—is n't it so, Miss Maverick? I see, I see; we must brace up the system, Miss Johns,—brace up the system."

And the kindly old gentleman prescribes his little tonics, of which Adèle takes some, and throws more out of the window.

Adèle does not mend, and the rumor is presently current upon the street that "Miss Adeel is in a decline." The spinster shows a solicitude in the matter which almost touches the heart of the French girl.

Weeks pass by, but still the tonics of the kindly old physician prove of little efficacy.

ILLNESS

Adèle has strength however for an occasional stroll with Rose, and, in the course of one of them, comes upon Madame Arles, whom she meets with a good deal of her old effusion. And Madame, touched by her apparent weakness, more than reciprocates it.

'But you suffer, you are unhappy, my child, —'t is the sun of Provence you need. Is n't it so, *mon ange?* No, no, you were never meant to grow up among these cold people. You must see the vineyards, and the olives, and the sea, Adèle; you must! you must!"

All this, uttered in a torrent, which, with its *tutoiements,* Rose can poorly comprehend.

Yet it goes straight to the heart of Adèle, and her tongue is loosened to a little petulant, fiery *roulade* against the severities of the life around her, which it would have greatly pained poor Rose to listen to in any speech of her own.

But such interviews, once or twice repeated, come to the knowledge of the watchful spinster, who clearly perceives that Adèle is chafing more and more under the wonted family regimen. With an affectation of tender solicitude, she volunteers to attend Adèle upon her short morning strolls, and she learns presently, with great triumph, that Madame Arles has estab-

DOCTOR JOHNS

lished herself at last under the same roof which gives refuge to the outcast Boody woman. Nothing more was needed to seal the opinion of the spinster, and to confirm the current village belief in the heathenish character of the French lady. Dame Tourtelot was shrewdly of the opinion that the woman represented some Popish plot for the abduction of Adèle, and for her incarceration in a nunnery,—a theory which Miss Almira, with her natural tendency to romance, industriously propagated.

Before July is ended a serious illness has declared itself, and Adèle is confined to her chamber. Madame Arles is among the earliest who come with eager inquiries, and begs to see the sufferer. But she is confronted by the indefatigable spinster. Madame withdraws, sadly; but the visit and the claim are repeated from time to time, until the stately civility of Miss Johns arouses her suspicions.

"You deny me, Madame. You do wrong. I love Adèle; she loves me. I know that I could comfort her. You do not understand her nature. She was born where the sky is soft and warm. You are all cold and harsh,—she has told me as much. I know how she suffers. I wish I could carry her back to France with me. I pray you, let me see her, good Madame!"

ILLNESS

"It is quite impossible, I assure you," said the spinster, in her most aggravating manner. "It would be quite against the wishes of my brother, the Doctor, as well as of Mr. Maverick."

"Monsieur Maverick! *Mon Dieu,* Madame! He is no father to her; he leaves her to die with strangers; he has no heart; I have better right: I love her. I must see her!"

And with a passionate step,—those eyes of hers glaring in that strange double way upon the amazed Miss Eliza,—she strides toward the door, as if she would overcome all opposition. But before she has gone out, that cruel pain has seized her and she sinks upon a chair, quite prostrated, and with hands clasped wildly over that burden of a heart.

"Too hard! too hard!" she murmurs, scarce above her breath.

The spinster is attentive, but is untouched.

The good Doctor is greatly troubled by the report of Miss Eliza. Can it be possible that Adèle has given a confidence to this strange woman that she has not given to them? Cold and harsh! Can Adèle, indeed, have said this? Has he not labored with a full heart? Has he not agonized in prayer to draw in this wandering lamb to the fold?

DOCTOR JOHNS

It touches him to the quick to think that her childlike, trustful confidence is at last alienated from him,—that her affection for him is so distempered by dread and weariness. For, unconsciously, he has grown to love her as he loves no one save his boy Reuben. Through her winning, playful talk, he has taken up that old trail of worldly affections which he had thought buried forever in Rachel's grave. That tender touch of her little fingers upon his cheek has seemed to say, "Life has its joys, old man!" The patter of her feet along the house has kindled the memories of other gentle steps that tread now silently in the courts of air. Those songs of hers,—how he has loved them!

And the good man, with such thoughts thronging on him, falls upon his knees, beseeching God to "be over the sick child, to comfort her, to heal her, to pour down His divine grace upon her, to open her blind eyes to the richness of His truth."

Rising from his attitude of prayer, and going toward the little window of his study to arrange it for the night, the Doctor sees a slight figure in black pacing up and down upon the opposite side of the way, and looking up from time to time to the light that is burning

SHORTCOMINGS OF REUBEN

in the window of Adèle. He knows on the instant who it must be, and fears more than ever the possible influence which this strange woman, who is so persistent in her attention, may have upon the heart of the girl.

Like most holy men, ignorant of the crafts and devices of the world, he no sooner blundered into a suspicion of some deep Devil's cunning than every footfall and every floating zephyr seemed to confirm it.

XXXVII

Shortcomings of Reuben

MEANTIME Reuben was gaining, month by month, in a knowledge of the world,—at least of such portion of it as came within the range of his vision in New York. He thought with due commiseration of the humble people of Ashfield. He wonders how he could have tolerated so long their simple ways. The Eagle Tavern, with its creaking sign-board, does not loom so largely as it once did upon the horizon of his thought.

He has put Phil through some of the

"sights:" for that great lout of a country lad (as Reuben could not help counting him, though he liked his big, honest heart for all that) had found him out, when he came to New York to take ship for the West Indies.

"I say, Phil," Reuben had said, as he marched his old schoolmate up Broadway, "it's rather a touch beyond Ashfield, this, is n't it? How do you think Old Boody's tavern and signboard would look along here?"

And Phil laughed, quietly.

"I should like to see old Deacon Tourtelot," continued Reuben, "with Huldy on his arm, sloping down Broadway. Would n't the old people stare?"

"I guess they would," Phil said, demurely.

"I wonder if they 'd knock off at sundown Saturday night," continued Reuben, mockingly.

And his tone somewhat hurt Phil, who had the memories of the old home — a very dear one to him — fresh upon him.

"And I suppose Miss Almiry keeps at her singing?"

'Yes," said Phil, straining a point in favor of his townswoman; "and I think she sings pretty well."

It seemed to him, in his honesty, that Reuben

SHORTCOMINGS OF REUBEN

was wantonly cutting asunder all the ties that once bound him to the old home. It pained him, moreover, to think—as he did, with a good deal of restiveness—that his blessed mother, and Rose perhaps, and the old Squire, his father, were among the Ashfield people at whom Reuben sneered so glibly. And when he parted with him upon the dock,—for Reuben had gone down to see him off,—it was with a secret conviction that their old friendship had come to an end, and that thenceforth they two could have no sympathies in common.

But in this Phil was by no means wholly right. The talk of Reuben was, after all, but the ebullition of a city conceit,—a conceit which is apt to belong to all young men at some period of their novitiate in city life.

On the very night after Reuben had parted from Phil, when he came late to his chamber, dazed with some new scene at the theater, and his brain flighty with a cup too much, it may well have happened, that in his fevered restlessness, as the clock near by chimed midnight, his thoughts ran back to that other chamber where once sweet sleep always greeted him,—to the overhanging boughs that rustled in the evening air at the window,—to the shaded street that stretched away between the silent houses,—to the song of the katydids, chattering their noisy chorus,—to the golden noons when light feet tripped along the village walks,—to the sunny smiles of Rose,—to the kindly entreaty of good Mrs. Elderkin,—and more faintly, yet more tenderly, than elsewhere, to a figure and face far remote, and so glorified by distance that they seem almost divine, a figure and face that are somehow associated with the utterance of his first prayer,—and with the tender vision before him, he mumbles the same prayer and falls asleep with it upon his lip.

Only on his lip, however,—and the next day, when he steals a half-hour for a stroll upon Broadway with that dashing girl, Miss Sophia Bowrigg, (she is really a stylish creature,) he has very little thought of the dreamy sentiments of the night before, which seemed for the time to keep his wilder vagaries in subjection, and to kindle aspirations toward a better life. It is doubtful, even, if he did not indulge in an artful compliment or two to the dashing Miss Sophia, the point of which lay in a cleverly covered contrast of herself with the humdrum manners of the fair ones of Ashfield. Yet, to tell truth, he is not wholly untouched by certain little rallying, coquettish

SHORTCOMINGS OF REUBEN

speeches of Miss Sophia in respect to Adèle, who, in her open, girl-like way, has very likely told the full story of Reuben's city attentions.

Reuben had, indeed, been piqued by the French girl's reception of his patronage, and he had been fairly carried off his feet in view of her easy adaptation to the ways of the city, and of her graceful carriage under all the toilet equipments which had been lavished upon her, under the advice of Mrs. Brindlock. A raw boy comes only by long aptitude into the freedom of a worldly manner; but a girl— most of all a French girl, in whom the instincts of her race are strong—leaps to such conquest in a day. Of course he had intimated to Adèle no wonder at the change; but he had thrust a stray glove of hers into his pocket, counting it only a gallant theft; and there had been days when he had drawn out that little relic of her visit from its hidden receptacle and smoothed it upon his table, and pressed it, very likely, to his lips, in the same way in which youth of nineteen or twenty are used to treat such feminine tokens of grace.

It was a dainty glove, to be sure. It conjured up her presence in its most alluring aspect. The rustle of her silk, the glow of her cheek, the coyness of her touch, whenever she

DOCTOR JOHNS

has dropped that delicate hand on his, came with the sight of it. He ventures, in a moment of gallant exuberance, to purchase a half-dozen of the same number of very charming tints, (to his eye,) and sends them as a gift to Adèle, saying,—

"I found your stray glove we had a search for in the carriage, but did not tell of it. I hope these will fit."

"They fit nicely," said Adèle, writing back to him,—"so nicely, I may be tempted to throw another old glove of mine some time in your way."

Miss Eliza Johns was of course delighted with this attention of Reuben's, and made it the occasion of writing him a long letter, (and her letters were very rare, by reason of the elaboration she counted necessary,) in which she set forth the excellence of Adèle's character, her "propriety of speech," her "lady-like deportment," her "cheerful observance of duty," and her "eminent moral worth," in such terms as stripped all romance from Reuben's recollection of her, and made him more than half regret his gallant generosity.

The Doctor writes to him regularly once a fortnight; of which missives Reuben reads as regularly the last third, containing, as it does

SHORTCOMINGS OF REUBEN

usually, a little home news or casual mention of Miss Rose Elderkin or of the family circle. The other two thirds, mainly expostulatory, he skips, only allowing his eye to glance over them, and catch such scattered admonitions as these:—"Be steadfast in the truth. . . . Be not tempted of the Devil; for if you resist him, he will flee from you. . . ."

Ah, how much of such good advice had been twisted into tapers for the lighting of Reuben's cigars! It is certain that he loved his father; it is certain that he venerated him; and yet, and yet, (he said to himself,) "I do wish he would keep this solemn stuff for his sermons. Who cares to read it? Who cares to hear it, except on Sundays?"

And when Mr. Brindlock wrote, as he took occasion to do about this period, regretting the extravagance of Reuben and the bad associations into which he had fallen, and urging the Doctor to impress upon him the advantages of regularity and of promptitude, and to warn him that a very advantageous business career which was opening upon him would be blighted by his present habits, the poor gentleman was fairly taken aback.

What admonition could the Doctor add to those which he had addressed to his poor son fortnightly for years past? Had he not unfolded the terrors of God's wrath upon sinners? However, the Doctor wrote to Reuben with even more than his usual unction. But he could not bring himself to warn his boy of the mere blight to his worldly career,—that was so small a matter! Yet he laid before him in graver terms than he had ever done before the weight of the judgment of an offended God. Reuben lighted his cigar with the latter, not unfeelingly, but indifferently.

"It ought to burn," he says. "There's plenty of brimstone in it!"

It would have crazed the minister of Ashfield to have heard the speech. In his agony of mind he went to consult Squire Elderkin, and laid before him the dire accounts he had heard.

"Ah, young men will be young men, Doctor. There's time for him to come out right yet. It's the blood of the old Major; it must have vent."

As the Doctor recalled what he counted his father's godless death, he shuddered. Presently he talked of summoning his boy home immediately.

"Well, Doctor," said the Squire, meditatively, "there are two sides to that matter. There are great temptations in the city, to be sure; but if God puts a man in the way of great temptations, I suppose He gives him strength to resist them. Is n't that good theology?"

The parson nodded assent.

"We can always resist, if we will, Squire," said he.

"Very good, Doctor. Suppose, now, you bring your boy home; he 'll fret desperately under your long lectures, and with Miss Eliza, and perhaps run off into deviltries that will make him worse than those of the city. You must humor him a little, Doctor; touch his pride; there 's a fine, frank spirit at the bottom; give him a good word now and then."

"I know no word so good as prayer," said the Doctor, gravely.

"That 's very well, Doctor, very well. Mrs. Elderkin gives him help that way; and between you and me, Doctor, if any woman's prayers can call down blessings, I think that little woman's can."

"An estimable lady,—most estimable!" said the Doctor.

"Pray, if you will, Doctor; it 's all right; and for my part, I 'll drop him a line, telling him the town feels an ownership in him, and hopes he 'll do us all credit. I think we can bring him out all right."

"Thank you,—thank you, Squire," said the Doctor, with an unusual warmth.

And he wrought fervently in prayer that night; may be, too, the hearty invocation of that good woman, Mrs. Elderkin, joined with his in the Celestial presence; and if the kindly letter of the Squire did not rank with the prayers, we may believe, without hardihood, that the recording angel took note of it, and gave credit on the account current of human charities.

XXXVIII

A New Experience

MR. BRINDLOCK had, may be, exaggerated somewhat the story of Reuben's extravagances, but he was anxious that a word of caution should be dropped in his ear from some other lips than his own. The allowance from the Doctor, notwithstanding all the economies of Miss Eliza's frugal administration, would have been, indeed, somewhat narrow, and could by no means have kept Reuben upon his feet in the ambitious city-career upon which he had entered. But Mr. Brindlock had taken a great

A NEW EXPERIENCE

fancy to the lad, and besides the stipend granted for his duties about the counting-room, had given him certain shares in a few private ventures which had resulted very prosperously,—so prosperously, indeed, that the prudent merchant had determined to hold the full knowledge of the success in reserve. The prospects of Reuben, however, he being the favorite nephew of a well-established merchant, were regarded by the most indifferent observers as extremely flattering; and Mr. Bowrigg was not disposed to look unfavorably upon the young man's occasional attentions to the dashing Sophia.

It was some time in the month of September, of the same autumn in which poor Adèle lay sick at the parsonage, that Reuben came in one night, at twelve or thereabout, to his home at the Brindlocks', (living at this time in the neighborhood of Washington Square,) with his head cruelly battered, and altogether in a very piteous plight. Mrs. Brindlock, terribly frightened,—in her woman's way,—was for summoning the Doctor at once; but Reuben pleaded against it; he had been in a row, that was all, and had caught a big knock or two. The truth was, he had been upon one of his frolics with his old boon companions; and it so happened that one had spoken sneeringly of the parson's son, in a way which to the fiery young fellow seemed to cast ridicule upon the old gentleman. And thereupon Reuben, though somewhat maudlin with wine, yet with the generous spirit not wholly quenched in him, had entered upon a glowing little speech in praise of the old gentleman and of his profession,—a speech which, if it were garnished with here and there an objectionable expletive, was very earnest and did him credit.

"Good for Reuben!" the party had cried out. "Get him a pulpit!"

"Hang me, if he would n't preach better now than the old man!" said one.

"And a deuced sight livelier," said another.

"Hold your tongue, you blackguard!" burst out Reuben.

And from this the matter came very shortly to blows, in the course of which poor Reuben was severely punished, though he must have hit some hard blows; for he was wondrously active, and not a few boxing lessons had gone to make up the tale of his city accomplishments.

Howbeit, he was housed now, in view of his black eye, for many days, and had ample time for reflection. In aid of this came a full sheet

A NEW EXPERIENCE

of serious expostulations from the Doctor, and that letter of advice which Squire Elderkin had promised, with a little warm-hearted postscript from good Mrs. Elderkin,—so unlike to the carefully modulated letters of Aunt Eliza! The Doctor's missive, very likely, did not impress him more than the scores that had gone before it; but there was a practical tact, and good-natured, common-sense homeliness, in the urgence of the Squire, which engaged all Reuben's attention; and the words of the good woman, his wife, were worth more than a sermon to him. "We all want," she writes, "to think well of you, Reuben; we *do* think well of you. Don't disappoint us. I can't think of the cheery, bright face, that for so many an evening shone amid our household, as any thing but bright and cheery now. We all pray for your well-being and happiness, Reuben; and I *do* hope you have not forgotten to pray for it yourself."

And with the memory of the kindly woman which this letter called up came a pleasant vision of the winsome face of Rose, as she used to sit, with downcast eyes, beside her mother in the old house of Ashfield,—of Rose, as she used to lower upon him in their frolic, with those great hazel eyes sparkling with indignation. And if the vision did not quicken any lingering sentiment, it at the least gave a mellow tint to his thought,—a mellowness which even the hardness of Aunt Eliza could not wholly do away.

"I feel it my duty to write you, Reuben," she says, "and to inform you how very much we have all been shocked and astonished by the accounts which reach us of your continued indifference to religious duties, and your reckless extravagance. Let me implore you to be frugal and virtuous. If you learn to save now, the habit will be of very great service when you come to take your stand on the arena of life. I am aware that the temptations of a great city are almost innumerable; but I need hardly inform you that you will greatly consult your own interests and mitigate our harassment of feeling by practising a strict economy with your funds, and by attending regularly at church. You will excuse all errors in my writing, since I indite this by the sick-bed of Adèle."

Adèle, then, is ill; and upon that point alone in the Aunt's letter the thought of Reuben fastens. Adèle is ill! He knows where she must be lying,—in that little room at the parsonage looking out upon the orchard; there

A NEW EXPERIENCE

are white hangings to the bed; careful steps go up and down the stair-way. There had never been much illness in the parson's home, indeed, but certain early awful days Reuben just remembers; there were white bed-curtains, (he recalls those,) and a face as white lying beneath; the nurse, too, lifting a warning finger at him with a low "hist!" the knocker tied over thickly with a great muffler of cloth, lest the sound might come into the chamber; and then, awful stillness. On a morning later, all the windows were suddenly thrown open, and strange men brought a red coffin into the house, which, after a day or two, went out borne by different people, who trod uneasily and awkwardly under the weight, but very softly; and after this a weary loneliness. All which drifting over the mind of Reuben, and stirring his sensibilities with a quick rush of vague, boyish griefs, induces a train of melancholy religious musings, which, if they do no good, can hardly, it would seem, work harm. Under their influence, indeed, (which lasted for several days,) he astonished his Aunt Mabel, on the next Sunday, by declaring his intention to attend church.

It is not the ponderous Dr. Mowry, fortunately or unfortunately, that he is called upon to listen to; but a younger man, of ripe age, indeed, but full of fervor and earnestness, and with a piercing magnetic quality of voice that electrifies from the beginning. And Reuben listens to his reading of the hymn,—

"Return, O wanderer! now return!"

with parted lips, and with an exaltation of feeling that is wholly strange to him. With the prayer it seems to him that all the religious influences to which he has ever been subject are slowly and surely converging their forces upon his mind; and, rapt as he is in the preacher's utterance, there come to him shadowy recollections of some tender admonition addressed to him by dear womanly lips in boyhood, which now, on a sudden, flames into the semblance of a Divine summons. Then comes the sermon, from the text, "My son, give me thine heart." There is no repulsive formality, no array of logical presentments to arouse antagonism of thought, but only inglowing enthusiasm, that transfuses the Scriptural appeal, and illuminates it with winning illustration. Reuben sees that the evangelist feels in his inmost soul what he utters; the thrill of his voice and the touching earnestness

A NEW EXPERIENCE

of his manner declare it. It is as if our eager listener were, by every successive appeal, placed in full *rapport* with a great battery of religious emotions, and at every touch were growing into fuller and fuller entertainment of the truths which so fired and sublimed the speaker's utterance.

All thought of God the Avenger and of God the Judge, which had been so linked with most of his boyish instructions, seemed now to melt away in an aureole of golden light, through which he saw only God the Father. And the first prayer he ever learned comes to his mind with a grace and a meaning and a power that he never felt before.

"Whether we obey Him," (it is the preacher we quote,) "or distrust Him, or revile Him, or forget Him, or struggle to ignore Him, always,—always He is our Father. And whatever we may do, however we may sin, however recreant we may be to early faith or early teaching, however unmoved by the voice of conscience,—which is smiting on your hearts as it is on mine to-day,—whatever we are, or whatever we may be, yet, ever while life is in us, that great, serene voice of the All-Merciful is sounding in our ears, 'My son, give me thine heart!'"

And Reuben says to himself, yet almost audibly, "I will."

The sermon was altogether such a one as to act with prodigious force upon so emotional a nature as that of Reuben. Yet we dare say there were gray-haired men in the church, and sallow-faced young men, who nodded their heads wisely and coolly, as they went out, saying, "An eloquent sermon, quite; but not much argument in it." As if all men were to plod to heaven on the vertebræ of an inexorable logic, and not—God willing—to be rapt away thitherward by the clinging force of a growing and confiding heart!

"Is this religion?" Reuben asked himself, as he went out of the church, with his pride all subdued. And the very atmosphere seemed to wear a new glory, and a new lien of brotherhood to tie him to every creature he met upon the thronged streets. All the time, too, was sounding in his ear (as if he had yielded full assent) the mellow and grateful cadence of the hymn,—

"Return, O wanderer! now return!"

XXXIX

Reuben Makes a Proselyte

REUBEN wrote to the Doctor, under the influence of this new glow of feeling, in a way that at once amazed and delighted the good old gentleman. And yet there were ill-defined, but very decided, terrors and doubts in his delight. Dr. Johns, by nature as well as by education, was disposed to look distrustfully upon a sudden conviction of duty which had its spring in any extraordinary exaltation of feeling, rather than in that full intellectual seizure of the Word, which it seemed to him could come only after a determined wrestling with those dogmas that to his mind were the aptest and compactest expression of the truth toward which we must agonize. The day of Pentecost showed a great miracle, indeed; but was not the day of miracles past?

The Doctor, however, did not allow his entertainment of a secret fear to color in any way his letters of earnest gratulation to his son. If God has miraculously snatched him from the ways that lead to destruction, (such was his thought,) let us rejoice.

DOCTOR JOHNS

"Be steadfast, my dear Reuben," he writes. "You have now a cross to bear. Do not dishonor its holy character; do not faint upon the way. Our beloved Adèle, as you have been told, is trembling upon the verge of the grave. May God in His mercy spare her, until, at least, she gain some more fitting sense of the great mission of His Son! It pains me beyond belief to find her indifferent to the godly counsels of your pious aunt, which she does not fail to urge upon her, 'in season and out of season;' and she has shown a tenacity in guarding that wretched relic of her early life, the rosary and crucifix, which, I fear, augurs the worst. Pray for her, my son; pray that all the vanities and idolatries of this world may be swept from her thoughts."

And Reuben, still living in that roseate atmosphere of religious meditation, is shocked by this story of the danger of Adèle. Is he not himself in some measure accountable? In those days when they raced through the Catechism together, did he never provoke her mocking smiles by his sneers at the ponderous language? Did he not tempt her to some mischievous sally of mirth, on many a day when they were kneeling in couple about the family altar?

REUBEN MAKES A PROSELYTE

And in the flush of his exalted feeling he writes her how bitterly he deplores all this, and borrowing his language from the sermons he now listens to with greed, he urges Adèle "to plant her feet upon the Rock of Ages."

Indeed, there is a fervor in his feeling which pushes him into such extravagances of expression as the Doctor would have found it necessary to qualify, if Adèle, poor child, had not been by far too weak for their comprehension.

The Brindlocks were, of course, utterly amazed at this new aspect in the character of their young *protégé*. Mr. Brindlock said, however, consolingly to his wife, "My dear, it's atmospheric, I think. It's a 'revival' season; there was such a one, I remember, in my young days."

(Mrs. Brindlock laughed at this quite merrily.)

"To be sure there was, my dear, and I was really quite deeply affected. Reuben will come out all right; we shall see him sitting down soon to good merchant habits again."

But the *animus* of the new tendency was far stronger than Brindlock had supposed; and within a month Reuben had come to a quiet rupture with his city patron. The smack of worldliness was too strong for him. He felt that he must go back to his old home, and place himself again under the instructions of the father whose counsels he had once spurned.

"You don't say you mean to become a parson?" said Mr. Brindlock, more than ever astounded.

"It is very likely," said Reuben.

"Well, Reuben, if you must, you must. But I don't see things in that light. However, my boy, we 'll keep our little private ventures astir; you may need them some day."

And so they parted.

Reuben had thought in his wild days, that, when he should go back to Ashfield for any lengthened stay, (for thus far his visits had been few and flying ones,) he should considerably astonish the old people there by his air and city cultivation. It is quite possible that he had laid by certain flaming cravats which he thought would have a killing effect in the country church, and anticipated a very handsome triumph by the easy swagger with which he would greet old Deacon Tourtelot and ask after the health of Miss Almira. But the hope of all such triumphs was now dropped utterly. Such things clearly belonged to the lusts of the eye and the pride of life. He even left behind him some of the most flashy articles of

REUBEN MAKES A PROSELYTE

his attire, with the request to Aunt Mabel that she would bestow them upon some needy person, or, in default of this, make them over to the Missionary Society for distribution among the heathen,—a purpose for which some of them, by reason of their brilliant colors, were certainly most admirably adapted.

All in Ashfield meet him kindly. Old Squire Elderkin, who chances to be the first to greet him as he alights from the coach, shakes him warmly by the hand, and taps him patronizingly upon the shoulder.

"Welcome home again, Reuben! Well, well, they thought you were given over to bad courses; but it's all right now, I hear; quite upon the other tack, eh, Reuben?"

And Reuben thanked him, thinking perhaps how odd it was that this worldly old gentleman, of whom he had thought, since his late revulsion of feeling, with a good deal of quiet pity, should commend what was so foreign to his own habit. There were, then, some streaks of good-natured worldliness which tallied with Christian duty. The serene, kindly look of Mrs. Elderkin was in itself the tenderest welcome; and it was an ennobling thought to Reuben, that he had at last placed himself (or fancied he had) upon the same moral plane

DOCTOR JOHNS

with that good woman. As for Rose, the joyous, frolicsome, charming Rose, whom he had thought at one time to electrify by his elegant city accomplishments,—was not even the graceful Rose a veteran in the Christian army in which he had but now enlisted? Why, then, should she show timidity and shyness at this meeting with him? Yet her little fingers had a quick tremor in them as she took his hand, and a swift change of color (he knew it of old) ran over her face like a rosy cloud.

"It is delightful to think that Reuben is safe at last," said Mrs. Elderkin, after he had gone.

'Yes, mamma," said Rose.

"It must be a great delight to them all at the parsonage."

"I suppose so, mamma; and yet it 's so very sudden. I wish Phil were here," said Rose again, in a plaintive little tone.

"I wish he were, my child; it might have a good influence upon him; and poor Adèle too; she must surely listen to Reuben, he is so earnest and impassioned."

Rose is working with nervous rapidity.

"But, my child," says the mother, "are you not sewing that breadth upon the wrong side?"

True enough, upon the wrong side,—so many weary stitches to undo!

REUBEN MAKES A PROSELYTE

Miss Eliza had shown a well-considered approval of Reuben's change of opinions; but this had not forbidden a certain reserve of worldly regret that he should give up so promising a business career. She had half hinted as much to the Doctor.

"I do not see, brother," she had said, "that his piety will involve the abandonment of mercantile life."

"His piety," said the Doctor, "if it be of the right stamp, will involve an obedience to conscience."

And there the discussion had rested. The spinster received Reuben with much warmth, in which her stately proprieties of manner, however, were never for one moment forgotten.

Adèle, who was now fortunately in a fair way of recovery, but who was still very weak, and who looked charmingly in her white chamber-dress, received him with a tender-heartedness of manner which he had never met in her before.

For a long time she had been hovering (how nearly she did not know) upon the confines of the other world; but with a vague sense that its mysteries might open upon her in any hour, she had, in her sane intervals, ranked together

DOCTOR JOHNS

the promises and penalties that had been set before her by the good Doctor; now worrying her spirit, as it confronted some awful catechismal dogma that it sought vainly to solve; and then, from sheer weakness and disappointment, seizing upon the symbol of the cross, (of which the effigy was always near at hand,) and by a kiss and a tear seeking to allay her fainting heart with the mystic company of the elect who would find admission to the joys of paradise. But the dogmas were vain, because she could not grapple them to her heart; the cross was vain, because it was an empty symbol; the kisses and the tears left her groping blindly for the key that would surely unlock for her the wealth of the celestial kingdom. In this attitude of mind, wearied by struggles and by fantasies, came to her the letter of Reuben,—the joyous outburst of a pioneer who had found the way.

She had listened, in those fatiguing and terrible days of illness, to psalms long drawn out, and wearily; but here was some wild bird that chanted a glorious carol in her ear,—a carol that seemed touched with heaven's own joy. And under its influence—exaggerated as it was by extreme youthful emotion—she seemed to see the celestial gates of jasper and pearl swing

REUBEN MAKES A PROSELYTE

open before her, and the beckonings of the great crowd of celestial inhabitants to enter and enjoy.

"I thank you very much for your letter, Reuben," said Adèle, and she looked eagerly into his face for traces of that triumph which so glittered throughout his letter.

And she did not look in vain; for, whether it were from the warm, electric touch of those white, thin fingers of hers, or the eager welcome in her eyes, or from more sacred cause, a great joy shone in his face,—a joy that from thenceforward they began to share in common. Not a doubt, not a penalty, not a mystic, blind utterance of the Catechism, but the glowing enthusiasm of Reuben invested it with cheery promise, or covered it with the wonderful glamour of his hope. Between these two young hearts—the one, till then, all doubt and weariness, and the other, just now, all impassioned exuberance—there came a grafting, by virtue of which the religious sentiment in Adèle shot away from all the severities around her into an atmosphere of peace and joy.

The Doctor saw it, and wondered at the abounding mercies of God. The spinster saw it, and rejoiced at the welding of this new link in the chain of her purposes. The village peo-

DOCTOR JOHNS

ple all saw it, and said among themselves, "If he has won her from the iniquities of the world, he can win her for a wife, if he will."

And the echoes of such speeches come, as they needs must, to the ear of Rose, without surprising her, so much do they seem the echo of her own thought; and if her heart may droop a little under it, she conceals it bravely, and abates no jot in her abounding love for Adèle.

"I wish Phil were here," she says in the privacy of her home.

"So do I, darling," says the mother, and looks at her with a tender inquisitiveness that makes the sweet girl flinch, and affect for a moment a noisy gayety, which is not in her heart.

XL

Death

MADAME ARLES did not forego either her solicitude or the persistence of her inquiry under the harsh rebuffs of the spinster. The village physician, too, had been addressed by this anxious lady with a tumult of questionings; and the old gentleman—upon whose sympathies the eager inquirer had won an easy approach—had taken hearty satisfaction in assuring her, that the poor girl was mending, was out of danger, in fact, and would be presently in a condition to report for herself.

After this, and through the long convalescence, Madame Arles was seen more rarely upon the village street. Yet the town gossips were busy with the character and habits of the "foreign lady." Her devotion to the little child of the outcast was searchingly discussed at all the tea-tables of the place; and it was special object of scandal that, neglectful of the Sabbath ministrations, she was frequently wandering about the fields in "meeting-time," attended by that poor wee thing of a child, upon whose head the good people all visited the sins of the parents. Dame Tourtelot enjoyed a good sharp fling at the "trollop."

"I allers said she was a bad woman," submitted the stout Dame; and her audience (consisting of the Deacon and Miss Almira) would have had no more thought of questioning the implied decision than of cutting down the meeting-house steeple.

"And I 'm afeard," continued the Dame,

"that Adeel is n't much better; she keeps a crucifix in her chamber!—need n't to look at me, Tourtelot!—Miss Johns told me all about it, and I don't think the parson should allow it. I think you oughter speak to the parson, Tourtelot."

The good Deacon scratched his head, over the left ear, in a deprecating manner.

"An I 've heerd this Miss Arles has been receivin' furren letters,—need n't to look at me, Tourtelot!—the postmaster told me;—and they 're filled with Popery, I ha'n't a doubt."

In short, the poor woman bore a sad reputation; and Doctor Johns, good as he was, took a little secret pride in such startling confirmation of his theories in respect to French character. He wrote to his friend Maverick, informing him that his suspicions in regard to Madame Arles were, he feared, "only too well founded."

Indeed, Miss Eliza and the Doctor (the latter from the best of motives) had scrupulously kept from Adèle all knowledge of Madame Arles's impatient solicitude during her illness.

When, therefore, Adèle, on one of her early walks with Reuben, after her recovery was fully established, encountered, in a remote part of the village, Madame Arles, trailing after

DEATH

her the little child of shame,—and yet darting toward the French girl, at first sight, with her old effusion,—Adèle met her coolly; so coolly, indeed, that the poor woman was overcome, and hurrying the little child after her, disappeared with a look of wretchedness upon her face that haunted Adèle for weeks and months. A moment of chilling indifference on the part of Adèle had worked stronger repulse than all the harsh rebuffs of the elder people; but of this the kind-hearted French girl was no way conscious; yet she *was* painfully conscious of a shadowy figure that still, from time to time, stole after her in her twilight walks, and that, if she turned upon it, shrank stealthily from observation. There was a mystery about the whole matter which oppressed the poor girl with a sense of terror.

Rumor, one day, brought the story, that the foreign woman who had been the subject of so much village scandal, lay ill, and was fast failing; and on hearing this, Adèle would have broken away from all the parsonage restraints, to offer what consolations she could; nor would the good Doctor have repelled her; but the rumor, if not false, was, in his view, grossly exaggerated; since, on the Sunday previous only, some officious member of his parish had

DOCTOR JOHNS

reported the Frenchwoman as strolling over the hills, decoying with her that little child of her fellow-lodger, which she had tricked out in the remnants of her French finery, and was thus wantoning throughout the holy hours of service.

A few days later, however, the Doctor came in with a serious and perplexed air; he laid his cane and hat upon the little table within the door, and summoned Adèle to the study.

"Adaly, my child," said he, "this unfortunate countrywoman of yours is really failing. I learn as much from the physician. She has asked to see you. She intimates that she has an important message to give you."

A strange tremor ran over the frame of Adèle.

"I fear, my child, that she is still bound to her idolatries; she has asked that you bring to her the little bauble of a rosary, which, I trust, Adaly, you have learned to regard as a vanity."

"Yet I have it still, New Papa; she shall have it;" and she turned to go.

"My child, I cannot bear that you should go as the messenger of a false faith, and to carry to her, as it were, the seal of her idolatries. You shall follow her wishes, Adaly; but I must attend you, my child, were it only to protest

DEATH

against such vanities, and to declare to her, if it be not too late, the truth as it is in the Gospel."

Adèle was only too willing; for she was impressed with a vague terror at thought of this interview, and of its possible revelations; and they set off presently in company. It was a chilly day of later autumn. Only a few scattered, tawny remnants of the summer verdure were hanging upon the village trees, and great rows of the dead and fallen leaves were heaped here and there athwart the path, where some high wall kept them clear of the winds; and as the walkers tramped through them, they made a ghostly rustle, and whole platoons of them were set astir to drift again until some new eddy caught and stranded them in other heaps. Adèle, more and more disturbed in mind, said,—

"It's such a dreary day, New Papa!"

"Is it the thought that one you know may lie dying now makes it dreary, my child?"

"Partly that, I dare say," returned Adèle; "and then the wind so tosses about these dead leaves. I wish it were spring."

"There is a country," said the parson, "where spring reigns eternal. I hope you may find it, Adaly; I hope your poor countrywoman may find it; but I fear, I fear."

"Is it, then, so dreadful to be a Romanist?"

"It is dreadful, Adaly, to doubt the free grace of God,—dreadful to trust in any offices of men, or in tithes of mint and anise and cumin. I have a conviction, my child," continued he, in a tone even more serious, "that the poor woman has not lived a pure life before God, or even before the world."

Adèle, trembling,—partly with the chilling wind, and partly with an ill-defined terror of—she knew not what,—nestled more closely to the side of the old gentleman; and he, taking her little hand in his, as tenderly as a lover might have done, said,—

"Adaly, at least *your* trust in God is firm, is it not?"

"It is! it is!" said she.

The house, as we have said, lay far out upon the river-road, within a strip of ill-tended garden-ground, surrounded by a rocky pasture. A solitary white-oak stood in the line of straggling wall that separated garden from pasture, and showed still a great crown of leaves blanched by the frosts, and shivering in the wind. An artemisia, with blackened stalks, nodded its draggled yellow blossoms at one angle of the house, while a little company of barn-door fowls stood closely grouped under

DEATH

the southern lea, with heads close drawn upon their breasts, idling and winking in the sunshine.

The young mother of the vagrant one who had attracted latterly so much of the solitary woman's regard received them with an awkward welcome.

"Miss Arles is poorly to-day," she said, "and she 's flighty. She keeps Arthur" (the child) "with her. You hear how she 's a-chatterin' now." (The door of her chamber stood half open.) "Arty seems to understand her. I 'm sure I don't."

Nor, indeed, did the Doctor, to whose ear a torrent of rapid French speech was like the gibberish of demons. Not so Adèle. There were sweet sounds to her ear in that swift flow of Provençal speech,—tender, endearing epithets, that seemed like the echo of music heard long ago.

"Ah, you 're a gay one! Now—put on your velvet cap—so. We 'll find a bride for you some day,—some day, when you 're a tall, proud man. Who 's your father, Arty? Pah! it 's nothing. You 'll make somebody's heart ache all the same,—eh, Arty, boy?"

"Do you understand her, Miss Maverick?" says the mother.

"Not wholly," said Adèle; and the two visitors stepped in noiselessly.

The child, bedizened with finery, was standing upon the bed where the sick woman lay, with a long feather from the cock's tail waving from his cap. Madame Arles, with the hot flush of the fever upon her, looked—saving the thinness—as she might have looked twenty years before. And as her flashing eye caught the new comers, her voice broke out wildly again,—

"Here's the bride, and here's the priest! Where's the groom? Where's the groom, I say?"

The violence of her manner made poor Adèle shiver.

The boy laughed as he saw it, and said,—

"She's afraid! *I'm* not afraid."

"Oh, no!" said the crazed woman, turning on him. "You're a man, Arty; men are not afraid,—you wanton, you wild one! Where's the groom?" said she again, addressing the Doctor, fiercely.

"My good woman," says the old gentleman, "we have come to offer you the consolations that are only to be found in the Gospel of Christ."

"Pah! you're a false priest!"—defiantly. "Where's the groom?"

DEATH

And Adèle, hoping to pacify the poor woman, draws from her reticule the little rosary, and holding it before the eyes of the sufferer, says, timidly,—

"My dear Madam, it is I,—Adèle; I have brought what you asked of me; I have come to comfort you."

And the woman, over whose face there ran instantly a marvellous change, snatched the rosary, and pressed it convulsively to her lips; then, looking for a moment yearningly, with that strange double gaze of hers, upon the face of Adèle, she sprang toward her, and, wreathing her arms about her, drew her fast upon her bosom,—

"Ma fille! ma pauvre fille!"

The boy slipped down from the bed,—his little importance being over,—and was gone. The Doctor's lips moved in silent prayer for five minutes or more, wholly undisturbed, while the twain were locked in that embrace. Then the old gentleman, stooping, said,—

"Adaly, will she listen to me now?"

And Adèle, turning a frightened face to him, whispered,—

"She 's sleeping; unclasp her hands; she holds me tightly."

The Doctor, with tremulous fingers, does her bidding.

Adèle, still whispering, says,—

"She's calm now, she'll talk with us when she wakes, New Papa."

"My poor child," said the Doctor, solemnly, and with a full voice, "she'll never awake again."

And Adèle turning,—in a maze of terror, as she thought of that death-clasp,—saw that her eyes had fallen open,—open, and fixed, and lusterless. So quietly Death had come upon his errand, and accomplished it, and gone; while without, the fowls, undisturbed, were still blinking idly in the sunshine under the lea of the wall, and the yellow chrysanthemums were fluttering in the wind.

XLI

Reuben's Struggle

IN the winter of 1838–39, Adèle, much to the delight of Dr. Johns, avowed at last her wish to join herself to the little church-flock over which the good parson still held serenely his office of shepherd. And as she told him quietly of her desire, sitting before him there in the

"*Ma fille! Ma pauvre fille!*"

study of the parsonage, without urgence upon his part, it was as if a bright gleam of sunshine had darted suddenly through the wintry clouds, and bathed both of them in its warm effulgence. The good man, rising from his chair and crossing over to her place, touched her forehead with as tender and loving a kiss as ever he had bestowed upon the lost Rachel.

He had seen too closely the development of her Christian faith to disturb her with various questionings. She rejoiced in this; for even then, with all the calm serenity of her trust, it was doubtful if her answers could have fully satisfied the austerities of his theological traditions. Even the little rosary, so obnoxious to the household of the parsonage, was, by its terrible association with the death-scene of Madame Arles, endeared to her tenfold; and she could not forbear the hope that the poor woman, at the very last, by that clinging kiss upon the image of Christ, told a prayer that might give access to His abounding mercy.

Meantime Reuben has a vague notion creeping over him, with fearfully chilling effect, that his sensibilities have been wrought upon rather than his reason; a confused sense of having yielded to enthusiasms which, if they once grow cool, will leave him to slump back into a mire worse than the old. He looked with something like envy upon the serene contentment of Adèle. He lived like an ascetic; he sought, by reading of all manner of exultant religious experience, to keep alive the ferment of the autumn. "If only death were near," he said to himself, "with what a blaze of hope one might go out!" But death was not near,—or, at least, life and its perplexing duties were nearer. If the glory of the promises and the tenderness of Divine entreaty were to be always dropping mellifluously on his ear, as upon that solemn Sunday of the summer, it might be well. But it is not thus; and even were the severe quiet of the Ashfield Sundays lighted up by the swift and burning words of such fiery evangelism, yet six solid workingdays roll over upon the heel of every Sunday, —in which he sees good Deacon Tourtelot in shirt-sleeves driving some sharp bargain for his two-year-old steers, or the stout Dame hectoring some stray peddler by the hour for the fall of a penny upon his wares, and wonders where their Christian largeness of soul is gone. Shall he consult the good Doctor? He is met straightway with an array of the old catechismal formulas, clearly stated, well argued, but brushing athwart his mind like a

REUBEN'S STRUGGLE

dusty wind. In this strait, he wanders over the hills in search of loneliness, and a volume of Tillotson he carries with him is all unread. Nature speaks more winningly, but scarce more helpfully.

Adèle, with a quick eye, sees the growing unrest, and with a great weight of gratitude upon her heart, says, timidly,—

"Can I help you, Reuben?"

"No, thank you, Adèle. I understand you; I'm in a boggle,—that's all."

The father, too, at a hint from Adèle, (whose perceptions are so much quicker,) sees at last how the matter stands."

"Reuben," he says, "these struggles of yours are struggles with the Great Adversary."

It was kindly said and earnestly said, but touched the core of the son's moral disquietude no more than if it were the hooting of an owl. It pains him grievously to think what humiliation would possess the old Doctor, if he but knew into what crazy currents his boy's thoughts were drifting over the pages of his beloved teachers.

But a man cannot live a deceit, even for charity's sake, without its making outburst some day, and wrecking all the fine preventive barriers which kept it in. The outburst came at last in the quiet of the Ashfield study. Reuben had been poring for hours—how wearily! how vainly!—over the turgid dogmas of one of the elder divines, when he suddenly dashed the book upon the floor.

"Confound the theologies! I'll have no more of them!"

The Doctor dropped his pen, and stared as if a serpent had stung him.

"My son! Reuben! Reuben!"

"I can't help it, father. It's the Evil One, perhaps. If it be, I'll cheat him, by making a clean breast of it. I can't abide the stuff; I can't see my way through it."

"My son, it is your sin that blinds you."

"Very likely," says Reuben.

"It was not thus with you three months ago, Reuben," continues the Doctor, in a softened tone.

"No, father, there was a strange light around me in those days. It seemed to me that the path lay clear and shining through all the maze. If Death had caught me then, I think I could have sung hosannas with the saints. It's faded dismally, father,—as if the Devil had painted it."

The old man shuddered.

"The muddle of the world and the theologies

REUBEN'S STRUGGLE

has come in since," continued Reuben, "and the base professions I see around me, and the hypocrisies and the cant, have taken away the glow. It's all a weariness and a confusion, and that's the solemn truth."

The Doctor said, measuredly, (as if the Book were before him,) —

"*'Some seeds fell upon stony places, where they had not much earth; and forthwith they sprung up, because they had no deepness of earth. And when the sun was up, they were scorched; and because they had no root, they withered away.'* Reuben! Reuben! we must agonize to enter into the strait gate!"

"It's a long agony," said Reuben; and he rose and paced back and forth for a time; then suddenly stopping before the Doctor, he laid his hand upon his shoulder, (the boy was of manly height now, and overtopped the old gentleman by an inch,) — "Father, it grieves me to pain you, — indeed it does; but truth is truth. I have told you my story; but if you wish it, I will live outwardly as if no such talk had passed."

"I would not have you practise hypocrisy, my son; but I would not have you withdraw yourself from any of the appointed means of grace."

And at this Reuben went out,—out far upon the hills, from which he saw the village roofs, and the spire, and the naked tree-tops, the fields all bare and brown, the smoke of a near house curling lazily into the sky; and the only sound that broke the solemn stillness was the drumming of a partridge in the woods or the harsh scream of a belated jay.

Never had Reuben been more kind or attentive to the personal wants of the old gentleman than on the days which followed upon this interview. There was something almost like a daughter's solicitude in his watchfulness. On the next Sunday the Doctor preached with an emotion that was but poorly controlled, and which greatly mystified his people. Twice in the afternoon his voice came near to failing. Reuben knew where the grief lay, but wore a composed face; and as he supported the old gentleman home after service, he said, (but not so loudly that Adèle would hear, who was tripping closely behind,)—

"Father, I grieve for you,—upon my soul I do; but it's fate."

"Fate, Reuben?" said the Doctor, but with a less guarded voice,—"fate? God only is fate!"

The Doctor was too much mortified by this

revelation of Reuben's present state of feeling to make it the subject of conversation, even with Miss Eliza, and much less with the elders of his flock. To Squire Elderkin, indeed, whose shrewd common sense he had learned to value even in its bearings upon the "weightier matters of the law," he had dropped some desponding reflections in regard to the wilful impetuosity of his poor son Reuben, from which the shrewd Squire at once suspected the difficulty.

"It 's the blood of the old Major," he said. "Let it work, Doctor, let it work!"

From which observation, it must be confessed, the good man derived very little comfort.

Miss Eliza, though she is not made a confidante in these latter secrets of the study, cannot, however, fail to see that Reuben's constancy to the Doctor's big folios is on the wane, and that symptoms of his old boyish recklessness occasionally show themselves under the reserve which has grown out of his later experiences. But her moral perceptions are not delicate enough to discover the great and tormenting wrangle of his thought. She ventures from time to time, as on his return, and from sharp sense of duty, some wiry, stereotyped religious reflections, which set his whole moral nature on edge. Nor is this the limit of her blindness: perceiving, as she imagines she does, the ripening of all her plans with respect to himself and Adèle, she thinks to further the matter by dropping hints of the rare graces of Adèle and of her brilliant prospects,—assuring him how much that young lady's regard for him has been increased since his *conversion,* (which word has to Reuben just now a dreary and most detestable sound,) and in a way which she counts playful, but which to him is *agaçant* to the last degree, she forecasts the time when Reuben will have his pretty French wife, and a rich one.

Left to himself, the youth would very likely have found enough to admire in the face and figure and pleasantly subdued enthusiasm of Adèle; but the counter-irritant of the spinster's speech drove him away on many an evening to the charming fireside of the Elderkins, where he spent not a few beguiling hours in listening to the talk of the motherly mistress of the household, and in watching the soft hazel eyes of Rose, as they lifted in eager wonderment at some of his stories of the town, or fell (the long lashes hiding them with other beauty) upon the work where her delicate fingers plied with a white swiftness that teased him into trains of thought which were not wholly French.

Adèle has taken a melancholy interest in decking the grave of the exiled lady, which she has insisted upon doing out of her own resources, and thus has doubled the little legacy which Madame Arles had left to the outcast woman and child with whom she had joined her fate, and who, with good reason, wept her death bitterly. Hour upon hour Adèle pondered over that tragic episode, tasking herself to imagine what message the dying woman could have had to communicate, and wondering if the future would ever clear up the mystery. With all the stimulus of her new Christian endeavor, Adèle sought to think charitably of Miss Eliza. Yet it was hard; always, that occasional cold kiss of the spinster had for Adèle an iron imprint, which drove her warm blood away, instead of summoning it to response.

For her, Miss Eliza's staple praises of Reuben, and her adroit stories of the admiration and attachment of Mrs. Brindlock for her nephew, were distasteful to the last degree. Coarse natures never can learn upon what fine threads the souls of the sensitive are strung.

As yet there was a ripe fulness in her heart that felt no wound,—at least no wound in which her hope rankled. Whether Reuben were present or away, her songs rose, with a sweeter, a serener, and a loftier cheer than of old under the roof of the parsonage; and, as of old, the Doctor laid down his book and listened, as if an angel sang.

XLII

A Revelation

In the summer of 1840 the Doctor received a letter from Maverick which overwhelmed him with consternation.

"My good friend Johns," he wrote, "I owe you a debt of gratitude which I can never repay; you have shown such fatherly interest in my dear child,—you have so guided and guarded her,—you have so abundantly filled the place which, though it was my duty, I had never the worthiness to fill, that I have no words to thank you.

"I hear,—from what sources it will be un-

A REVELATION

necessary for me now to explain,—that a close intimacy has grown up latterly between your son Reuben and my dear Adèle, and that this intimacy has provoked village rumors of the possibility of some nearer tie. These rumors may be, perhaps, wholly untrue; but the knowledge of them, vague as they are, has stimulated me to a task which I ought far sooner to have accomplished, and which, as a man of honor, I can no longer defer.

"I go back to the time when I first paid you a visit at your parsonage. I never shall forget the cheery joyousness of that little family scene at your fireside, the winning modesty and womanliness of your lost Rachel, and the serenity and peace that lay about your household. It was to me, fresh from the vices of Europe, like some charming Christian idyl, in whose atmosphere I felt myself not only an alien, but a profane intruder; for, at that very time, I was bound by one of those criminal *liaisons* to which so many strangers on the Continent are victims. Your household and your conversation prompted a hope and a struggle for better things. But, my dear Johns, the struggle was against a whole atmosphere of vice. And it was only when I had broken free of entanglement, that I learned, with a dreary pang, that I was the father of a child,—my poor, dear Adèle!"

The Doctor crumpled the letter in his hand, and smote upon his forehead. Never, in his whole life, had he known such strange revulsion of feeling. With returning calmness he smooths the letter upon his desk, and continues:—

"I expect your condemnation, of course; yet listen to my story throughout. That child I might have left to the tender mercies of the world, might have ignored it, and possibly forgotten its existence. Many a man, with fewer stains on his conscience than I have, would have done this, and met the world and old friends cheerily. But then the memory of you and of your teachings somehow kindled in me what I counted a worthier purpose. I vowed that the child should, if possible, lead a guileless life, and should no way suffer, so far as human efforts could prevent, for the sins of the parents. The mother assented, with what I counted a guilty willingness, to my design, and I placed her secretly under the charge of the old godmother of whom Adèle must often have spoken.

"But I was no way content that she should grow up under French influences, and to the

A REVELATION

future knowledge (inevitable in these scenes) of the ignominy of her birth. And if that knowledge were ever to come, I could think of no associations more fitted to make her character stanch to bear it than those that belong to the rigid and self-denying virtues which are taught in a New England parish. Is it strange that I recurred at once to your kindness, Johns? Is it strange that I threw the poor child upon your charity?

"It is true, I used deceit,—true that I did not frankly reveal the truth; but see how much was at stake! I knew in what odium such trespasses were held in the serenity of your little towns; I knew that, if you, with Spartan courage, should propose acceptance of the office, your family would reject it. I knew that your love of truth would be incapable of the concealments or subterfuges which might be needed to protect the poor child from the tongue of scandal. In short, I was not willing to take the risk of a repulse. 'Such deceit as there may be,' I said, 'is my own. My friend Johns can never impute it as a sin to Adèle.' I am sure you will not now. Again, I felt that I was using deceit (if you will allow me to say it) in a good cause, and that you yourself, when once the shock of discovery should be past, could never reprimand yourself for your faithful teachings to an erring child, but must count her, in your secret heart, only another of the wandering lambs which it was your duty and pleasure to lead into the true fold. Had she come to you avowedly as the child of sin, with all the father's and mother's guilt reeking upon her innocent head, could you have secured to her, my dear Johns, that care and consideration and devotion which have at last ripened her Christian character, and made her proof against slander?"

Here the Doctor threw down the letter again, and paced up and down the room.

"The child of sin! the child of sin! Who could have thought it? Yet does not Maverick reason true? Does not Beelzebub at times reason true? Adaly! my poor, poor Adaly!"

"It seemed to me," the letter continued, "that there might possibly be no need that either you or my poor child should ever know the whole truth in this matter; and I pray (with your leave) that it may be kept from her even now. You will understand, perhaps, from what I have said, why my visits have been more rare than a fatherly feeling would seem to demand; to tell truth, I have feared the familiar questionings of her prattling girl-

A REVELATION

hood. Mature years shrink from perilous inquiry, I think, with an instinct which does not belong to the freshness of youth.

"But from your ears, in view of the rumors that have come to my hearing, I could not keep the knowledge longer. I cannot, my dear Johns, read your heart, and say whether or not you will revolt at the idea of any possible family tie between your son and my poor Adèle. But whatever aspect such possibility may present to your mind, I can regard it only with aversion. Whatever your Christian forgiveness or your love for Adèle (and I know she is capable of winning your love) may suggest, I can never consent that any stain should be carried upon your family record by any instrumentality of mine. I must beg, therefore, that, if the rumor be true, you use all practicable means, even to the use of your parental authority, in discountenancing and forbidding such intimacy. If necessary to this end, and Reuben be still resident at the parsonage, I pray you to place Adèle with Mrs. Brindlock, or other proper person, until such time as I am able to come and take her once more under my own protection.

"If you were a more worldly man, my dear Johns, I should hope to win your heartier cooperation in my views by telling you that recent business misfortunes have placed my whole estate in peril, so that it is extremely doubtful if Adèle will have any ultimate moneyed dependence beyond the pittance which I have placed in trust for her in your hands. Should it be necessary, in furtherance of the objects I have named, to make communication of the disclosures in this letter to your son or to Miss Johns, you have my full liberty to do so. Farther than this, I trust you may not find it necessary to make known the facts so harmful to the prospects and peace of my innocent child.

"I have thus made a clean breast to you, my dear Johns, and await your condemnation. But let not any portion of it, I pray, be visited upon poor Adèle. I know with what wrathful eyes you, from your New England stand-point, are accustomed to look upon such shortcomings; and I know, too, that you are sometimes disposed to 'visit the sins of the fathers upon the children;' but I beg that your anathemas may all rest where they belong, upon my head, and that you will spare the motherless girl you have taught to love you."

Up and down the study the Doctor paced, with a feverish, restless step, which in all the

A REVELATION

history of the parsonage had never been heard in it before.

"Such untruth!" is his exclamation. "Yet no, there has been no positive untruth; the deception he admits."

But the great fact comes back upon his thought, that the child of sin and shame is with him. All his old distrust and hatred of the French are revived on the instant; the stain of their iniquities is thrust upon his serene and quiet household. And yet what a sweet face, what a confiding nature God has given to this creature conceived in sin! In his simplicity, the good Doctor would have fancied that some mark of Cain should be fixed on the poor child.

Again, the Doctor had somewhere in his heart a little of the old family pride. The spinster had ministered to it, coyly indeed by word, but always by manner and conduct. How it would have shocked the stout Major, or his good mother, even, to know that he had thus fondled and fostered the vagrant offspring of iniquity upon his hearth! A still larger and worthier pride the Doctor cherished in his own dignity,—so long the honored pastor of Ashfield,—so long the esteemed guide of this people in paths of piety.

DOCTOR JOHNS

What if it should appear that, during almost the entire period of his holy ministrations, he had, as would seem, colluded with an old acquaintance of his youth—a brazen reprobate—to shield him from the shame of his own misdeeds, and to cover with the mantle of respectability and with all the pastoral dignities this French-speaking child, who, under God, was the seal of the father's iniquities?

As he paced back and forth, there was a timid knock at the door; and in a moment more Adèle, blooming with health, and radiant with hope, stood before him. Her face had never beamed with a more wondrous frankness and sweetness.

XLIII

The Spinster's Indignation

THE foreign letters rarely came singly; and Adèle had already accomplished the reading of her own missive, in which Maverick had spoken of his having taken occasion to address, by the same mail, a line to the Doctor on matters of business, "in regard to which,"

THE SPINSTER'S INDIGNATION

(he had said,) "don't, my dear Adèle, be too inquisitive, even if you observe that it is cause of some perplexity to the good Doctor. Indeed, in such case, I hope you will contribute to his cheer, as I am sure you have often done. We owe him a large debt of gratitude, my child, and I rely upon you to add your thankfulness to mine, and speak for both."

"You look troubled, New Papa," said Adèle. "Can I help you? Eh, Doctor?"

And she came toward him in her playful manner, and patted the old gentleman on the shoulder, while he sat with his face buried in his hands.

"I don't think papa writes very cheerfully, do you? Eh,—Doctor—Benjamin—Johns?' (Tapping him with more spirit.)—"Why, New Papa, what does this mean?"

For the Doctor had raised his head now, and regarded her with a look of mingled yearning and distrust that was wholly new to her.

"Pray, New Papa, what is it?"

The old gentleman—so utterly guileless—was puzzled for an answer; but his ingenuity came to his relief at length.

"No, Adaly, your father does not write cheerfully,—certainly not; he speaks of the probable loss of his fortune."

DOCTOR JOHNS

Now Adèle, with her parsonage training, had really very little idea of fortune.

"That means I won't be rich, New Papa, I suppose. But I don't believe it; he will have money enough, I 'm sure. It don't disturb me, New Papa,—not one whit."

The Doctor was so poor a hand at duplicity that he hardly knew what to say, but meantime was keeping his eye with the same dazed look upon the charming Adèle.

"You look so oddly, New Papa,—indeed you do! You have some sermon in your head, now have n't you, that I have broken in upon? —some sermon about—about—let us see."

And she moved toward his desk, where the letter of Maverick still lay unfolded.

The Doctor, lost in thought, did not observe her movement until she had the letter fairly in her hand; then he seized it with a suddenness of gesture that instantly caught the attention of Adèle.

A swift, deep color ran over her face.

"It is for my eye only, Adaly," said the Doctor, excitedly, folding it and placing it in his pocket.

Adèle, with her curiosity strangely piqued, said,—

"I remember now, papa told me as much."

THE SPINSTER'S INDIGNATION

"What did he tell you, my child?"

"Not to be too curious about some business affairs of which he had written you."

"Ah!" said the Doctor, with a sigh of relief.

"But why should n't I be? Tell me, New Papa," (toying now with the silvered hair upon the forehead of the old gentleman,) "is he really in trouble?"

"No new trouble, my child,—no new trouble."

For a moment Adèle's thought flashed upon that mystery of the mother she had never seen, and an uncontrollable sadness came over her.

"Yet if there be bad news, why should n't I know it?" said she. "I must know it some day."

"'Sufficient unto the day is the evil thereof,'" said the Doctor, gravely. "And if bad news should ever come to you, my dear Adaly,— though I have none to tell you now,—may you have strength to bear it like a Christian!"

"I will! I can!" said she, with a great glow upon her face.

Never more than in that moment had the heart of the old gentleman warmed toward the little stranger.

When Reuben came presently to summon

DOCTOR JOHNS

Adèle to their evening engagement at the Elderkins', the Doctor followed their retreating figures, as they strolled out of the parsonage-gate, with a new and strange interest. Most inscrutable and perplexing was the fact, that this outcast child, whom scarce one in his parish would have been willing to admit to the familiarities of home,—this daughter of infidel France, about whose mind the traditions of the Babylonish harlot had so long lingered,—who had never known motherly counsel or a father's reproof,—that she, with the stain of heathenism upon her skirts, should have grown into the possession of such a holy, placid, and joyous trust. And there was his poor son beside her, the child of so many hopes, reared, as it were, under the very droppings of the altar, still wandering befogged in the mazes of error, if indeed, he were not in his secret heart a scoffer. Now that such a result was wholly impracticable and impossible, it did occur to him that perhaps no helpmeet for Reuben could so surely guide him in the way of truth. But of any perplexity of judgment on this score he was now wholly relieved. If his own worldly pride had not stood in the way, (and **he** was dimly conscious of a weakness of this kind,) the wish of Maverick was

THE SPINSTER'S INDIGNATION

authoritative and final. The good man had not the slightest conception of how matters might really stand between the two young parties; he had discovered the anxieties of Miss Eliza in regard to them, and had often queried with himself if too large a taint of worldliness were not coloring the manœuvres of his good sister. For himself he chose rather to leave the formation of all such ties in the hands of Providence; and entertained singularly old-fashioned notions in regard to the sacredness of the marriage-bond and the mystery of its establishment.

In view, however, of possible eventualities, it was necessary that he should come to a full understanding with the spinster in regard to the state of affairs between Adèle and Reuben, and that he should make disclosure to her of the confessions of Maverick. For the second time in his life the Doctor dreaded the necessity of taking his sister into full confidence. The first was on that remarkable occasion—so long past by—when he had declared his youthful love for Rachel, and feared the opposition which would grow out of the spinster's family pride. Now, as then, he apprehended some violent outbreak.

After due reflection on the letter of Maverick,

DOCTOR JOHNS

the Doctor stepped softly to the stairs, and said,—

"Eliza, may I speak with you for a few moments in the study?"

There was something in the parson's tone that promised an important communication; and Miss Johns presently appeared and seated herself, work in hand, over against the parson, at the study-table. Older than when we took occasion to describe her appearance in the early portion of this narrative, and—if it could be—more prim and stately. A pair of delicately bowed gold spectacles were now called into requisition by her, for the nicer needlework on which she specially prided herself. Yet her eye had lost none of its apparent keenness, and inclining her head slightly, she threw an inquiring glance over her spectacles at the Doctor, who was now as composed as if the startling news of the day had been wholly unheard.

"Eliza," said he, "you have sometimes spoken of the possibility of an attachment between Adaly and our poor Reuben."

"Yes, I have, Benjamin," said the spinster, with an air of confidence that seemed to imply full knowledge of the circumstances.

"Do you see any strong indications of such attachment, Eliza?"

THE SPINSTER'S INDIGNATION

"Well, really, Benjamin," said she,—holding her needle to the light, and bringing her spectacles to bear upon the somewhat difficult operation (at her age) of threading it,—"really, I think you may leave that matter to my management."

"The letter which I have received to-day from Mr. Maverick alludes to a rumor of such intimacy."

"Really!"—and the lady eyes the Doctor with a look of keen expectation.

"Mr. Maverick," continued the Doctor, "in referring to the matter, speaks of the probable loss of his fortune."

"Is it possible, brother? Loss of his fortune!" And the spinster gives over attention to her work, while she taps with her thimble, reflectively, upon the elbow of her chair. "I don't think, Benjamin," said she, "that Reuben has committed himself in any way."

"That is well, perhaps, Eliza; it is quite as I had supposed."

"And so the poor man's fortune is gone!" continued the spinster plaintively.

"Not gone absolutely, Eliza. Maverick's language is, that his estate is in great peril," returned the Doctor.

"Ah!" The spinster is thoughtful and silent

for a while, during which the thimble-finger is also quiet. "Does your friend Maverick speak approvingly of such an attachment, brother?"

"By no means, Eliza; he condemns it in the strongest terms."

Miss Johns is amazed at this revelation; and having taken off her golden-bowed spectacles, she passes them in a nervous way, from end to end, upon the Doctor's table.

"Benjamin," says she presently, with a shrewd look and her sharpest tone, "I don't think his fortune is in any peril whatever. I think Reuben Johns is a good match for Miss Adèle Maverick, any day."

"Tut, tut, Eliza! we must not glorify ourselves vainly. If Maverick disapproves, and Reuben shows no inclination, our course is both plain and easy."

"But I am not so sure about the inclination, Benjamin," said the spinster, sharply; and she replaced her spectacles.

"If that is the case, I am very sorry," said the parson.

The good man had hoped that by only a partial revelation of the contents of the letter he might divert his sister effectually from any matrimonial schemes she might have in hand,

THE SPINSTER'S INDIGNATION

and so spare himself the pain of a full disclosure. It was quite evident to him, however, that his plan had miscarried. There was nothing for it but to lay before her the whole disagreeable truth.

When the Doctor commenced the reading of the letter, Miss Johns resumed her needlework with a resolute composure that seemed to imply, "The Johns view of the case has been stated; let us now listen to what Mr. Maverick may have to say."

For a while her fingers plied nimbly; but there came a pause,—an exclamation of amazement, and her work (it was a bit of embroidery for poor Adèle) was dashed upon the floor.

"Benjamin, this is monstrous! The French hussy! Reuben, indeed!"

The Doctor returned composedly to his reading.

"No, brother, I want to hear no more. What a wretch this Maverick must be!"

"A sinner, doubtless, Eliza; yet not a sinner before all others."

The spinster was now striding up and down the room in a state of extraordinary excitement. With a strange inconsequence, she seized the letter from the Doctor's hands, and read it through to the end.

DOCTOR JOHNS

"I am bewildered, Benjamin. To think that the Johns name should be associated with such shame and guilt!"

"Whosoever exalteth himself shall be abased," murmured the Doctor.

But the spinster was in no mood for listening to Scriptural applications.

"And that he should dare to ask us to cloak for him this great scandal!" continued she, wrathfully.

"For the child's sake, Eliza,—for poor Adaly."

"While I am mistress of your household, brother, I shall try to maintain its dignity and respectability. Do you consider, Benjamin, how much these are necessary to your influence?"

"Without doubt, Eliza; yet I cannot perceive how these would suffer by dealing gently with this unfortunate child. A very tender affection for her has grown upon me, Eliza; it would sadden me grievously, if she were to go out from among us bearing unkind thoughts."

"And is your affection strong enough, Benjamin, to make you forget all social proprieties, and the honorable name of our family, and to wish her stay here as the wife of Reuben?"

THE SPINSTER'S INDIGNATION

The Doctor may have winced a little at this; and possibly a touch of worldly pride entered into his reply.

"In this matter, Eliza, I think the wish of Maverick is to be respected."

"Pah! For my part, I respect much more the Johns name."

As the spinster retired to her room, after being overheated in the discussion, in which the calmness of the Doctor, and the news he had communicated, contributed almost equally to her frenzy, she cast a look, in passing, upon the bed-chamber of Adèle. There were all the delicate fixtures, in which she had taken such a motherly pride,—the spotless curtains, the cherished vases, and certain toilet adornments,—her gifts,—by each one of which she had hoped to win a point in the accomplishment of her ambitious project. In the flush of her disappointment she could almost have torn down the neatly adjusted drapery, and put to confusion this triumph of her housewifely skill. But cooler thoughts succeeded; and, passing on into her own chamber, she threw herself into her familiar rocking-chair and entered upon a long train of reflections, whose result will very likely have their bearing upon the development of our story.

XLIV

Philip Elderkin

ABOUT this time, Phil Elderkin had come back from his trip to the West Indies,—not a little bronzed by the fierce suns he had met there, but stalwart as ever, with his old free, frank manner, to which he had superadded a little of that easy confidence and self-poise which come of wild intercourse with the world. The old Squire took a pride he had never anticipated in walking down the street arm in arm with his stalwart son, (whose support, indeed, the old gentleman was beginning to need,) and in watching the admiring glances of the passers-by, and of such old cronies as stopped to shake hands and pass a word or two with the Squire's youngest boy.

Even the Doctor had said, "You have reason to be proud of your boy, Squire. I trust that in time he may join piety to prudence."

"Hope he may, hope he may, Doctor," said the Squire. "Fine stout lad, is n't he, Doctor?"

Of course Phil had met early with Reuben, and with the fresh spirit of their old school-

PHILIP ELDERKIN

days. Phil had very likely been advised of the experiences which had brought Reuben again to Ashfield, and of the questionable result,—for even this had become subject of village gossip; but of such matters there was very coy mention on the part of young Elderkin. Phil's world-knowledge had given him wise hints on this score. And as for Reuben, the encounter with such frank, outspoken heartiness and manliness as belonged to his old school-friend was, after his weary mental struggle of the last few months, immensely refreshing:

"Phil, my good fellow, your coming is a great god-send to me. I 've been worrying at the theologies here; but it 's blind work. I think I shall get back to business again."

"But you have n't made it blind for Adèle, Reuben,—so they tell me."

"And it is true. Faith, Phil, if I could win her beautiful trust I would give my right arm, indeed, I would."

Sister Rose had, of course, met Phil on his return most gushingly. There is something very beautiful in that warm sisterly affection which at a certain age can put no bounds to its admiring pride. There is a fading away of it as the years progress, and as the sisters drop into little private clamorous circles of their own, and look out upon other people through the spectacles of their husband's eyes,—as they are pretty apt to do; but for a long period following upon the school age it is very tender and beautiful. If Phil had been coarse, or selfish, or awkward, or ten times the sinner in any way that he was, Rose would most surely have found some charming little excuse for each and every sin, and delighted in reflecting upon him the glow of her own purity.

Of course she insists coyly upon his making the village rounds with her. Those intellectual ladies, the Misses Hapgood, must have an opportunity of admiring his grand air, and the easy manner he has brought back with him of entering a parlor, or of passing the compliments of the day; and, indeed, those respectable old ladies do pay him the honor of keeping him in waiting, until they can arrange their best frontlets, and present themselves in their black silks and in kerchiefs wet with lavender.

Then with what a bewildering success the traveller, under convoy of the delighted Rose, comes down upon the family of the Tourtelots! What an elaborate toilet Almira matures for his reception! and how the Dame nervously

PHILIP ELDERKIN

dusts and redusts her bombazine at sight of his grand manner, as she peeps through the half-opened blinds!

The Deacon is not, indeed, so much "taken off the hooks" by Phil, but entertains him in the old way.

"Pooty well on 't for beef cattle in Cuby, Philip?"

And Rose's eyes glisten, as Brother Philip goes on to set forth some of the wonders of the crops, and the culture.

"Waäl, they 're smart farmers, I 've heerd," says the Deacon; "but we 're makin' improvements here in Ashfield. Doän't know as you 've seen Square Wilkinson's new string o' wall he 's been a-buildin' all the way between his home pastur' and the west medders?"

Phil had not.

"Waäl, it 's wuth seein'. I doän't *know* what they pretend to have in Cuby; but in my opinion there a'n't such another string o' stone fence, not in the whole caounty!"

And Phil has had his little private talks with Rose,—about Adèle, among other people.

"She is more charming than ever," Rose had said.

"I suppose so."

And there had been a pause here.

DOCTOR JOHNS

"I suppose Reuben is as tender upon her as ever," Phil had said at last, in his off-hand way.

"He has been very devoted; but I'm not sure that it means anything, Phil, dear."

"I should think it meant a great deal," said Phil.

"I mean," continued Rose, reflectingly, and with some embarrassment of speech, "I don't think Adèle speaks of Reuben as if—as I should—think"—

"As you would, Rose,—is that it?"

"For shame, Phil!"

And Phil begged pardon with a kiss.

"Do you think, Phil," said Rose, concealing a little fluttering of the heart under very smoothly spoken words, "do you think that Reuben really loves Adèle?"

"Think so? To be sure, Rose. How can he help it? It's enough for me to see her as I do, odd whiles in our parlor, or walking up and down the garden with you, Rose; if I were to meet her every night and morning, as Reuben must, I should go mad."

"Aha!" said Rose, laughingly; "that's not the way lovers talk,—at least, not in books. I think you are safe, Phil. And yet" (with a soberer air) "I did think, Phil, one while, that

PHILIP ELDERKIN

you thought very, very often, and a great deal, of Adèle; and I was not sorry."

"Did you, Rose?" said Phil, eagerly; "did you truly? Then I'll tell you a secret, Rose, —mind, Rose, a great secret, never to be lisped, —not to mother even. I did love Adèle as far back as I can remember. You know the strange little French hat she used to wear? Well, I used to draw it on my slate at school, Rose; it was all I could draw that belonged to her. Many's the time when, if a boy came near, I would dash in some little flourishes about it, and call it a basket or a coal-scoop; but all the while, for me, her little dark eyes were shining under it. But there was Reuben,—and he beat me in reading and writing, and everything, I think, but fisticuffs."

"Did he?" said Rose, with the prettily arched brow which mostly accompanied only her mischievous sallies; and it seemed to Phil afterward that she would have resented the statement, if he had made it concerning any other young fellow in Ashfield.

"Yes, indeed," continued he. "I knew he must beat me out and out with Adèle. Do you remember, Rose, how you told me once that he had sent a gift of furs to her? Well, Rose, I had my own little gift hidden away for her for that same New-Year's Day, and I burned it. Those furs kept me awake an awful time. And when I went away, Rose, I prayed that I might learn to forget her; but there was never a letter of yours that came with her name in it, (and most of them had it, you know,) but I saw her as plainly as ever, with her arm laced in yours, as I used to see you many a time from my window, strolling down the garden. And now that I have come back, Rose, it's the same confounded thing. By Jove, I feel as if I could pitch into Reuben, as I used to do at school. But then—he's a good fellow."

"I'm sure he is," said Rose. "But, Phil," continued she, meditatively, "it seems to me, if I were a man, and loved a woman as you love Adèle, I should find some way of letting her know it."

"Would you, Rosy? Do you think there's a ghost of a chance?"

"I don't know, Phil; Adèle is not one who talks of such things."

"Nor you, I think, Rose."

Now it happened that this private conversation took place upon the same day on which had transpired the interview we have already chronicled between the Doctor and Miss Johns. Reuben and Adèle were to pass the evening at

PHILIP ELDERKIN

the Elderkins'. Adèle was not of a temper to be greatly disturbed by the rumor at which the Doctor had hinted of a lost fortune. (We write, it must be remembered, of a time nearly thirty years gone by.) Indeed, as she tripped along beside Reuben, it seemed to him that she had never been in a more jocular and vivacious humor. A reason for this (and it is what, possibly, many of our readers may count a very unnatural one) lay in the letter which she had that day received from her father, in which Maverick, in alluding to a possible *affaire de cœur* in connection with Reuben, had counselled her, with great earnestness, to hold her affections in reserve, and, above all, to control most rigidly any fancy which she might entertain for the son of their friend the Doctor.

It amused Adèle; for Reuben had been so totally undemonstrative in matters of sentiment, (possibly keeping his deeper feelings in reserve,) that Adèle had felt over and over a girl's mischievous propensity to provoke it. Not that she was in any sense heartless; not that she did not esteem him, and feel a keen sense of gratitude; but his kindest and largest favors were always attended with such demureness and reticence of manner as piqued her womanly vanity. For these reasons there was something exhilarating to her in the intimation conveyed by Maverick's letters, that she was the party, after all, upon whose decision must rest the peace of mind of the two, and that she must cultivate the virtue of treating him with coolness.

Possibly it would have been an easy virtue to cultivate, even though Reuben's attentions had shown the warmth which the blood of nineteen feminine years craves in a lover; but as the matter stood, there was something amusing to her in Maverick's injunction. As if there were any danger! As if there could be! Should it grow serious some day, it would be time enough then to consider her good papa's injunction; very possibly she would pay the utmost heed to it, since a respect for Mr. Maverick's opinions and advice was almost a part of Adèle's religion.

XLV

The Spinster's Policy

WE left Miss Eliza Johns in her chamber, swaying back and forth in her rocking-chair, and resolutely confronting the dire news which

THE SPINSTER'S POLICY

the Doctor had communicated. What was to be done?

Adèle was to be discarded, but not suddenly. All her art must be employed to disabuse Reuben of any lingering tenderness. The Doctor's old prejudice against French blood must be worked to its utmost. But there must be no violent clamor,—above all, no disclosure of the humiliating truth. Maverick (the false man!) must be instructed that it would be agreeable to the Johns family—nay, that their sense of dignity demanded—that he should reclaim his child at an early day.

She was not the woman to sleep upon her plans, when once they were decided on; and she had no sooner forecast her programme than she took advantage of the lingering twilight to arrange her toilet for a call upon the Elderkins. Of course she led off the Doctor in her trail. The spinster's "marching orders," as he jocularly termed them, the good man was as incapable of resisting as if he had been twenty years a husband.

In a few swift words she unfolded her design.

"And now, Benjamin, don't, pray, let your sentiment get the better of you, in regard to this French girl. Think of the proprieties in

DOCTOR JOHNS

the case, Benjamin,—the proprieties,"—which she enforced by a little shake of her forefinger.

Whenever it came to a question of the "proprieties," the Doctor was conscious of his weakness.

What, indeed, can any man do, when a woman bases herself on the "proprieties"?

It was summer weather, and the windows of the hospitable Elderkin mansion were wide open. As the Doctor and spinster drew near, little gusts of cheery music came out to greet their ears. For, at this time, Miss Almira had her rival pianos about the village; and the pretty Rose had been taught a deft way of touching the "first-class" instrument, which the kind-hearted Squire had bestowed upon her. Indeed, if it must be told, little sparkling waltzes had from time to time waked the parlor solitude, and the kind Mistress Elderkin had winked at little furtive parlor-dances on the part of Rose and Adèle,—they had so charmed the old Squire, and set all his blood (as he said, with a gallant kiss upon the brow of Mrs. Elderkin) flowing in the old schoolboy currents. Now it happened upon this very evening, that the Squire, though past seventy now, was in the humor to see a good old-fashioned frolic; so while Rose was rattling

THE SPINSTER'S POLICY

off some crazy waltz, Phil, at a hint from the old gentleman, had taken possession of Adèle, and was showing off with a good deal of grace, and more spirit, the dancing-steps of which he had had experience with the Spanish senoritas.

Dame Tourtelot, who chanced to be present, wore a long face, which (it is conceivable) the hearty old Squire enjoyed as much as the dancing. But Mrs. Elderkin must have looked with a warm maternal pride upon the fine athletic figure of her boy, as he went twirling down the floor with that graceful figure of Adèle.

Upon the very midst of it, however, the Doctor and Miss Johns came in like a cloud. The fingers of Rose rested idly on the keys. Adèle, who was gay beyond her wont, alone of all the company could not give over her light-heartedness on the instant: so she makes away to greet the Doctor,—Miss Johns standing horrified.

"New Papa, you have surprised us. Phil was showing me some new steps. Do you think it very, very wrong?"

"Adaly! Adaly!"

"Ah, you dear old man, it is n't wrong; say it is n't wrong."

By this time the Squire has come forward.

DOCTOR JOHNS

"Ah, Doctor, young folks will be young folks; but I think you won't have a quarrel with Mrs. Elderkin yonder. My dear," (addressing Mrs. Elderkin,) "you must set this matter right with the Doctor. We must keep our young people in his good books."

"The good books are not kept by me, Squire," said the parson.

Reuben, who had been loitering about Rose, and who, to do him justice, had seen Phil's gallant attention to Adèle without one spark of jealousy, was especially interested in this interruption of the festivities. In his present state of mind, he was most eager to know how far the evening's hilarity would be imputed as a sin to the new convert, and how far religious severities (if she met any) would control the ardor of Adèle. The Doctor's face softened, even while he talked with the charming errant, —Reuben observed that; but with Aunt Eliza the case was different. Never had he seen such a threatening darkness in her face.

"We have interrupted a ball, I fear," she said to the hostess, in a tone which was as virulent as a masculine oath.

"Oh! no! no!" said Mrs. Elderkin. "Indeed, now, you must not scold Adèle too much; 't was only a bit of the Squire's foolery."

THE SPINSTER'S POLICY

"Oh, certainly not; she is quite her own mistress. I should be very sorry to consider myself responsible for all her tastes."

Reuben, hearing this, felt his heart leap toward Adèle in a way which the spinster's praises had never provoked.

Dame Tourtelot here says, in her most aggravating manner,—

"I think she dances beautifully, Miss Johns. She dooz yer credit, upon my word she dooz."

And thereupon there followed a somewhat lively altercation between those two sedate ladies,—in the course of which a good deal of stinging mockery was covered with unctuous compliment. But the spinster did not lose sight of her chief aim, to wit, the refusal of all responsibility as attaching to the conduct of Adèle, and a most decided intimation that the rumors which associated her name with Reuben were unfounded, and were likely to prove altogether false.

This last hint was a revelation to the gossiping Dame; there had been trouble, then, at the parsonage; things were clearly not upon their old footing. Was it Adèle? Was it Reuben? Yet never had either shown greater cheer than on this very night. But the Dame none the less eagerly had communicated her story, before the evening closed, to Mrs. Elderkin,—who received it doubtingly,—to Rose, who heard it with wonder and a pretty confusion,—and to the old Squire, who said only

"Pooh! pooh! it 's a lover's quarrel; we shall be all straight to-morrow."

Adèle, by her own choice, was convoyed home, when the evening was over, by the good Doctor, and had not only teased him into pardon of her wild mirth, before they had reached the parsonage-gate, but had kindled in him a glow of tenderness that made him utterly forgetful of the terrible news of the day. Reuben and the spinster, as they followed, talked of Rose; never had Aunt Eliza spoken so warmly of her charms; but before him was tripping along, in the moonlight, the graceful figure of Adèle, clinging to the old gentleman's arm, and it is doubtful if his eye did not feast more upon that vision than his ear upon the new praises of the spinster.

Yet, for all that, Rose was really charming. The young gentleman, it would seem, hardly knew his own heart; and he had a wondrous dream that night. There was a church, (such as he had seen in the city,) and a delicately gloved hand, which lay nestling in his; and Mr. Maverick, oddly enough, appeared to give away

THE SPINSTER'S POLICY

a bride, and all waited only for the ceremony, which the Doctor (with his old white hat and cane) refused to perform; whereat Phil's voice was heard bursting out in a great laugh; and the face of Rose, too, appeared; but it was only as a saint upon a painted window. And yet the face of the saint upon the window was more distinct than any thing in his dream.

The next morning found Miss Eliza harsh and cold. Even the constrained smile with which she had been used to qualify her "good-morning" for Adèle was wanting; and when the family prayers were said, in which the good Doctor had pleaded, with unction, that the Christian grace of charity might reign in all hearts, the poor girl had sidled up to Miss Eliza, and put her hand in the spinster's,—

"You think our little frolic last night to be very wrong, I dare say?"

"Oh, no," said the spinster. "I dare say Mr. Maverick and your French relatives would approve."

It was not so much the language as the tone which smote on poor Adèle, and brought the tears welling into her eyes.

Reuben, seeing it all, and forgetful of the

good parson's plea, gnawed his lip to keep back certain very harsh utterances.

"Don't think of it, Ady," said he, watching his chance a little later; "the old lady is in one of her blue moods to-day."

"Do you think I did wrong, Reuben?" said Adèle, earnestly.

"I? Wrong, Adèle? Pray, what should I have to say about the right or wrong? and I think the old ladies are beginning to think I have no clear idea of the difference between them."

"You have, Reuben! you have! And, Reuben, (more tenderly,) "I have promised solemnly to live as you thought a little while ago that you would live. And if I were to break my promise, Reuben, I know that you would never renew yours."

"I believe you are speaking God's truth, Adèle," said he.

The summer months pass by, and for Adèle the little table at the parsonage had become as bleak and cheerless as the autumn. Miss Johns maintained the rigid severity of manner, with which she had undertaken to treat the outcast child, with a constancy that would have done credit to a worthier intent. Even the good Doctor was unconsciously oppressed by it, and

THE SPINSTER'S POLICY

by the spinster's insistence upon the due proprieties he was weaned away from his old tenderness of speech; but every morning and every evening his voice trembled with emotion as he prayed for God's grace and mercy upon all sinners and outcasts.

He had written to Maverick, advising him of the great grief which his confession had caused him, and imploring him to make what reparation he yet might do, by uniting in the holy bonds of matrimony with the erring mother of his child. He had further advised him that his apprehensions with regard to Reuben were, so far as was known, groundless. He further wrote,—"Upon consultation with Miss Johns, who is still at the head of our little household, I am constrained to ask that you take as early a time as may be convenient to relieve her of the further care of your daughter. Age is beginning to tell somewhat upon my sister; and the embarrassment of her position with respect to Adèle is a source, I believe, of great mental distress."

All which the good Doctor honestly believed,—upon Miss Eliza's averment,—and in his own honest way he assured his friend, that, though his sins were as scarlet he should still implore Heaven in his favor, and should part from Adèle—whenever the parting might come—with real grief, and with an outpouring of his heart.

As for Reuben, a wanton levity had come over him in those latter days of summer that galled the poor Doctor to the quick, and that strangely perplexed the observant spinster. It was not the mischievous spirit of his boyhood revived again, but a cold, passionless, determined levity, such as men wear who have secret griefs to conceal. He talked in a free and easy way about the Doctor's Sunday discourses, that fairly shocked the old people of the parish; rumor said that he had passed some unhallowed jokes with the stolid Deacon Tourtelot about his official duties; and it was further reported that he had talked open infidelity with a young physician who had recently established himself in Ashfield, and who plumed himself—until his tardy practice taught him better—upon certain arrogant physiological notions with regard to death and disease that were quite unbiblical. Long ago the Doctor had given over open expostulation; every such talk seemed to evoke a new and more airy and more adventurous demon in the backslidden Reuben. The good man half feared to cast his eye over the books he might

THE SPINSTER'S POLICY

be reading. If it were Voltaire, if it were Hume, he feared lest his rebuke and anathema should give a more appetizing zest.

But he prayed—ah, how he prayed! with the dead Rachel in his thought—as if (and this surely cannot be Popishly wicked)—as if she, too, in some sphere far remote, might with angel voice add tender entreaty to the prayer, whose burden, morning after morning and night after night, was the name and the hope of her boy.

And Adèle? Well, Reuben pitied Adèle,—pitied her subjection to the iron frowns of Miss Eliza; and almost the only earnest words he spoke in those days were little quiet words of good cheer for the French girl. And when Miss Eliza whispered him, as she did, that the poor child's fortune was gone, and her future insecure, Reuben, with a brave sort of antagonism, made his words of cheer and good-feeling even more frequent. But about his passing and kindly attentions to Adèle there was that air of gay mockery which overlaid his whole life, and which neither invited nor admitted of any profound acknowledgment. His kindest words—and some of them, so far as mere language went, were exuberantly tender—were met always by a half-saddened air of thankfulness and a little restrained pressure of the hand, as if Adèle had said,—"Not in earnest yet, Reuben—earnest in nothing!"

XLVI

A Phrenzy

It would have been strange, if Adèle had not some day formed her ideal of a lover. Who cannot recall the sweet illusions of those tripping youthful years, when, for the first time, Sir William Wallace strode so gallantly with waving plume and glittering falchion down the pages of Miss Porter,—when the sun-browned Ivanhoe dashed so grandly into that famous tilting-ground near to Ashby-de-la-Zouch, and brought the wicked Sir Brian de Bois-Guilbert to a reckoning,—when we wished the disinherited knight better things than the cold love of the passionless Rowena, and sighed over the fate of poor Fergus MacIvor? With all these characters, and many other such, Adèle had made acquaintance, in company with her dear Rose, and by the light of

A PHRENZY

them, they had fashioned such ideals in their little heads as do not often appear in the flesh. Not that the two friends always agreed in their dreamy fancies; but for either, a hero must have been handsome and brave and true and kind and sagacious and learned. If only a few hundred of men should be patterned after the design of a young girl of sixteen or eighteen, what an absurd figure we old sinners should cut in the comparison!

But the ideal of our friend Adèle had not been constant. Three years back, the open, frank, brave front which Phil Elderkin wore had almost reached it; and when Rose had said,—as she was wont to say, in her sisterly pride,—"He's a noble fellow," there had been a little tingling of the heart in Adèle, which seemed to echo the words. Afterward had come that glimpse of the world which her journey and intercourse with Maverick had afforded; and the country awkwardness of the Elderkins had somehow worked an eclipse of his virtues. Reuben, indeed, had comeliness, and had caught at that time some of the graces of the city; but Reuben was a *tease,* and failed in a certain quality of respect for her, (at least, she fancied it,) in default of which she met all his favors with a sisterly tenderness, in which there was none of the reserve that tempts passion to declare itself.

Later, when Reuben so opened the way to her belief, and associated himself so intimately with the culmination of her religious faith, he seemed to her for a time the very impersonation of her girlish fancy,—so tender, so true, so trustful. Her religious enthusiasm blended with and warmed her sentiment; and never had she known such hours of calm enjoyment, or such hopeful forecast of her worldly future, as in those golden days when the hearts of both were glowing (or seemed to be) with a common love. It was not that this sentiment in her took any open form of expression; her instinctive delicacy so kept it under control that she was but half conscious of its existence. But it was none the less true that the sad young pilgrim, who had been a brother, and who had unlocked for her the Beautiful Gate, wore a new aspect. Her heart was full of those glittering estimates of life, which come at rare intervals, in which duties and affections all seem in delightful accord, working each their task, and glowing through all the reach of years, until the glow is absorbed in the greater light which shines upon Christian graves. But Reuben's desertion from the faith

A PHRENZY

broke this phantasm. *Her* faith, standing higher, never shook; but the sentiment which grew under its cover found nothing positive whereby to cling, and perished with the shock. Besides which, her father's injunction came to the support of her religious convictions, and made her disposition to shake off that empty fancy tenfold strong. Had Reuben, in those days of his exaltation, made declaration of his attachment, it would have met with a response that could have admitted of no withdrawal, and her heart would have been leashed to his, whatever outlawry might threaten him. She thanked Heaven that it had not been thus. Her ideal was still sustained and unbroken; but it no longer found its type in the backsliding Reuben. It is doubtful, indeed, if her sentiment at this period, by mere force of rebound, and encouraged by her native charities and old proclivities, did not rally about young Elderkin, who had equipped himself with many accomplishments of the world, and who, if he made no pretensions to the faith she had embraced, manifested an habitual respect that challenged her gratitude.

As for Reuben, after his enthusiasm of the summer had vanished, he felt a prodigious mortification in reflecting that Adèle had been so closely the witness of his short-lived hallucination. It humiliated him bitterly to think that all his religious zeal had proved in her regard but the empty crackling of a fire of thorns. No matter what may be a youth's sentiment for girlhood, he never likes it to be witness of any thing disparaging to his sturdy resolution and manly purpose. But Adèle had seen him shake like a reed under the deepest emotions that could give tone to character; and in his mortification at the thought, he transferred to her a share of the resentment he felt against himself. It had been a relief to treat her with a dignified coolness, and to meet all her tender inquiries, which she did not forbear, with an icy assurance of manner that was more than half affected,—yet not unkind, but assiduously and intensely and provokingly civil.

Seeing this, the Doctor and Miss Eliza had given over any fear of a possibly dangerous interest on the part of Reuben; and yet keen observers might well have scented a danger in this very studied indifference, if they reflected that its motive lay exclusively in a mortified pride. We are not careful to conceal our mortifications from those whose regard we rate humbly.

At any rate, it happened that, with the com-

A PHRENZY

ing of the autumn months, Reuben, still flaunting drearily on a sea of religious speculation, and veering more and more into open mockery of the beliefs of all about him, grew weary of his affectations with respect to Adèle. He fretted under the kindly manner with which she met his august civilities. They did not wound her sensibilities, as he hoped they might have done. Either this disappointment or the need of relief provoked a change of tactics. With a sudden zeal that was half earnest and half a freak of vanity, he devoted himself to Adèle. The father's sympathy with him was just now dead; that of the aunt had never been kindled to such a degree as to meet his craving; with the Elderkins he was reluctant to unfold his opinions so far as to demand sympathy. As for Adèle, if he could light up again the sentiment which he once saw beaming in her face, he could at least find in it a charming beguilement of his unrest. She had a passion for flowers: every day he gathered for her some floral gift; every day she thanked him with a kindness that meant only kindness. She had a passion for poetry: every day he read to her such as he knew she must admire; every day she thanked him with a warmth upon which he could build no hopes.

DOCTOR JOHNS

Both the Doctor and Miss Eliza were disturbed by this new zeal of his. At the instance of the spinster, the Doctor undertook to lay before Reuben the information conveyed in the letter of Maverick, and that gentleman's disapproval of any association between the young people looking to marriage. It was not an easy or an agreeable task for the Doctor; and he went about it in a very halting manner.

"Your Aunt Eliza has observed, Reuben, that you have lately become more pointed in your attentions to Adaly.

"I dare say, father; worries her, does n't it?"

"We do not know how far these attentions may be serious, Reuben."

"Nor I, father."

The Doctor was shocked at this new evidence of his son's indifference to any fixed rule of conduct.

"How long is it, father," continued Reuben, "since Aunt Eliza has commenced her plottings against Adèle?"

"Not plottings against her, I trust, Reuben."

"Yes, she has, father. She's badgering her in her quiet way incessantly,—as far back as when she caught sight of her in that dance at the Elderkins'. For my part, I think it was a charming thing to see."

A PHRENZY

"We have graver reasons for our anxiety in regard to your relations with her, my son; and not the least of them is Mr. Maverick's entire disapproval of any such attachment."

And thereupon the Doctor had proceeded to lay before Reuben (who now showed a most lively interest) a full revelation of the facts announced in Maverick's letter.

The son had a strong smack of the father's family pride, and the strange news was bewildering to him; but in his present state of distrust, he felt a strong disposition to protest against all the respectable conventionalities that hedged him in. A generous instinct in him, too, as he thought of the poor girl under the ban of the towns folk, craved some chivalric expression; and whatever sentiment he may really have entertained for her in past days took new force in view of the sudden barriers that rose between him and the tender, graceful, confiding, charming Adèle, whose image had so long and (as he now thought) so constantly dwelt in the dreamy mirage of his future. Under the spur of these feelings, he presently gave over his excited walk up and down the study, and, coming close to the Doctor, whispered, with a grave earnestness that made the old gentleman recognize a man in his boy. —

DOCTOR JOHNS

"Father, I have doubted my own feelings about Adèle: now I do not. I love her; I love her madly. I shall protect her; if she will marry me," (and he touched the Doctor on the shoulder with a quick, nervous tap of his hand,) "I shall marry her,—God bless her!"

And Reuben, by the very speech, as well as by the thoughts that had gone before, had worked himself into a passion of devotion.

"Be careful, my son," said the old gentleman; "remember how your enthusiasm has betrayed you in a still more serious matter."

Reuben smiled bitterly.

"Don't reproach me with that, father. It seems to me that I am acting now more on the side of the Christian charities than either you or Aunt Eliza."

And with this he strode out, leaving the Doctor in an agony of apprehension.

A moment after, Miss Eliza, who was ever on the alert, and without whose knowledge a swallow could not dart into the chimneys of the parsonage, came rustling into the study.

"Well, Benjamin, what does Reuben say?"

"Given over to his idols, Eliza,—given over to his idols. We can only pray God to have him in His holy keeping."

It would be impossible to fathom all the

A PHRENZY

emotions of Reuben during that interview with his father. It would be wrong to say that the view of future marriage had not often held up its brilliant illusions before him; it would be wrong to say that they had never been associated with the charming vivacity of Adèle, as well as, at other times, with the sweet graces of Rose Elderkin. But these illusions had been of a character so transitory, so fleeting, that he had come to love their brilliant changes, and to look forward with some dread to the possible permanence of them, or such fixedness as should take away the charming drift of his vagaries. If, in some wanton and quite impossible moment, the modest Rose had conquered her delicacy so far as to put her hand in his, and say, "Will you be my husband?" he would not have been so much outraged by her boldness as disturbed by the reflection that a pleasant little dream of love was broken up, and that his thought must come to that practical solution of a *yes* or *no* which would make an end of his delightful doubts and yearnings. The positive and the known are, after all, so much less under imaginative measure, than the uncertain and the dreamy!

And if he could have taken the spinster's old tales of Adèle's regard for him and devotion

DOCTOR JOHNS

to him at their highest truth, (which he never did, because of the girl's provoking familiarity and indifference,) he would have felt a great charm in his life cut off. Yet now he wanders in search of her with his heart upon his lip and a great fire in his brain. Not a little pride in affronting opinion may have kindled the glow of his sudden resolve. There was an audacity in it that tempted and regaled him. Why should he, whose beliefs were so uncertain, who had grown into doubts of that faith on which all the conventional proprieties about him reposed,—why should he not discard them, and obey a single, strong, generous instinct? When a man's religious sensibilities suffer recoil as Reuben's had done, there grows up a new pride in the natural emotions of generosity; the humane instincts show exceptional force; the skeptics become the teachers of an exaggerated philanthropy.

Did he love her beyond all others? Yesterday he could not have told; to-day, under the fervor of his audacity and of his pride, his love blazes up in a fiery flame. It seethes around the memory of her lithe, graceful figure in a whirl of passion. Those ripe red lips shall taste the burning heat of his love and tenderness. He will guard, cherish, protect, and the iron aunt may protest, or the world talk as it will. "Adèle! Adèle!" His heart is full of the utterance, and his step wild with tumultuous feeling, as he rushes away to find her,—to win her,—to bind together their destinies forever!

XLVII

Will She?

IT was a mellow evening of later October. Mists hung in all the hollows of the hills. Within the orchard, where Adèle was strolling, a few golden apples still shone among the bronzed leaves. She saw Reuben coming swiftly through the garden; but his eager step faltered as he came near her. Even the serene look of girlhood has a power in it to make impassioned confidence waver, and enthusiasms suffer recoil. He meets her at last with an assumption of his every-day manner, which she cannot but see presently is underlaid with a tempest of struggling feeling to which he is a stranger. He has taken her hand and placed it within his arm,—a little coquettish device to which he was wont; but he keeps the little hand in his with a nervous clasp that is new, and that makes her tremble all the more when his speech grows impassioned, and the easy compliments of his past days of frolicsome humor take a depth of tone which makes her heart thrill strangely. Meantime, they had come to the garden-end of the walk.

"It 's late, Reuben, and I must go in-doors," said she, with a quiet that she did not feel.

"We 'll take one more turn, Adèle; you *must*." And her hand trembled in the eager clasp he fastened upon it.

Not once did it come into her mind that Reuben was to make a declaration of passion for her. She had feared only some burst of feeling in the direction of the spinster, or of the Doctor, which should compromise him even more seriously. When, therefore, he burst forth, as he did presently, with a passionate avowal of his love, she was overwhelmed with confusion.

"This is so sudden, so strange, Reuben! indeed it is!"

Tenderly as she may have felt toward him in days gone, and gratefully as she always felt, this sudden attempt to carry by storm the very citadel of her affections was not alone a sur-

WILL SHE?

prise, but seemed like sacrilege. The mystery and doubt that overhung the relations between her own father and mother—and which she felt keenly—had made her regard with awe any possible marriage of her own, investing the thought of it with a terrible sanctity, and as something to be approached only with a reverent fear. If in this connection she had ever thought of Reuben, it was in those days when he seemed so earnest in the faith, and when their feelings were blent by some superhuman agency. But at his divergence into the paths of skepticism, it seemed to her simple and intense faith that thenceforth their pilgrimages must be wholly distinct: his—and she trembled at the thought of it—through some terrible maze of error, where she could not follow; and hers—by God's grace—straight to the city whose gates are of pearl.

When, therefore, she had replied to the passionate address of Reuben, "You must not talk thus," it was with a tear in her eye.

"It grieves you, then, Adèle?"

"Yes, it grieves me, Reuben. Our paths are different now;" and she bethought herself of her father's injunction, which seemed to make her duty still plainer, and forbade her to encourage that parley with her heart which—

DOCTOR JOHNS

with her hand still fast in Reuben's, and his eyes beaming with a fierce heat upon her—she was beginning to entertain.

"Adèle, tell me, can I go on?"

"Indeed, indeed, you must not, Reuben!"—and withdrawing her hand suddenly, she passed it over brow and eyes, as if to rally her thoughts to measure the situation.

"You are weeping, Adèle?" said Reuben.

"No, not weeping," said she, dashing the merest film of mist from her eyes, "but so troubled!—so troubled!" And she looked yearningly, but vainly, in his face for that illumination which had belonged to his enthusiasm of the summer.

They walked for a moment in silence,—he, with a scowl upon his face. Seeing this, Adèle said, plaintively,—

"It seems to me, Reuben, as if this might be only a solemn mockery of yours."

"You doubt me, then?" returned he like a flash.

"Do you not doubt yourself, Reuben? Have you never doubted yourself?" This with a glance that pierced him through.

"Good Heavens! are you turned preacher?" said he, bitterly. "Will you measure a heart by its dogmatic beliefs?"

WILL SHE?

"For shame, Reuben!"

And for a time both were silent. At last Adèle spoke again,—

"There is a sense of coming trouble that oppresses me strangely,—that tells me I must not listen to you, Reuben."

"I know it, Adèle; and it is for this I would cherish you, and protect you against all possible shame or indignities——"

"Shame! Indignities! What does this mean? What do you know, Reuben?"

Reuben blushed scarlet. His speech had outrun his discretion; but seizing her hand, and pressing it more tenderly than ever, he said,—

"Only this, Adèle: I see that a coolness has grown up toward you in the parsonage; the old prejudice against French blood may revive again; besides which, there is, you know, Adèle, that little family cloud——"

"Is this the old, kind Reuben,—my brother,—who reminds me of a trouble so shadowy I cannot fairly measure it?" And Adèle covered her face with her hands.

"Forgive me, Adèle, for God's sake!"

"There *is* a cloud, Reuben; thank you for the word," said Adèle, recovering herself; "and there is, I fear, an even darker cloud upon your faith. Until both are passed, I can never listen to such talk as you would urge upon me,—never! never!"

And there was a spirit in her words now that awed Reuben.

"Would you impute my unbelief to me as a crime, Adèle? is this your Christian charity? Do you think that I enjoy this fierce wrestling with doubts? or, having them, would you bid me play false and conceal them? What if I am a final castaway, as your good books tell us some must be, would you make me a castaway before my time, and balk all my hopes in life? Is this your charity?"

"I would not,—you know I would not, Reuben."

"Listen to me, Adèle. If there be any hope of making my way out of this weary wrangle, it seems to me that it would be in the constant presence of your simple, exultant faith. Will you be my teacher, Adèle?"

"Teacher,—yes, with all my heart, Reuben."

"Then be mine," said he, seizing her hand again, "from this very hour!"

An instant she seemed to waver; then came over her the memory of her father's injunction,—the mystery, too, that overshadowed her own life.

WILL SHE?

"I cannot,—I cannot, Reuben!"

"Is this final?" said he, calmly.

"Final."

She sighed it rather than spoke aloud; the next instant she had slipped away through the shrubbery, with a swift, cruel rustle of her silken dress, toward the parsonage.

Reuben lingered in the orchard until he saw the light flashing through the muslin hangings of her window. She had gone early to her chamber. She had kissed the crucifix that was her mother's with a fervor that sprang as much from devotion as from sentiment. She had sobbed out her prayer, and with sobs had buried her sweet face in the pillow.

Could Reuben have seen or conceived all this, he might have acted differently.

As it was, he entered the Doctor's study an hour later, with the utmost apparent coolness.

"Well, father," said he, "I have offered marriage to your motherless and pious French *protégée,* and she declines."

"My poor son!" said the Doctor.

But his sympathy was not so much with any possible feeling of disappointment as with the chilling heartlessness and unbelief that seemed to boast themselves in his speech.

"It will be rather dull in Ashfield now, I

DOCTOR JOHNS

fancy," continued Reuben, "and I shall slip off to New York to-morrow and take a new taste of the world."

And the Doctor (as if to himself) said despairingly, " *'Whom He will He hardeneth.'* "

"But, father," said Reuben, (without notice of the old gentleman's ejaculation,) "don't let Aunt Eliza know of this,—not a word, or she will be fearfully cruel to the poor child."

There was a grave household in the parsonage next morning. Reuben rebelled in heart, in face, and in action against the tediously long prayer of the parson, though the old gentleman's spirit was writhing painfully in his pleadings. The aunt was more pious and austere than ever. Adèle, timid and shrinking, yet with a beautiful and a trustful illumination in her eye, that for days, and weeks, and months, lingered in the memory of the parson's son.

Later in the day Reuben went to make his adieus to the Elderkins. The old Squire was seated in his door busied with the "Weekly Courant," which had just come in.

"Aha, Master Reuben," (this was his old-fashioned way,) "you 're looking for that lazy fellow, Phil, I suppose. You 'll find him upstairs with his cigar and his Spanish, I 'll venture."

WILL SHE?

Reuben made his way up to Phil's chamber after the unceremonious manner to which he had been used in that hospitable home, while a snatch of a little songlet from Rose came floating after him along the stairs. It was very sweet. But what were sweet songlets to him now? It being a mild autumn day, Phil sat at the open window, from which he had many a time seen the old Doctor jogging past in his chaise, and sometimes the tall Almira picking her maidenly way along the walk with her green parasol daintily held aloft with thumb and two fingers, while from the lesser fingers dangled a little embroidered bag which was the wonder of all the school-girls. Other times, too, from this eyrie of his, he had seen Adèle tripping past, with Reuben beside her, and had wondered what their chat might be, while he had feasted his eyes upon her fair figure.

Reuben was always a welcome visitor, and was presently in full flow of talk, and puffing nervously at one of Phil's choice Havanas (which in that day were true to their titles).

"I 'm off, Phil," said Reuben at last, breaking in upon his host's ecstasy over a ballad he had been reciting, with what he counted the true Castilian magniloquence.

"Off where?" said Phil.

DOCTOR JOHNS

"Off to the city. I 'm weary of this do-nothing life,—weary of the town, weary of the good people."

"There 's nothing you care for, then, in Ashfield?" said Phil. And at that moment a little burst of the singing of Rose came floating up the stair,—so sweet! so sweet!

"Care for? Yes," said Reuben, "but they are all so good! so devilish good!"—and he puffed at his cigar with a nervous violence.

"I thought there would have been at least one magnet that would have kept you here," said Phil.

"What magnet, pray?" says Reuben,—somewhat calm again.

"There she goes," says Phil, looking out of the window. And at that moment Adèle tripped by, with the old Doctor walking gravely at her side.

"Humph!" said Reuben, with a composure that was feigned, "she 's too much of a Puritan for me, Phil: or rather, I 'm too little of a Puritan for her."

Philip looked at his companion keenly. And Reuben, looking back at him as keenly, said, after a silence of a few moments,—

"I don't think you 'll ever marry her either, Phil."

WILL SHE?

"Marry!" said Phil, with a deep, honest blush,—"who talks of that?"

"You, in your heart, Phil. Do you think I am blind? Do you think I have not seen that you have loved her, Phil, ever since you knew what it was to love a woman? Do you think, that, as a boy, you ever imposed upon me with your talk about the tavern-keeper's daughter? Good Heavens! Phil, I think there were never two men in the world who talked their thoughts plainly to each other! Do you think I do not know that you have played the shy lover, because with your big heart you have yielded to what you counted a prior claim of mine,—because Adèle was one of us at the parsonage?"

"In such affairs," said Phil, with some constraint and not a little wounded pride, "I don't think men are apt to recognize prior claims."

Reuben replied only by a faint sardonic smile.

"You're a good fellow, Phil, but you won't marry her."

"Of course, then, you know why," said Phil, with something very like a sneer.

"Certainly," said Reuben. "Because you can't affront the world, because you are bound by its conventionalities and respectabilities, as I am not. I spurn them."

"Respectabilities!" said Phil, in amazement. "What does this mean? Just now she was a Puritan."

"It means, Phil," (and here Reuben reflected a moment or two, puffing with savage energy,) "it means what I can't wholly explain to you. You know her French blood; you know all the prejudices against the faith in which she was reared; you know she has an instinct and will of her own. In short, Phil, I don't think you 'll ever marry her; but if you can, you may."

"*May!*" said Phil, whose pride was now touched to the quick. "And what authority have you, pray?"

"The authority of one who has loved her," said Reuben, with a fierce, quick tone, and dashing his half-burnt cigar from the window; "the authority of one who, if he had chosen to perjure himself and profess a faith which he could not entertain, and wear sanctimonious airs, might have won her heart."

"I don't believe it!" said Phil, with a great burst of voice. "There 's no hypocrisy could win Adèle."

Reuben paced up and down the chamber, then came and took the hand of his old friend:—

"Phil, you 're a noble-hearted fellow. I never thought any one could convict me of injustice to Adèle. You have done it. I hope you 'll always defend her; and whatever may betide, I hope your mother and Rose will always befriend her. She may need it."

Again there was a little burst of song from below, and it lingered upon the ear of Reuben long after he had left the Elderkin homestead.

The next day he was gone,—to try his new taste of the world.

XLVIII

Café de l'Orient

IT was in no way possible for the simple-hearted Doctor to conceal from the astute spinster the particular circumstances which had hurried Reuben's departure, and the knowledge of them made her humiliation complete. During all the latter months of Reuben's stay she had not scrupled to drop occasional praises of him in the ear of Adèle, as in the old times. It was in agreement with her rigid notions of retribution, that this poor social outlaw should love vainly; and a baffling disappointment would have seemed to the spinster's narrow mind a highly proper and most logical result of the terrible ignominy which overhung the unconscious victim. Indeed, the innocent unconsciousness of any thing derogatory to her name or character which belonged to Adèle, and her consequent cheery mirthfulness, were sources of infinite annoyance to Miss Eliza.

The Doctor showed all his old, grave kindness; but he was sadly broken by his anxieties with respect to his son; nor was he ever demonstrative enough to supply the craving of Adèle's heart, under her present greed for sympathy. Even the villagers looked upon her more coldly since the sharpened speech of the spinster had dropped widely, but very quietly, its damaging innuendoes, and since her well-calculated surmises,—that French blood was, after all, not to be wholly trusted. It was clear to the towns-people that all was at an end between Adèle and Reuben,—clear that she had fallen away from the old favor in which she once stood at the parsonage; and Miss Eliza, by her adroit hints, and without any palpable violation of truth, found means of associating these results with certain suspicious circumstances which had come to light respecting the poor girl's character,—circumstances for which she herself (Miss Eliza was kind enough to say) was not altogether accountable, perhaps, but yet sufficient to warrant a little reserve of confidence, and *of course* putting an end to any thought of intimate alliance with "the Johns family." She even whispered in her most insidious manner into the ear of old Mistress Tew,—who, being somewhat deaf, was the most inveterate village gossip,—that "it was hard for the poor thing, when Reuben left so suddenly."

Adèle writes in these times to her father, that he need put himself in no fear in regard to marriage. "I have had an *éclaircissement*" (she says) "with friend Reuben. His declaration of attachment (I think I may tell *you* this, dear papa) was so wholly unexpected that I could not count it real. He seemed actuated by some sudden controlling sympathy (as he often is) that I could not explain; and had it been otherwise, your injunction, dear papa, and the fact that he has become a bitter skeptic in regard to our most holy religion, would have made me pause. He dropped a hint, too, of the mystery attaching to my family, (not unkindly, for he is, after all, a dear, good hearted fellow,) which kindled not a little indignation in me; and I told him—with some of the pride, I think, I must have inherited from you, papa—that, until that mystery is cleared, I would marry neither him nor another. Was I not right?

"I want so much to be with you again, dear papa,—to tell you all I hope and fear,—to feel your kiss again! Miss Johns, whom I have tried hard to love, but cannot, is changed wofully in her manner toward me. I feel it is only my home now by sufferance,—not such a home as you would choose for me, I am sure. The Doctor—good soul—is as kind as he knows how to be, but I want—oh, how I want! —to leap into your arms, dear papa, and find home there. Why can I not? I am sure— over and over sure—that I could bring some sunlight into a home of yours, if you would but let me. And when you come, as you say you mean to do soon, do not put me off with such stories as you once told me, of 'a lean Savoyard in red wig and spectacles, and of a fat Frenchman with bristly mustache' (you see I remember all); tell me I may come to be the mistress of your parlor and your *salon,* and I will keep all in such order, that, I am sure, you will not want me to leave you again;

and you will love me so much that I shall never want to leave you.

"Indeed, indeed, it is very wearisome to me here. The village people seem all of them to have caught the coolness of Miss Johns, and look askance at me. Only the Elderkins show their old kindness, and it is unfailing. Do not, I pray, disturb yourself about any 'lost fortune' of which you wrote to the Doctor, but never—cruel papa!—a word to me. I am rich: I can't tell you how many dollars are in the Savings Bank for me,—and for you, if you wish them, I have so little occasion to spend anything. But I have committed the extravagance of placing a beautiful tablet over the grave of poor Madame Arles, and, much to the horror of the good Doctor, insisted upon having a little cross inscribed upon its front. You have never told me, dear papa, if you received the long account I gave you of her sudden death, and how she died without ever telling me any thing of herself,—though I believe it was in her mind to do so, at the last."

No, of a truth, such letter had never been received by Maverick, and he cursed the mails royally for it, since it might have prevented the need of any such disclosure as he had made to his friend Johns. When the present missive

DOCTOR JOHNS

of Adèle came to him, he was entering the brilliant Café de L'Orient at Marseilles, in company with his friend Papiol. The news staggered him for a moment.

"Papiol!" said he, "*mon ami,* Julie is dead!"

"*Parbleu!* And among your Puritans, yonder? She must have made a piquant story of it all!"

"Not a word, Papiol! She has kept her promise bravely."

"*Tant mieux:* it will give you good appetite, *mon ami.*"

For a moment the better nature of Maverick had been roused, and he turned a look of loathing upon the complacent Frenchman seated by him (which fortunately the stolid Papiol did not comprehend). For a moment, his thought ran back to a sunny hill-side near to the old town of Arles, where lines of stunted, tawny olives crept down the fields,—where fig-trees showed their purple nodules of fruit,—where a bright-faced young peasant-girl, with a gay kerchief turbaned about her head with a coquettish tie, lay basking in the sunshine. He heard once more the trip of her voice warbling a Provençal song, while the great ruin of the Roman *arène* came once more to his vision, with its tufting shrubs and battered arches rising grim and gaunt into the soft Southern sky; the church-bells of the town poured their sweet jangle on his ear again, the murmur of distant voices came floating down the wind, and again the pretty Provençal song fluttered on the balmy air; the coquettish turban was in his eye, the plump, soft hand of the pretty Provençal girl in his clasp, and her glossy locks touched his burning cheek. So much, at least, that was Arcadian; and then (in his glowing memory still) the loves, the jealousies, the delusions, the concealments, the faithlessness, the desertion, the parting! And now,—now the chief actress in this drama that had touched him so nearly lay buried in a New England grave, with his own Adèle her solitary mourner!

"It was your friend the Doctor who gave the good woman absolution, I suppose," said Papiol, tapping his snuff-box, and gathering a huge pinch between thumb and finger.

"Not even that comfort, I suspect," said Maverick.

"Bah! pauvre femme!"

And the philosopher titillated his nostril until he sneezed again and again.

"And the Doctor," continued Papiol,—"does he suspect nothing?"

DOCTOR JOHNS

"Nothing. He has counselled me to make what amends I may by marrying—you know whom."

"*Pardieu!* he is a good innocent, that old friend of yours!"

"Better than you or I, Papiol."

"That goes without saying, my friend. And *la petite,*—the little bright-eyes,—what of her?"

"She is unsuspicious, but hints at a little cloud that overshadows her domestic history, and tells her lover that it shall be cleared up before she will marry him, or any other."

"Ta, ta! It's an inquisitive sex, Maverick! I could never quite understand how Julie should have learned that her little one was still alive, and been able to trace her as she did. I think the death was set forth in the 'Gazette,'—eh, Maverick?"

"It certainly was," said Maverick,—"honestly, for the child's good."

"Ha!—honestly,—*bon!* I beg pardon, *mon ami.*"

And Papiol took snuff again.

"Set forth in the 'Gazette,' *en règle,* and came to Julie's knowledge, as I am sure; and she sailed for the East with her brother, who was a small trader in Smyrna, I believe,—poor

CAFÉ DE L'ORIENT

woman! To tell truth, Papiol, had she been alive, loving Adèle as I do, I believe I should have been tempted to follow the parson's admonition, cost what it might."

"And then?"

"And then I should give *petite* an honest name to bear,—honest as I could, at least; and would have lavished wealth upon her, as I mean to do; and made the last half of my life better than the first."

"Excellent! most excellent! considering that the lady is dead, *pauvre femme!* And now, my dear fellow, you might go over to your country and play the good Puritan by marrying Mees Eliza,—*hein?*"

And he called out obstreperously:

"*Garçon!*"

"*Voici, Messieurs!*"

"*Absinthe,—deux verres.*"

And he drummed with his fat fingers upon the edge of the marble slab.

"*Mon Dieu!*" said Maverick, with a sudden pallor on his face, "who is she?"

The eyes of Papiol fastened upon the figure which had arrested the attention of Maverick, —a lady of, may be, forty years, fashionably and gracefully attired, with olive-brown complexion, hair still glossy black, and attended

DOCTOR JOHNS

by a strange gentleman with a brusk and foreign air.

"Who is she?" says Maverick, in a great tremor. "Do the dead come to haunt us?"

"You are facetious, my friend," said Papiol.

But in the next moment the lady opposite had raised her eyes, showing that strange double look which had been so characteristic of Madame Arles, and poor Papiol was himself fearfully distraught.

"It's true! it's true, *mon ami!*" he whispered his friend. "It's Julie!—*elle même,*—Julie!"

Maverick, too, had met that glance, and he trembled like a leaf. He gazed upon the stranger like one who sees a spectre. And she met his glance, boldly at the first; then the light faded from her eyes, her head drooped, and she fell in a swoon upon the shoulder of her companion.

LIX

Adèle Leaves the Parsonage

At about the date of this interview which we have described as having taken place beyond the seas,—upon one of those warm days of early winter, which, even in New England, sometimes cheat one into a feeling of spring,—Adèle came strolling up the little path that led from the parsonage gate to the door, twirling her muff upon her hand, and thinking—thinking—

The chance villagers, seeing her lithe figure, her well-fitting pelisse, her jaunty hat, her blooming cheeks, may have said, "There goes a fortunate one!" But if the thought of poor Adèle took one shape more than another, as she returned that day from a visit to her sweet friend Rose, it was this: "How drearily unfortunate I am!" And here a little burst of childish laughter breaks on her ear. Adèle, turning to the sound, sees that poor outcast woman who had been the last and most constant attendant upon Madame Arles coming down the street, with her little boy frolicking beside her. Obeying an impulse she was in no mood to resist, she turns back to the gate to greet them; she caresses the boy; she has kindly words for the mother, who could have worshipped her for the kiss she has given to her outcast child.

"I likes you," says the sturdy urchin, sidling closer to the parsonage gate, over which Adèle leans. "You 's like the French ooman."

Whereupon Adèle, in the exuberance of her kindly feelings, can only lean over and kiss the child again.

Miss Johns, looking from her chamber, is horrified. Had it been summer, she would have lifted her window and summoned Adèle. But she never forgot—that exemplary woman—the proprieties of the seasons, any more than other proprieties; she tapped upon the glass with her thimble, and beckoned the innocent offender into the parsonage.

"I am astonished, Adèle!"—these were her first words; and she went on to belabor the poor girl in fearful ways,—all the more fearful because she spoke in the calmest possible tones.

Adèle made no reply,—too wise now for that; but she winced, and bit her lips severely, as the irate spinster "gave Miss Maverick to understand that an intercourse which might possibly be agreeable to her French associa-

ADÈLE LEAVES THE PARSONAGE

tions could never be tolerated at the home of Dr. Johns."

No reply, as we have said,—unless it may have been by an impatient stamp of her little foot, which the spinster could not perceive.

But it is the signal, in her quick, fiery nature, of a determination to leave the parsonage, if the thing be possible. From her chamber, where she goes only to arrange her hair and to wipe off an angry tear or two, she walks straight into the study of the parson.

"Doctor," (the "New Papa" is reserved for her tenderer or playful moments now), "are you quite sure that papa will come for me in the spring?"

"He writes me so, Adaly. Why?"

Adèle seeks to control herself, but she cannot wholly. "It 's not pleasant for me any longer here, New Papa,—indeed it is not;"— and her voice breaks utterly.

"But, Adaly!—child!" says the Doctor, closing his book.

"It 's wholly different from what it once was; it 's irksome to Miss Eliza,—I know it is; it 's irksome to me. I want to leave. Why does n't papa come for me at once? Why should n't he? What is this mystery, New Papa? Will you not tell me?"—and she comes toward him, and lays her hand upon his shoulder in her old winning, fond way. "Why may I not know? Do you think I am not brave to bear whatever must some day be known? What if my poor mother be unworthy? I can love her! I can love her!"

"Ah, Adaly," said the parson, "whatever may have been her unworthiness, it can never afflict you more; I believe that she is in her grave, Adaly."

Adèle sunk upon her knees, with her hands clasped as if in prayer.

From the day when Maverick had declared her unworthiness, Adèle had cherished secretly the hope of some day meeting her, of winning her by her love, of clasping her arms about her neck and whispering in her ear, "God is good, and we are all God's children!" But in her grave!

The Doctor has not spoken without authority; since Maverick, in his reply to the parson's suggestions respecting marriage, has urged that the party was totally unfit, to a degree of which the parson himself was a witness; and by further hints he had served fully to identify, in the mind of the old gentleman, poor Madame Arles with the mother of Adèle. "Adaly, my child, you are very dear to me"

ADÈLE LEAVES THE PARSONAGE

said he; and she stood by him now, toying with those gray locks of his, in a caressing manner. "If it be your wish to change your home for the little time that remains, it shall be. I have your father's authority to do so."

"Indeed I do wish it, New Papa;"—and she dropped a kiss upon his forehead,—upon the forehead where so few tender tokens of love had ever fallen, or ever would fall.

The Doctor talked over the affair with Miss Eliza, who avowed herself as eager as Adèle for a change in her home, and suggested that Benjamin should take counsel with his old friend, Mr. Elderkin; it is quite possible that she shrewdly anticipated the result of such a consultation.

Certain it is that the old Squire caught at the suggestion in a moment.

"The very thing, Doctor! I see how it is. Miss Eliza is getting on in years; a little irritable, possibly,—though a most excellent person, Doctor,—most excellent! and there being no young people in the house, it's a little dull for Miss Adèle,—eh, Doctor? Grace, you know, is not with us this winter; so your lodger shall come straight to my house, and she shall take the room of Grace, and Rose will be delighted, and Mrs. Elderkin will be delighted;

DOCTOR JOHNS

and as for Phil, when he happens with us,—as he does only off and on now,—he 'll be falling in love with her, I have n't a doubt; or, if he does n't, I shall be tempted to myself. She 's a fine girl, eh, Doctor?"

"She 's a good Christian, I believe," said the Doctor gravely.

"I have n't a doubt of it," said the Squire; "and I hope that a bit of a dance about Christmas time, if we should fall into that wickedness, would n't harm her on that score, —eh, Doctor?"

"I should wish, Mr. Elderkin, that she maintain her usual propriety of conduct, until she is again in her father's charge."

"Well, well, Doctor, you shall talk with Mrs. Elderkin of that matter."

So, it is all arranged. Rose is overjoyed, and can hardly do enough to make the new home agreeable to Adèle; while the mistress of the house—mild, and cheerful, and sunny, diffusing content every evening over the little circle around her hearth—wins Adèle to a new cheer.

Phil is away at her coming; but a week after he bursts into the house on a snowy December night, and there is a great stamping in the hall, and a little grandchild of the house

ADÈLE LEAVES THE PARSONAGE

pipes from the half-opened door, "It's Uncle Phil!" and there is a loud smack upon the cheek of Rose, who runs to give him welcome, and a hearty, honest grapple with the hand of the old Squire, and then another kiss upon the cheek of the old mother, who meets him before he is fairly in the room,—a kiss upon her cheek, and another, and another. Phil loves the old lady with an honest warmth that kindles the admiration of poor Adèle, who, amid all this demonstration of family affection, feels herself more cruelly than ever a stranger in the household,—a stranger, indeed, to the interior and private joys of any household.

Yet such enthusiasm is, somehow, contagious; and when Phil meets Adèle with a shake of the hand and a hearty greeting, she returns it with an out-spoken, homely warmth, at thought of which she finds herself blushing a moment after. To tell truth, Phil is rather a fine-looking fellow at this time,—strong, manly, with a comfortable assurance of manner,—a face beaming with *bonhomie,* cheeks glowing with that sharp December drive, and a wild, glad sparkle in his eye, as Rose whispers him that Adèle has become one of the household. Phil, meantime, dashes on, in his own open, frank way, about his drive, and the state of the ice in the river, and some shipments he had made from New York to Porto Rico,—on capital terms, too.

"And did you see much of Reuben?" asks Mrs. Elderkin.

"Not much;" and Phil (glancing that way) sees that Adèle is studying her crimsons; "but he tells me he is doing splendidly in some business venture to the Mediterranean with Brindlock; he could hardly talk of any thing else. It 's odd to find him so wrapped up in money-making."

"I hope he 'll not be wrapped up in any thing worse," said Mrs. Elderkin, with a sigh.

"Nonsense, mother!" burst in the old Squire; "Reuben 'll come out all right yet."

"He says he means to know all sides of the world, now," says Phil, with a little laugh.

"He 's not so bad as he pretends to be, Phil," answered the Squire. "I knew the Major's hot ways; so did you, Grace (turning to the wife). It 's a boy's talk. There 's good blood in him."

And the two girls,—yonder, the other side of the hearth,—Adèle and Rose, have given over their little earnest comparison of views about the colors, and sit stitching, and stitching, and thinking—and thinking—

L

Philip's Chances

PHIL had at no time given over his thought of Adèle, and of the possibility of some day winning her for himself, though he had been somewhat staggered by the interview already described with Reuben. It is doubtful, even, if the quiet *permission* which this latter had granted (or, with an affectation of arrogance, had seemed to grant) had not itself made him pause. There are some things which a man never wants any permission to do; and one of those is—to love a woman.

But now, when on coming back, he found her in his own home,—so tenderly cared for by mother and by sister,—so coy and reticent in his presence, the old fever burned again. It was not now a simple watching of her figure upon the street that told upon him; but her constant presence; her fresh, fair face every day at table; the tapping of her light feet along the hall; the little musical bursts of laughter (not Rose's,—oh, no!) that came from time to time floating through the open door of his chamber. For an honest lover, propinquity is always dangerous,—most of all, in one's own home. The sister's caresses of the charmer, the mother's kind looks, the father's playful banter, and the whisk of a silken dress (with a new music in it) along the balusters you have passed night and morning for years, have a terrible executive power.

In short, Adèle had not been a month with the Elderkins before Phil was tied there by bonds he had never known the force of before.

And how was it with Adèle?

That strong, religious element in her,—abating no jot in its fervor,—which had found a shock in the case of Reuben, met none with Philip. He had slipped into the mother's belief and reverence, not by any spell of suffering or harrowing convictions, but by a kind of insensible growth toward them, and an easy, deliberate, moderate living by them, which more active and incisive minds cannot comprehend.

It would have been strange if the calm, mature repose of Phil's manner,—never disturbed except when Adèle broke upon him suddenly and put him to a momentary confusion, of which the pleasant fluttering of her own heart gave account,—strange, if this had not won upon her regard,—strange, if it had not given

PHILIP'S CHANCES

hint of that cool, masculine superiority in him, with which even the most ethereal of women like to be impressed. Nor will it seem strange, if, by contrast, it made the excitable Reuben seem more dismally afloat and vagrant. Yet how could she forget the passionate pressure of his hand, the appealing depth of that gray eye of the parson's son, and the burning words of his that stuck in her memory like thorns?

Phil, indeed, might have spoken in a way that would have driven the blood back upon her heart; for there was a world of passionate capability under his calm exterior. She dreaded lest he might. She shunned all provoking occasion, as a bird shuns the grasp of even the most tender hand, under whose clasp the pinions will flutter vainly.

When Rose said now, as she was wont to say, after some generous deed of his, "Phil is a good, kind, noble fellow!" Adèle affected not to hear, and asked Rose, with a bustling air, if she was "quite sure that she had the right shade of brown" in the worsted work they were upon.

So the Christmas season came and went. The Squire cherished a traditional regard for its old festivities, not only by reason of a general festive inclination that was very strong in him, but from a desire to protest in a quiet way against what he called the pestilent religious severities of a great many of the parish, who ignored the day because it was a high holiday of the Popish Church, and in that other, which, under the wing of Episcopacy, was following, in their view, fast after the Babylonish traditions. There was Deacon Tourtelot, for instance, who never failed on a Christmas morning—if weather and sledding were good—to get up his long team (the restive two-year-olds upon the neap) and drive through the main street, with a great clamor of "Haw, Diamond!" and "Gee, Buck and Bright!"—as if to insist upon the secular character of the day. Even the good Doctor pointed his Christmas prayer with no special unction. What, indeed, were anniversaries, or a yearly proclamation of peace and good-will to men, with those who, on every Sabbath morning, saw the heavens open above the sacred desk, and heard the golden promises expounded, and the thunders of coming retribution echo under the ceiling of the Tabernacle?

The Christmas came and went with a great lighting-up of the Elderkin house; and there were green garlands which Rose and Adèle have plaited over the mantel, and over the stiff

PHILIP'S CHANCES

family portraits; and good Phil—in the character of Santa Claus—has stuffed the stockings of all the grandchildren, and—in the character of the bashful lover—has played like a moth about the blazing eyes of Adèle.

Yet the current of the village gossip has it, that they are to marry. Miss Eliza, indeed, shakes her head wisely, and keeps her own counsel. But Dame Tourtelot reports to old Mistress Tew,—"Phil Elderkin is goin' to marry the French girl."

"Haöw?" says Mrs. Tew, adjusting her tin trumpet.

"Phil Elderkin—is—a-goin' to marry the French girl," screams the Dame.

"Du tell! Goin' to settle in Ashfield?"

"I don't know."

"No! Where, then?" says Mistress Tew.

"I don't KNOW," shrieks the Dame.

"Oh!" chimes Mrs. Tew; and, after reflecting awhile and smoothing out her cap-strings, she says,—"I've heerd the French gurl keeps a cross in her chamber."

"*She* DOOZ," explodes the Dame.

"I want to know! I wonder the Squire don't put a stop to 't."

"Doän't believe *he would if he* COULD," says the Dame, snappishly.

"Waäl, waäl! it's a wicked world we 're a-livin' in, Miss Tourtelot." And she elevates her trumpet, expectantly.

LI

Concerning a Colleague

IN the days which our narrative has now reached, the Doctor has grown feeble. His pace has slackened, and there is an occasional totter in his step. There are those among his parishioners who say that his memory is failing. On one or two Sabbaths of the winter he has preached sermons scarce two years old. There are acute listeners who are sure of it. And the spinster has been horrified on learning that, once or twice, the old gentleman—escaping her eye—has taken his walk to the post-office, unwittingly wearing his best cloak wrong-side out; as if—for so good a man—the green baize were not as proper a covering as the brown camlet.

The parson is himself conscious of these short-comings, and speaks with resignation of the growing infirmities which, as he modestly

CONCERNING A COLLEAGUE

hints, will compel him shortly to give place to some younger and more zealous expounder of the faith. His parochial visits grow more and more rare. All other failings could be more easily pardoned than this; but in a country parish like Ashfield, it was quite imperative that the old chaise should keep up its familiar rounds, and the occasional tea-fights in the outlying houses be honored by the gray head of the Doctor or by his evening benediction. Two hour-long sermons a week and a Wednesday evening discourse were very well in their way, but by no means met all the requirements of those steadfast old ladies whose socialities were both exhausting and exacting. Indeed, it is doubtful if there do not exist even now, in most country parishes of New England, a few most excellent and notable women, who delight in an overworked parson, for the pleasure they take in recommending their teas, and plasters, and nostrums. The more frail and attenuated the teacher, the more he takes hold upon their pity; and in losing the vigor of the flesh, he seems to their compassionate eyes to grow into the spiritualities they pine for. But he must not give over his visitings; *that* hair-cloth shirt of penance he must wear to the end, if he would achieve saintship.

Now, just at this crisis, it happens that there is a tall, thin, pale young man—Rev. Theophilus Catesby by name, and nephew of the late Deacon Simmons (now unhappily deceased)—who has preached in Ashfield on several occasions to the "great acceptance" of the people. Talk is imminent of naming him colleague to Dr. Johns. The matter is discussed, at first, (agreeably to custom,) in the sewing-circle of the town. After this, it comes informally before the church brethren. The duty to the Doctor and to the parish is plain enough. The practical question is, how cheaply can the matter be accomplished?

The salary of the good Doctor has grown, by progressive increase, to be at this date some seven hundred dollars a year,—a very considerable stipend for a country parish in that day. It is understood that the proposed colleague would expect six hundred. The two joined made a somewhat appalling sum for the people of Ashfield. They tried to combat it in a variety of ways,—over tea-tables and barnyard gates, as well as in their formal conclaves; earnest for a good thing in the way of preaching, but earnest for a good bargain, too.

"I say, Huldy," said the Deacon, in discussion of the affair over his wife's fireside,

CONCERNING A COLLEAGUE

"I would n't wonder if the Doctor 'ad put up somethin' handsome between the French girl's boardin', and odds and ends."

"What if he ha'n't, Tourtelot? Miss Johns 's got property, and what 's *she* goin' to do with it, I want to know?"

On this hint the Deacon spoke, in his next encounter with the Squire upon the street, with more boldness.

"It 's my opinion, Squire, the Doctor's folks are pooty well off, now; and if we make a trade with the new minister, so 's he 'll take the biggest half o' the hard work of the parish, I think the old Doctor 'ud worry along tol'able well on three or four hundred a year; heh, Squire?"

"Well Deacon, I don't know about that;— don't know. Butcher's meat is always butcher's meat, Deacon."

"So it is, Squire; and not so dreadful high, nuther. I 've got a likely two-year-old in the yard, that 'll dress about a hundred to a quarter, and I don't pretend to ask more 'n twenty-five dollars; know any body that wants such a critter, Squire?"

These discussions come to the ear of Reuben, who writes back in a very brusk way to the Doctor: "Why on earth, father, don't you cut all connection with the parish? Don't let the 'minister's pay' be any hindrance to you, for I am getting on swimmingly in my business ventures,—thanks to Mr. Brindlock; I enclose a check for two hundred dollars, and can send you one of equal amount every quarter, without feeling it. Why should n't a man of your years have rest?"

Correspondence between the father and son is not infrequent in these days; for, since Reuben has slipped away from home control utterly,—being now well past one and twenty,— the Doctor has forborne that magisterial tone which, in his old-fashioned way, it was his wont to employ. Under these conditions, Reuben is won into more communicativeness,— even upon those religious topics which are always prominent in the Doctor's letters; indeed, it would seem that the son rather enjoyed a little logical fence with the old gentleman, and a passing lunge, now and then, at his severities.

"I see the honesty of your faith, father," he writes, "though there seems a strained harshness in it when I think of the complacency with which you must needs contemplate the irremediable perdition of such hosts of outcasts. In Adèle, too, there seems a beautiful singleness of trust; but I suppose God made the birds to live in the sky.

NEWS FROM MAVERICK

"You need not fear my falling into what you call the Pantheism of the moralists; it is every way too cold for my hot blood. It seems to me that the moral icicles with which their doctrine is fringed (and the fringe is the beauty of it) must needs melt under any passionate human clasp,—such clasp as I should want to give (if I gave any) to a great hope for the future. I should feel more like groping my way into such hope by the light of the golden candlesticks of Rome even. But do not be disturbed, father; I fear I should make, just now, no better Papist than Presbyterian."

The Doctor reads such letters in a maze. Can it indeed be a son of his own loins who thus bandies language about the solemn truths of Christianity? "How shall I give thee up, Ephraim!"

LII

News from Maverick

IN the early spring of 1842,—we are not quite sure of the date, but it was at any rate shortly after the establishment of the Reverend Theo-

DOCTOR JOHNS

philus Catesby at Ashfield,—the Doctor was in the receipt of a new letter from his friend Maverick, which set all his old calculations adrift.

"I find, my dear Johns," he writes, "that my suspicions in regard to a matter of which I wrote you very fully in my last were wholly untrue. How I could have been so deceived, I cannot even now fairly explain; but nothing is more certain, than that the person calling herself Madame Arles (since dead, as I learn from Adèle) was not the mother of my child. My mistake in this will the more surprise you, when I state that I had a glimpse of this personage (unknown to you) upon my visit to America; and though it was but a passing glimpse, it seemed to me—though many years had gone by since my last sight of her—that I could have sworn to her identity. And coupling this resemblance, as I very naturally did, with her devotion to my poor Adèle, I could form but one conclusion.

"The mother of my child, however, still lives. I have seen her. You will commiserate me in advance with the thought that I have found her among the vile ones of what you count this vile land. But you are wrong, my dear Johns. So far as appearance and present conduct go, no more reputable lady ever crossed your own threshold. The meeting was accidental, but the recognition on both sides absolute and, on the part of the lady, so emotional as to draw the attention of the *habitués* of the café where I chanced to be dining. Her manner and bearing, indeed, were such as to provoke me to a renewal of our old acquaintance, with honorable intentions,—even independent of those suggestions of duty to herself and to Adèle which you have urged.

"But I have to give you, my dear Johns, a new surprise. All overtures of my own toward a renewal of acquaintance have been decisively repulsed. I learn that she has been living for the past fifteen years or more with her brother, now a wealthy merchant of Smyrna, and that she has a reputation there as a *dévote* and is widely known for the charities which her brother's means place within her reach. It would thus seem that even this French woman, contrary to your old theory, is atoning for an early sin by a life of penance.

"And now, my dear Johns, I have to confess to you another deceit of mine. This woman —Julie Chalet when I knew her of old, and still wearing the name—has no knowledge that she has a child now living. To divert all inquiry, and to insure entire alienation of my little girl from all French ties, I caused a false mention of the death of Adèle to be inserted in the 'Gazette' of Marseilles. I know you will be very much shocked at this, my dear Johns, and perhaps count it as large a sin as the grosser one; that I committed it for the child's sake will be no excuse in your eye, I know.

"If Julie, the mother of Adèle, knew to-day of her existence,—if I should carry that information to her,—I am sure that all her rigidities would be consumed like flax in a flame. Shall I do so? I ask you as one who, I am sure, has learned to love Adèle, and who, I hope, has not wholly given over a friendly feeling toward me. Consider well, however, that the mother is now one of the most rigid of Catholics; I learn that she is even thinking of conventual life. I know her spirit and temper well enough to be sure that, if she were to meet the child again which she believes lost, it would be with an impetuosity of feeling and a devotion that would absorb every aim of her life. This disclosure is the only one by which I could hope to win her to any consideration of marriage; and with a mother's rights and a mother's love, would she not sweep away all that Protestant faith which you, for so many

NEWS FROM MAVERICK

years, have been laboring to build up in the mind of my child? And inasmuch as I am making you my father confessor, I may as well tell you, my dear Johns, that no particular self-denial would be involved in a marriage with Mademoiselle Chalet. For myself, I am past the age of sentiment; my fortune is now established; neither myself nor my child can want for any luxury. The mother, by her present associations and by the propriety of her life, is above all suspicion; and her air and bearing are such as would be a passport to friendly association with refined people here or elsewhere. You may count this a failure of Providence to fix its punishment upon transgressors: I count it only one of those accidents of life which are all the while surprising us.

"There was a time when I would have had ambition to do otherwise; but now, with my love for Adèle established by my intercourse with her and by her letters, I have no other aim, if I know my own heart, than her welfare. It should be kept in mind, I think, that the marriage spoken of, if it ever take place, will probably involve, sooner or later, a full exposure to Adèle of all the circumstances of her birth and history. I say this will be involved, because I am sure that the warm affections of Mademoiselle Chalet will never allow of the concealment of her maternal relations, and that her present religious perversity (if you will excuse the word) will not admit of further deceits. I tremble to think of the possible consequences to Adèle, and query very much in my own mind, if her present blissful ignorance be not better than reunion with a mother through whom she must learn of the ignominy of her birth. Of Adèle's fortitude to bear such a shock, and to maintain any elasticity of spirits under it, you can judge better than I.

"I propose to delay action, my dear Johns, and of course my sailing for America, until I shall hear from you."

Our readers can surely anticipate the tone of the Doctor's reply. He writes:

"Duty, Maverick, is always duty. The issues we must leave in the hands of Providence. One sin makes a crowd of entanglements; it is never weary of disguises and deceits. We must come out from them all, if we would aim at purity. From my heart's core I shall feel whatever shock may come to poor, innocent Adèle by reason of the light that may be thrown upon her history; but if it be a light that flows from the performance of Christian duty, I shall never fear its revelations. If we had been always true, such dark corners would never have existed to fright us with their goblins of terror. It is never too late, Maverick, to begin to be true.

"I find a strange comfort, too, in what you tell me of that religious perversity of Mademoiselle Chalet which so chafes you. I have never ceased to believe that most of the Romish traditions are of the Devil; but with waning years I have learned that the Divine mysteries are beyond our comprehension, and that we cannot map out His purposes by any human chart. The pure faith of your child, joined to her buoyant elasticity,—I freely confess it,— has smoothed away the harshness of many opinions I once held.

"Maverick, do your duty. Leave the rest to Heaven."

LIII

Clear but Dark

REUBEN, meantime, is leading a dashing life in the city. The Brindlock family have taken him to their arms again as freely and heartily as if he had never entered the fold over which the good Doctor exercised pastoral care, and as if he had never strayed from it again.

"I told you 't would be all right, Mabel," said Mr. Brindlock to his wife; and neither of them ever rallied him upon his bootless experience in that direction.

But the kindly aunt had not foreborne (how could she?) certain pertinent inquiries in regard to the pretty Miss Maverick, under which Reuben had shown considerable disposition to flinch. Mrs. Brindlock drew her own conclusions, but was not greatly disturbed by them. Why should she be, indeed? Reuben, with his present and most promising establishment in business, and with a face and air that insured him a cordial welcome in that circle of wealthy acquaintances which Mrs. Brindlock especially cultivated, was counted a *bon parti,* independent of his position as presumptive heir to a large share of the Brindlock estate.

Once or twice since his leave of Ashfield he has astonished the good people there by a dashing visit. It is even possible that he may have entertained agreeably the fancy of dazing the eyes of both Rose and Adèle with the glitter of his city distinctions. But their admiration, if they felt any, was not flatteringly ex-

CLEAR BUT DARK

pressed. Adèle, indeed, was always graciously kind, and, seeing his confirmed godlessness, tortured herself secretly with the thought that, but for her rebuff, he might have made a bitter fight against the bedevilments of the world, and lived a truer and purer life. All that, however, was irrevocably past. As for Rose, if there crept into her little prayers a touch of sentiment as she pleaded for the backslidden son of the minister, her prayers were none the worse for it. Such trace of sentimental color —like the blush upon her fair cheek—gave a completed beauty to her appeals.

Reuben saw that Phil was terribly in earnest in his love, and he fancied, with some twinges, that he saw indications on the part of Adèle of its being not wholly unacceptable. Rose, too, seemed not disinclined to receive the assiduous attentions of the young minister, who had become a frequent visitor in the Elderkin household, and who preached with an unction and an earnestness that touched her heart, and that made her sigh despondingly over the outcast son of the old pastor. Watching these things with a look studiedly careless and indifferent, Reuben felt himself cut off more than ever from such charms or virtues as might possibly have belonged to continued association

DOCTOR JOHNS

with the companions of his boyhood. There were moments—mostly drifting over him in silent night-hours, within his old chamber at the parsonage—when it seemed to him that he had made a losing game of it. The sparkling eyes of Adèle, suffused with tears,—as in that memorable interview of the garden,—beam upon him, promising, as then, other guidance; they gain new brilliance, and wear stronger entreaty, as they shine lovingly upon him from the distance—growing greater and greater—which now lies between them. Her beauty, her grace, her tenderness, now that they are utterly beyond reach, are tenfold enticing; and in that other sphere to which, in his night reverie, they seem translated, the joyous face of Rose, like that of an attendant angel, looks down regretfully, full of a capacity for love to which he must be a stranger.

He is wakened by the bells next morning,—a Sunday morning, may be. There they go,—he sees them from the window,—the two comely damsels, picking their way through the light, fresh-fallen snow of March. Going possibly to teach the catechism; he sneers at this thought, for he is awake now. Has the world no richer gift in store for him? That Sophia Bowrigg is a great fortune, a superb dancer,

CLEAR BUT DARK

a gorgeous armful of a woman. What if they were to join their fortunes and come back some day to dazzle these quiet townsfolk with the splendor of their life? His visits in Ashfield grow shorter and more rare. We shall not meet him there again until we meet him for the last time.

Mr. Catesby is an "acceptable preacher." He unfolds the orthodox doctrines with more grace than had belonged to the manner of the Doctor. The old ladies befriend him and pet him in their kindly way; and if at times his speculative humor (which he is not wholly without) leads him beyond the bounds of the accepted doctrines, he compounds the matter by strong assertion of those sturdy generalities which lie at the bottom of the orthodox creed.

But his self-control is not so apparent in his social intercourse; and before he has been three months in Ashfield, he has given tongue to gossip, and all the old ladies comment upon his enslavement to the pretty Rose Elderkin. Young clergymen have this way of falling, at sight, into the toils, which is vastly refreshing to middle-aged observers. An incident only of his recreative pursuits in this direction belongs to our narrative.

Upon one of the botanical excursions of

DOCTOR JOHNS

later spring which he had inaugurated, and to which the maidenly modesty of Rose had suggested that Adèle should make a party; the young Catesby (who was a native of Eastern Massachusetts) had asked in his *naïve* manner after her family connections. An uncle of his had known a Mr. Maverick, who had long been a resident of Europe.

"It may possibly be some relation of yours, Miss Maverick," said the young minister.

"Do you recall the first name?" said Rose.

Mr. Catesby hesitated in that interesting way in which lovers are wont to hesitate. No, he did not remember; but he was a jovial, generous-hearted man, (he had heard his uncle often describe him,) who must be now some fifty or sixty years old.—"Frank Maverick, to be sure, I have the name."

"Why, it is my father," said Adèle with a swift, happy rush of color to her face.

"Oh no, Miss Maverick," said the young Catesby with a smile, "that is quite impossible. The gentleman of whom I speak, and my uncle visited him only three years ago, is a confirmed bachelor, and he had rallied him, I remember, upon never having married."

The color left the cheeks of Adèle.

"Frank, did you say?" persisted Rose.

CLEAR BUT DARK

"Frank was the name," said the innocent young clergyman; "and he was a merchant, if I remember rightly, somewhere upon the Mediterranean."

"It's very strange," said Rose, turning to Adèle.

And Adèle, all her color gone, had the fortitude to pat Rose lovingly upon the shoulder, and to say, with a forced smile. "Life is very strange, Rose."

But from this time till they reached home,— fortunately not far away,—Adèle said nothing more. Rose remarked the unwonted pallor in her cheeks.

"You are tired, Adèle," said she; "you are so pale!"

"Child," said Adèle, tapping her again, in a womanly way that was strange to her companion, "you have color for us both."

At this, her reserve of dignity and fortitude being now well-nigh spent, she rushed away to her chamber. What wonder if she sought the little crucifix, sole memento of the unknown mother, and glued it to her lips, as she fell upon her knees by the bedside, and uttered such a prayer for help and strength as she had never uttered before?

"It is true! it is true! I see it now. The

child of shame! The child of shame! O my father, my father! what wrong have you done me!"

There is not a doubt in her mind where the truth lies. In a moment her thought has flashed over the whole chain of evidence. The father's studied silence; her alienation from any home of her own; the mysterious hints of the Doctor; and the strange communication of Reuben,—all come up in stately array and confound her with the bitter truth. There is a little miniature of her father which she kept among her choicest treasures. She seeks it now. Is it to throw it away in scorn? No, no, no! Our affections are after all not submissible to strict moral regimen. It is with set teeth and a hard look in her eye that she regards it at first; then her eyes suffuse with tears while she looks, and she kisses it passionately again and again.

"Can there be some horrible mistake in all this?" she asks herself. At the thought she slips on hat and shawl and glides noiselessly down the stairs, (not for the world would she have been interrupted!) and walks swiftly away to her old home at the parsonage.

Dame Tourtelot meets her and says, "Good evening, Miss Adeel."

And Adèle, in a voice so firm that it does not seem her own, says, "Good evening, Mrs. Tourtelot." She wonders greatly at her own calmness.

LIV

Clearer and Darker

THE DOCTOR is alone in his study when Adèle comes in upon him, and she has reached his chair and dropped upon her knees beside him before he has time to rise.

"New Papa, you have been so kind to me! I know the truth now,—the mystery, the shame;"—and she dropped her head upon his knees.

"Adaly, Adaly, my dear child!" said the old man with a great tremor in his voice, "what does this mean?"

She was sobbing, sobbing.

"Adaly, my child, what can I do for you?"

"Pray for me, New Papa!" and she lifted her eyes upon him with a tender, appealing look.

"Always, always, Adaly!"

"Tell me, New Papa,—tell me honestly,—is it not true that I can call no one mother,—that I never could?"

The Doctor trembled: he would have given ten years of his life to have been able to challenge her story, to disabuse her mind of the belief which he saw was fastened past all recall. "Adaly," said he, "Christ befriended the Magdalen,—how much more you, then, if so be you are the unoffending child of"—

"I knew it! I knew it!" and she fell to sobbing again upon the knee of the old gentleman, in a wild, passionate way.

In such supreme moments the mind reaches its decisions with electrical rapidity. Even as she leaned there, her thought flashed upon that poor Madame Arles who had so befriended her,—against whom they had cautioned her, who had shown such intense emotion at their first meeting, who had summoned her at the last, and who had died with that wailing cry, *"Ma fille!"* upon her lip. Yes, yes, her mother indeed, who died in her arms! (She can never forget that death-clasp.)

She hints as much to the Doctor, who, in view of the recent communication from Maverick, will not gainsay her.

When she moved away at last, as if for a

CLEARER AND DARKER

leave-taking, silent and humiliated, the old man said to her, "My child, are you not still my Adaly? God is no respecter of persons; His ministers should be like Him."

Whereupon Adèle came and kissed him with a warmth that reminded him of days long past.

She rejoiced in not having encountered the gray, keen eyes of the spinster. She knew they would read unfailingly the whole extent of the revelation that had dawned upon her. That the spinster herself knew the truth, and had long known it, she was sure; and she recalled with a shudder the look of those uncanny eyes upon the evening of their little frolic at the Elderkins'. She dreaded the thought of ever meeting them again, and still more the thought of listening to the stiff, cold words of consolation which she knew she would count it her duty to administer.

It was dusk when she left the Doctor's door; he would have attended, but she begged to be alone. It was an April evening, the chilliness of the earth just yielding to the coming summer; the frogs clamorous in all the near pools, and filling the air with the harsh uproar of their voices; the delicate grass-blades were just thrusting their tips through the brown

DOCTOR JOHNS

web of the old year's growth, and in sunny, close-trodden spots showing a mat of green; while the fleecy brown blossoms of the elm were tufting all the spray of the embowering trees. Here and there a village loiterer greeted her kindly. They all knew Miss Adèle. "They will all know it to-morrow," she thought, "and then—then"—

With a swift but unsteady step she makes her way to the little grave-yard; she had gone there often, and there were those who said wantonly that she went to say her prayers before the little cross upon the tomb-stone she had placed over the grave of Madame Arles. Now she threw herself prone upon the little hillock, with a low, sharp cry of distress, like that of a wounded bird,—"My mother! my mother!"

Every word, every look of tenderness which the dead woman had lavished, she recalls now with a terrible distinctness. Those loud, vague appeals of her delirium come to her recollection with a meaning in them that is only too plain; and then the tight, passionate clasp, when, strained to her bosom, relief came at last. Adèle lies there unconscious of the time, until the night dews warn her away; she staggers through the gate. Where next? She

CLEARER AND DARKER

fancies they must know it all at the Elderkins', —that she has no right there. Is she not an estray upon the world? Shall she not—as well first as last—wander forth, homeless as she is, into the night? And true to these despairing thoughts, she hurries away farther and farther from the town. The frogs croak monotonously in all the marshes, as if in mockery of her grief. On some near tree an owl is hooting, with a voice that is strangely and pitifully human. Presently an outlying farm-house shows its cheery, hospitable light through the window-panes, and she is tempted to shorten her steps and steal a look into the room where the family sits grouped around the firelight. No such sanctuary for her ever was or ever can be. Even the lowing of a cow in the yard, and the answering bleat of a calf within the barn, seem to mock the outcast.

On she passes, scarce knowing whither her hurrying steps are bearing her, until at last she spies a low building in the fields away upon her right, which she knows. It is the home of that outlawed woman where Madame Arles had died. Here at least she will be met with sympathy, even if the truth were wholly known; and yet perhaps last of all places would she have it known there. She taps at the door;

she has wandered out of her way, and asks for a moment's rest. The little boy of the house, when he has made out the visitor by a few furtive peeps from behind the mother's chair, comes to her fawningly and familiarly; and as Adèle looks into his bright, fearless eyes, a new courage seems to possess her. God's children, all of us; and He careth even for the sparrows. She will conquer her despairing weakness; she will accept her cross and bear it resolutely. By slow degrees she is won over by the frolicsome humor of the curly-pated boy, who never once quits her side, into cheerful prattle with him. And when at last, fairly rested, she would set off on her return, the lone woman says she will see her safely as far as the village street; the boy, too, insists doggedly upon attending them; and so, with her hand tightly clasped in the hand of the lad, Adèle makes her way back into the town. Along the street she passes, even under the windows of the parsonage, with her hand still locked in that of the outlawed boy; and she wonders if in broad day the same courage would be meted to her? They only part when within sight of the broad glow of light from the Elderkin windows; and here Adèle, taking out her purse, counts out the half of her money and places it in the hands of the boy.

"We will share and share alike, Arthur," said she. "But never tell who gave you this."

"But, Miss Maverick, it 's too much," said the woman.

"No, it 's not," said the boy, clutching it eagerly.

With a parting good-night, Adèle darted within the gate, and opened softly the door, determined to meet courageously whatever rebuffs might be in store for her.

LV

Confidences

ROSE has detailed the story of the occurrence, with the innocent curiosity of girlhood, to the Squire and Mrs. Elderkin (Phil being just now away). The Squire, as he hears it, has passed a significant look across to Mrs. Elderkin.

"It 's very queer, is n't it?" asked Rose.

"Very," said the Squire, who had for some time cherished suspicions of certain awkward relations existing between Maverick and the mother of Adèle, but never so decided as this story would seem to warrant. "And what said Adèle?" continued he.

"It disturbed her, I think, papa; she did n't seem at all herself."

"Rose, my dear," said the kindly old gentleman, "there is some unlucky family difference between Mr. and Mrs. Maverick, and I dare say the talk was unpleasant to Adèle; if I were you, I would n't allude to it again; don't mention it, please, Rose."

If it could be possible, good Mrs. Elderkin greeted Adèle as she came in more warmly than ever. "You must be careful, my dear, of these first spring days of ours; you are late to-night."

"Yes," says Adèle, "I was gone longer than I thought. I rambled off to the churchyard, and I have been at the Doctor's."

Again the old people exchanged glances.

Why does she find herself watching their looks so curiously? Yet there is nothing but kindness in them. She is glad Phil is not there.

The next morning the Squire stepped over at an early hour to the parsonage, and by an adroit question or two, which the good Doctor

CONFIDENCES

had neither the art nor the disposition to evade, unriddled the whole truth with respect to the parentage of Adèle. The Doctor also advised him of the delusion of the poor girl with respect to Madame Arles, and how he had considered it unwise to attempt any explanation until he should hear further from Mr. Maverick, whose recent letter he counted it his duty to lay before Mr. Elderkin.

"It's a sad business," said he.

And the Doctor,—*"The way of the wicked is as darkness; they know not at what they stumble."*

The Squire walks home in a brown study. Like all the rest, he had been charmed with the liveliness and grace of Adèle; over and over he has said to his boy, "How fares it, Phil? Why, at your age, my boy, I should have had her in the toils long ago."

Since her domestication under his own roof, the old gentleman's liking for her had grown tenfold strong; he had familiarized himself with the idea of counting her one of his own flock. But, the child of a French—

"Well, well, we will see what the old lady may say," reflected he. And he took the first private occasion to lay the matter before Mrs. Elderkin.

"Well, mother, the suspicions of last night are all true,—true as a book."

"God help the poor child, then!" said Madam, holding up her hands.

"Of course He 'll do that, wife. But what say you to Phil's marriage, now?"

The old lady reflected a moment, lifting her hand to smooth the hair upon her temple, as if in aid of her thought, then said,—"Giles, you know the world better than I; you know best what may be well for the boy. I love Adèle very much; I do not believe that I should love her any less if she were the wife of Phil. But you know best, Giles; you must decide."

"There 's a good woman!" said the Squire; and he stayed his pace up and down the room to lay his hand approvingly upon the head of the old lady, touching as tenderly those gray locks as ever he had done in earlier years the ripples of golden brown.

In a few days Phil returns,—blithe, hopeful, winsome as ever. He is puzzled, however, by the grave manner of the Squire, when he takes him aside, after the first hearty greetings, and says, "Phil, my lad, how fares it with the love-matter? Have things come to a crisis, eh?"

CONFIDENCES

"What do you mean, father?" and Phil blushes like a boy of ten.

"I mean to ask, Philip," said the old gentleman, measuredly, "if you have made any positive declaration to Miss Maverick."

"Not yet," said Phil, with a modest frankness.

"Very good, my son, very good. And now, Phil, I would wait a little,—take time for reflection; don't do any thing rashly. It's an important step to take."

"But, father," says Phil, puzzled by the old gentleman's manner, "what does this mean?"

"Philip," said the Squire, with seriousness that seemed almost comical by its excess, "would you really marry Adèle?"

"To-morrow, if I could," said Phil.

"Tut, tut, Phil! It's the old hot blood in him!" (He says this, as if to himself.) "Philip, I would n't hurry the matter, my boy."

And thereupon he gives him in his way a story of the revelations of the last few days.

At the first, Phil is disposed to an indignant denial, as if by no possibility any indignity could attach to the name or associations of Adèle. But in the whirl of his feeling he remembered that interview with Reuben, and

DOCTOR JOHNS

his boast that Phil could not affront the conventionalities of the world. It confirmed the truth to him in a moment. Reuben then had known the whole, and had been disinterestedly generous. Should he be any less so?

"Well, father," said Phil, after a minute or two of silence, "I don't think the story changes my mind one whit. I would marry her tomorrow, if I could," and he looked the Squire fairly and squarely in the face.

"Gad, boy," said the old gentleman, "you must love her as I loved your mother!"

"I hope I do," said Phil,—"that is, if I win her. I don't think she's to be had for the asking."

"Aha! the pinch lies there, eh?" said the Squire, and he said it in better humor than he would have said it ten days before. "What's the trouble, Philip?"

"Well, sir, I think she always had a tenderness for Reuben; I think she loves him now in her heart."

"So, so! The wind lies there, eh? Well, let it bide, my boy; let it bide awhile."

And there the discourse of the Squire ended.

Meantime, however, Rose and Adèle are having a little private interview above stairs,

CONFIDENCES

which in its subject-matter is not wholly unrelated to the same theme.

"Rose," Adèle had said, as she fondled her in her winning way, "your brother Phil has been very kind to me."

"He always meant to be," said Rose with a charming glow upon her face.

"He always *has* been," said Adèle; "but, dear Rose, I know I can talk as plainly to you as to another self almost."

"You can,—you can, Ady," said she.

"I have thought," continued Adèle, "though I know it is very unmaidenly in me to say it, that Phil was disposed sometimes to talk even more warmly than he has ever talked, and to ask me to be a nearer friend to him even than you, dear Rose. May be it is only my own vanity that leads me sometimes to suspect this."

"Oh, I hope it may be true!" burst forth Rose.

"I hope *not*," said Adèle, with a voice so gravely earnest that Rose shuddered.

"O Ady, you don't mean it! you who are so good, so kind! Phil's heart will break."

"I don't think that," said Adèle, with a faint hard smile, in which her womanly vanity struggled with her resolution. "And whatever might have been, that which I have hinted at *must* not be now, dear Rose. You will know some day why—why it would be ungrateful in me to determine otherwise. Promise me, darling, that you will discourage any inclination toward it, wherever you can. Promise me, dear Rose!"

"Do you really, truly mean it?" said the other, with a disappointment she but poorly concealed.

"With all my heart, I do," said Adèle.

And Rose promised, while she threw herself upon the neck of Adèle and said, "I am so sorry! It will be such a blow to poor Phil."

After this, things went on very much in their old way. To the great relief of Adèle there was no explosive village demonstration of the news which had come home so cruelly to herself. The Doctor had given an admonition to the young minister, and the old Squire had told him, in a pointed and confidential way, that he had heard of his inquiries and assertions with respect to Mr. Maverick, and begged to hint that the relations between the father and mother of Adèle were not of the happiest, and it was quite possible that Mr. Maverick had assumed latterly the name of a bachelor; it was not, however, a very profita-

CONFIDENCES

ble subject of speculation or of gossip, and if he valued the favor of the young ladies he would forbear all allusion to it. A suggestion which Mr. Catesby was not slow to accept religiously, and scrupulously to bear in mind.

Phil was as hot a lover as ever, though for a time a little more distant: and the poor fellow remarked a new timidity and reserve about Adèle, which, so far from abating, only fed the flame; and there is no knowing to what reach it might have blazed out, if a trifling little circumstance had not paralyzed his zeal.

From time to time, Phil had been used to bring home a rare flower or two as a gift for Adèle, which Rose had always lovingly arranged in some coquettish fashion, either upon the bosom or in the hair of Adèle; but a new and late gift of this kind—a little tuft of the trailing arbutus which he has clambered over miles of woodland to secure—is not worn by Adèle, but by Rose, who glances into the astounded face of Phil with a pretty, demure look of penitence.

"I say, Rose," says he, seizing his chance for a private word,—"that 's not for you."

"I know it, Phil; Adèle gave it to me."

"And that 's her favorite flower."

"Yes, Phil," and there is a shake in her

voice now. "I think she's grown tired of such gifts, Phil;"—whereat she glances keenly and pitifully at him.

"*Truly,* Rose?" says Phil, with the color on a sudden quitting his cheeks.

"Truly,—truly, Phil,"—and in spite of herself the pretty hazel eyes are brimming full, and, under pretence of some household duty, she dashes away. For a moment Phil stands confounded. Then, through his set teeth, he growls, "I was a fool not to have known it!"

LVI

Adèle—Reuben—Maverick

Adèle sees clearly now the full burden of Reuben's proposal to cherish and guard her against whatever indignities might threaten; she sees more clearly than ever the rich, impulsive generosity of his nature reflected, and it disturbs her grievously to think that she had met it only with reproach. The thought of the mad, wild, godless career upon which he may have entered, and of which the village gossips are full, is hardly more afflictive to her than her recollection of that frank, self-sacrificing generosity, so ignobly requited. She longs in her heart to clear the debt,—to tell him what grateful sense she has of his intended kindness. But how? Should she,—being what she is,—even by a word, seem to invite a return of that devotion which may be was but the passion of an hour, and which it were fatal to renew? And yet—and yet—so brave a generosity shall not be wholly unacknowledged. She writes:—

"Reuben, I know now the full weight of the favor you promised to bestow upon me when I so blindly reproached you with intrusion upon my private griefs. Forgive me, Reuben! I thank you now, late as it is, with my whole heart. It is needless to tell you how I came to know what, perhaps, I had better never have known, but which must always have overhung me as a dark cloud. This knowledge, dear Reuben, which separates us so surely and so widely, takes away the embarrassment I might have felt in telling you of my lasting gratitude, and (if as a sister I may say it) my love. If your kind heart could so overflow with pity then, you will surely pity me the more now; yet not *too much,* Reuben, for my pride is as strong as ever. The world was made for me, as much as it was made for others; and if I bear its blight, I will find some flowers yet to cherish. I do not count it altogether so grim and odious a world,—even under the broken light which shines upon it for me,—as in your last visits you seemed disposed to reckon it.

"How is it with the cloud that lay in those times upon you? Is there any light? Ah, Reuben, when I recall those days in which long ago your faith in something better beyond this world than lies in it seemed to be so much stronger and firmer than mine, and when your trust was so confident as to make mine stronger, it seems like a strange dream to me, all the more when now you, who should reason more justly than I, believe in 'nothing,' (was not that your last word?)—and yet, dear Reuben, I cling,—I cling. Do you remember the old hymn I sung in those days:—

' Ingemisco tanquam reus.'

Even your good father, who was so troubled by the Romish hymns, said it must have been written by a good man."

Much more she writes in this vein, but returns ever and again to that noble generosity of his,—her delicacy struggling throughout with her tender gratitude,—yet she fails not to show a deep, earnest undercurrent of affection, which surely might develop under sympathy into a very fever of love. Will it not touch the heart of Reuben? Will it not divert him from the trail where he wanders blindly?

God send that the letter may reach him safely.

For a long time Adèle has not written to Reuben, and it occurs to her, as she strolls away toward the village post, that to mail it herself may possibly provoke new town gossip. In this perplexity she presently encounters her boy friend, Arthur, who for a handful of pennies, and under an injunction of secrecy, cheerfully undertakes the duty. To the house of the lad's mother, far away as it was, Adèle had wandered frequently of late, and had borne away from time to time some trifling memento of the dead one whose memory so endeared the spot. It happens that she continues her stroll thither on this occasion; and the poor woman, toward whom Adèle's charities have flowed with a profusion that has astounded the Doctor, repays some new gift by placing in her hands a little embroidered kerchief, "too fine for such as she," which had belonged to Madame Arles. A flimsy bit of muslin daintily embroidered; but there is a name stitched upon its corner, for which Adèle treasures it past all reckoning,—the name of *Julie Chalet*.

It was as if the dead one had suddenly come back and whispered it in her ear,—Julie Chalet. The spring birds sung the name in chorus as she walked home; and on the gravestone, under the cross, she seemed to see it cut upon the marble,—Julie Chalet.

Adèle has written to her father, of course, in those days when the first shock of the new revelation had passed. How could she do otherwise?

"I think I now understand," she writes, "the reason of your long absence from me. Whatever other griefs I bear, I will not believe that it has been from lack of affection for me. I recall that day, dear papa, when, with my head lying on your bosom, you said to me, 'She is unworthy; I will love you for both.' You must! But was she, papa, so utterly unworthy? I think I have known her; nay, I feel almost sure,—sure that these arms held her in the moment when she breathed adieu to the world. If ever bad, I am sure that she must have grown into goodness. I cannot, I will not, think otherwise. I can tell you so many of her kind deeds as will take away your condemnation. In this hope I live, dear papa.

"I have found her true name too, at last,—Julie Chalet,—is it not so? I wonder with what feeling you will read it; will it be with awakened fondness? will it be loathing? I tremble while I ask. You shall go with me (will you not?) *to her grave;* and there a kind Heaven will put in our hearts what memories are best.

"I know now the secret of your caution in respect to Reuben; you have been unwilling that *your child* should bring shame to the household of a friend! Trust to me,—trust to *me,* papa. Yet I have never told you—what I have since learned—of the unselfish devotion of Reuben, which declared itself when he knew all,—all. Would I not be almost tempted to thank him with—myself? Yet, if I have written him with an almost unmaidenly warmth, I have called to his mind the great gulf that *must* lie between us.

"Is the old godmother, of whom you used to speak, still alive? It seems that I should love to hang about her neck in memory of days gone; it seems that I should love the warm

DOCTOR JOHNS

sky under which I was born,—I am sure I should love the olive-orchards, and the vines, and the light upon the sea. I feel as if I were living in chains now. When, when will you come to break them, and set me free?"

In those days of May, when the leaflets were unfolding, and when the downy bluebells were lifting their clustered blossoms filled with a mysterious fragrance, like the breath of young babes, Adèle loved to linger in the study of the parsonage; more than ever the good Doctor seemed a "New Papa,"—more than ever his eye dwelt upon her with a parental smile. It was not that she loved Rose less, that she lingered here so long; but she could not shake off the conviction that some day soon Rose might shrink from her.

The Doctor was always gravely kind. "Have courage, Adaly, have courage!" he was wont to say; "God orders all things right."

And somehow, when she hears him say it, she believes it more than ever.

Ten days, a fortnight, and a month pass, and there is no acknowledgment from Reuben of her grateful letter. He does not count it worth his while, apparently, to break his long silence; or, possibly, he is too much engrossed with livelier interests to give a thought to this episode of his old life in Ashfield. Adèle is disturbed by it; but the very disturbance gives her new courage to combat faithfully the difficulties of her position. "One cheering word I would have thought he might have given me," said she.

The appeal to her father, too, has no answer. Before it reaches its destination, Maverick has taken ship for America; and, singularly enough, it is fated that the letter of Adèle should be first opened and read—by her mother.

LVII

Maverick is Married

SOME time in mid-May of this year Maverick writes:—

"My dear Johns,—I shall again greet you, God willing, in your own home, some forty days hence, and I shall come as a repentant Benedick; for I now wear the dignities of a married man. Your kind letter counted for a great deal toward my determination; but I will not affect to conceal from you, that my tender interest in the future of Adèle counted for a great deal more. As I had supposed, the communication to Julie (which I effected through her brother) that her child was still living, and living motherless, woke all the tenderness of her nature. I cannot say that the sudden change in her inclinations was any way flattering to me; but knowing her recent religious austerities, I was prepared for this. I shall not undertake to describe to you our first interview, which I can never forget. It belongs to those heart-secrets which cannot be spoken of; but this much I may tell you,— that, if there was no kindling of the old and wayward love, there grew out of it a respect for her present severity and elevation of character that I had never anticipated. At our age, indeed (though, when I think of it, I must be many years your junior), a respect for womanly character most legitimately takes the place of that disorderly sentiment which twenty years ago blazed out in passion.

"We have been married according to the rites of the Romish Church. If I had proposed other ceremony, more agreeable to your views, I am confident that she would not have listened to me. She is wrapped as steadfastly in her creed as ever you in yours. To

MAVERICK IS MARRIED

do otherwise in so sacred a matter—and with her it wore solely that aspect—than as her Church commands, would have been to do foully and vainly. The only trace of worldliness which I see in her is her intense yearning toward our dear Adèle, and her passionate longing to clasp the child once more to her heart. Nor will I conceal from you that she hopes, with all the fervor of a mother's hope, to wean her from what she counts the heretical opinions under which she has been reared.

"You will naturally ask, my dear Johns, why I do not combat this; but I am too old and too far spent for a fight about creeds. I should have made a lame fight on that score at any day; but now my main concern, it would seem, should be to look out personally for the creed which has the most of mercy in it. If I seem to speak triflingly, my dear Johns, I pray you to excuse me; it is only my business way of stating the actual facts in the case. As for Madame Maverick, I am sure you will find no trifling in her (if you ever meet her); she is terribly in earnest. Yet I should do wrong if I were to represent her as always severe, even upon such a theme; there certainly belongs to her a tender, appealing manner (reminding of Adèle in a way that brings tears to my eyes) but it is always bounded by allegiance to her sworn faith. My home near to Marseilles, which has been but a gypsy home for so many years, she has taken under her hand, and by its new appointments and order has convicted me of the losses I have felt so long. True, you might object to the *oratoire;* but in all else I am confident you would approve, and in all else felicitate Adèle.

"Madame Maverick will not sail with me for America; although the marriage, under French law, may have admitted Adèle to all rights and even social immunities, yet I have represented that another law and custom rule with you. Whatever opprobrium might attach to the mother, Julie, with her exalted religious sentiment, would not weigh for a moment; but as regards Adèle, she manifests a strange tenderness. But while she assents— with some reluctance, I must admit—to this plan of deferring her meeting with Adèle, she insists in a way that I find it difficult to combat, upon her child's speedy return. That her passionate love will insure entire devotion on the part of Adèle, I cannot doubt. And how the anti-Romish faith instilled in the dear girl by your teachings, as well as by her associations, may withstand the earnest attack of

MAVERICK IS MARRIED

Madame Maverick, I cannot tell. I have a fear it may lead to some dismal complications. You know what the earnestness of your own faith is; but I don't think you yet know the earnestness of an opposing faith, with a Frenchwoman to back it. Even as I write, she comes to cast a glance at my work, and says, 'Monsieur Maverick' (she called me Frank once), 'what are you saying there to the heretical Doctor?'

"Whereupon I translate for her ear a sentence or two. 'Tell him,' says she, 'that I thank him for his kindness; tell him besides, that I can in no way better atone for the guiltiness of the past, than by bringing back this wandering lamb into the true fold. Only when we kneel before the same altar, her hand in mine, can I feel that she is truly my child.'

"I fear greatly this zeal may prove infectious.

"And now, my dear Johns, in regard to the revelation to Adèle of what is written here, I must throw myself on your charity. For Heaven's sake, tell the story as kindly as you can. See to it, I pray, that my name don't become a bugbear in the village. I have pretty broad shoulders, and could bear it, if I only were to be sufferer; but I am sure 't would react fearfully on the sensibilities of poor Adèle. Do me this favor, Johns, and you will find me a more willing listener in what is to come. I can't promise, indeed, to accept all your dogmas; there is a thick crust of the world on me, and I doubt if you could force them through it; but, for Adèle's sake, I think I could become a very orderly and presentable person, even for a New England meeting-house. I will make a beginning now by turning over the little property which you hold for Adèle, in trust, for disbursement in your parish charities. The dear child won't need it, and the parish may."

The Doctor was happy to be relieved of the worst part of the revelation; but he had yet to communicate the fact that the mother was still alive, and (what was to him worst of all) that she was imbruted with the delusions of the Romish Church. He chose his hour, and, meeting her upon the village street, asked her into his study.

"Adaly, your father is coming. He will be here within a month."

"At last! at last!" said she, with a cry of joy.

"But, Adaly," continued he, with great gravity, "I have perhaps led you into error.

MAVERICK IS MARRIED

Your mother, Adaly,—your mother is still living."

"Living!" and an expression almost of radiance shot over the fair face. But in an instant it was gone. Was not the poor lady she had so religiously mourned over her mother? That death embrace and the tomb were, then, only solemn mockeries! With a frightful alertness her thought ran to them,—weighed them. "New Papa," said she, approaching him with a gravity that matched his own, "is this some new delusion? Is it true? Has he written me?"

"He has not written you, my child; but I have a letter, informing me of his marriage, and begging me to make the revelation to you as kindly as I might."

"Marriage! marriage to whom?" says Adèle, her eyes flashing fire, and her lips showing a tempest of scarce controllable feeling.

"Marriage to your mother, Adaly. He would be just at last."

"O my God!" exclaimed Adèle, with a burst of tears. "It's false! I shall never see my mother again in this world. I know it! I know it!"

"But, Adaly, my child, consider!" said the old gentleman.

Adèle did not heed him. She was lost in her own griefs. She could only exclaim, "O my father! my father!"

The old Doctor was greatly moved: he laid down his spectacles, and paced up and down the room. The earnestness of her doubt made him almost believe that he was himself deceived.

"Can it be? can it be?" he muttered, half under breath, while Adèle sat drooping in her chair. "May be the instinct of the poor girl is right, after all," thought he,—"sin is so full of disguises."

At this moment there is a sharp tap at the door, and Miss Eliza steps in, the bearer of a letter from Reuben.

LVIII

New Complications

A LETTER from Reuben indeed has come; but not for Miss Adèle. The Doctor is glad of the relief its perusal will give him. Meantime Miss Eliza, in her stately, patronizing manner, and with a coolness that was worse than a

NEW COMPLICATIONS

sneer, says, "I hope you have pleasant news from your various friends abroad, Miss Maverick?"

Adèle lifted her eyes with a glitter in them that for a moment was almost serpent-like; then, as if regretting her show of vexation, and with an evasive reply, bowed her head again to brood over the strange suspicions that haunted her. Miss Johns, totally unmoved, thinking all the grief but a righteous dispensation for the sin in which the poor child had been born,—next addressed the Doctor, who had run his eye with extraordinary eagerness through the letter of his son.

"What does Reuben say, Benjamin?"

"His 'idols,' again, Eliza; 't is always the 'flesh-pots of Egypt.'"

And the Doctor reads: "There is just now rare promise of a good venture in our trade at one of the ports of Sicily, and we have freighted two ships for immediate dispatch. At the last moment our supercargo has failed us, and Brindlock has suggested that I go myself; it is short notice, as the ship is in the stream, and may sail to-morrow, but I rather fancy the idea, and have determined to go. I hope you will approve. Of course, I shall have no time to run up to Ashfield to say good-by. I shall try for a freight back from Naples, otherwise shall make some excuse to run across the Straits for a look at Vesuvius and the matters thereabout. St. Paul, you know, voyaged in those seas, which will interest you in my trip. I dare say I shall find where he landed; it's not far from Naples, Mrs. Brindlock tells me. Give love to the people who ever ask about me in Ashfield. I enclose a check of five hundred dollars for parish contingencies till I come back; hoping to find you clean out of harness by that time." (The Doctor cannot for his life repress a little smile here.) "Tell Adèle I shall see her blue Mediterranean at last, and will bring her back an olive leaf, if I find any growing *within reach*. Tell Phil I love him, and that he deserves all the good he will surely get in this world, or in any other. Ditto for Rose. Ditto for good old Mrs. Elderkin, whom I could almost kiss for the love she's shown me. What high old romps have n't we had in her garden! Eh, Adèle? (I suppose you'll show her this letter, father.)

"Good-by, again.

"N. B. We hope to make a cool thirty thousand out of this venture!"

Adèle had half roused herself at the hearing

NEW COMPLICATIONS

of her name, but the careless, jocular mention of it, (so it seemed at least,) in contrast with the warmer leave-taking of other friends, added a new pang to her distress. She wished, for a moment, that she had never written her letter of thanks. What if she wished—in that hour of terrible suspicion and of vain search after any object upon which her future happiness might rest—that she had never been born?

"It will be of service to Reuben, I think, Benjamin," said Aunt Eliza; "I quite approve,"—and slipped away noiselessly.

The Doctor was still musing,—the letter in his hand,—when Adèle rose, and, approaching him, said in her gentlest way, "It's a great grief to you, New Papa, I know it is, but 'God orders all things well'—except for me."

"Adaly! my child, I am shocked!"

She had roused the preacher in him unwittingly.

"I can't listen now," said she, impatiently; "and tell me,—you must,—did papa give you the name of this—new person he is to marry?"

"Yes, Adaly, yes," but he has forgotten it; and searching for the previous letter, he presently finds it, and sets it before her,—"Mademoiselle Chalet."

"Chalet!" screams she. "There is some horrible mistake, New Papa. More than ever I am in the dark,—in the dark!" And with a hasty adieu she rushed away, taking her course straight for the house of that outlawed woman, with whom now, more than ever, she must have so many sympathies in common. Her present object, however, was to learn if any more definite evidence could be found that the deceased lady—mother still, in her thought—bore the name of Chalet. She found the evidence. One or two little books (devotional books they prove to be), which the mistress of the house had thrown by as valueless, were brought out, upon the fly-leaves of which the keen eyes of Adèle detected the name,—crossed and recrossed indeed, as if the poor woman would have destroyed all traces of her identity,—but still showing when held to the light a portion of the name she so cherished in her heart,—Chalet.

Adèle was more than ever incensed at thought of the delusion or the deception of her father. But, by degrees, her indignation yielded to her affection. He was himself to come, he would make it clear; this new mother —whom she was sure she should not love—

NEW COMPLICATIONS

was to remain; the Doctor had told her this much. *She* would have rushed to her arms; no fear of idle tongues could have kept her back. And though she yearned for the time when she should be clasped once more in her father's arms, she dreaded the thought of crossing the seas with him upon such empty pilgrimage. She half wished for some excuse to detain her here,—some fast anchor by which her love might cling, within reach of that grave where her holier affections had centered.

This wish was confirmed by the more cordial manner in which she was received by the Elderkins, and, indeed, by the whole village, so soon as the Doctor had made known the fact—as he did upon the earliest occasion—that Mr. Maverick was speedily to come for Adèle, and to restore her to the embraces of a mother whom she had not seen for years.

Even the spinster, at the parsonage, was disposed to credit something to the rigid legal aspects which the affair was taking, and to find in them a shelter for her wounded dignities. Nor did she share the inquietude of the Doctor at thought of the new and terrible religious influences to which Adèle must presently be exposed. 'T was right, in her exalted view, that she should struggle and agonize and wrestle with Satan for much time to come, before she should fully cleanse her bedraggled skirts of all taint of heathenism, and stand upon the high plane with herself, among the elect.

"It is satisfactory to reflect, Benjamin," said she, "that during her residence with us the poor girl has been imbued with right principles; at least I trust so."

And as she spoke, the exemplary old lady plucked a little waif of down from her bombazine dress, and snapped it away jauntily upon the air,—even as throughout her life, she had snapped from her the temptations of the world. And when, in his Scriptural reading that very night, the Doctor came upon the passage, *"Woe unto you, Pharisees!"* the mind of the spinster was cheerfully intent upon the wretched sinners of Judea.

LIX

A Trust for Phil

THE news of Maverick's prospective arrival, and the comments of the good Doctor,—as we have said,—shed a new light upon the position of Adèle. Old Squire Elderkin, with a fatherly interest, was not unaffected by it; indeed, the Doctor had been communicative with him to a degree that had enlisted very warmly the old gentleman's sympathies.

"Better late than never, Doctor," had been his comment; and he had thought it worth his while to drop a hint or two in the ear of Phil.

"I say, Phil, my boy, I gave you a word of caution not long ago in regard to—to Miss Maverick. There were some bad stories afloat, my boy; but they are cleared up,—quite cleared up, Phil."

"I 'm glad of it, sir," says Phil.

"So am I,—so am I, my boy. She 's a fine girl, Phil, eh?"

"I think she is, sir."

"The deuce you do! Well, and what then?"

Phil blushed, but the smile that came on his face was not a hearty one.

"Well, Phil?"

"I said she was a fine girl, sir," said he, measuredly.

"But she 's an uncommon fine girl, Phil, eh?"

"I think she is, sir."

"Well?"

Phil was twirling his hat in an abstracted way between his knees. "I don't think she 's to be won very easily," said he at last.

"Nonsense, Phil! Faint heart never won. Make a bold push for it, my boy. The best birds drop at a quick shot."

"Do they?" said Phil, with a smile of incredulity that the old gentleman did not comprehend.

He found, indeed, a much larger measure of hope in a little hint that was let fall by Rose two days after. "I would n't despair if I were you, Phil," she had whispered in his ear.

Phil, indeed, had never given over most devoted and respectful attentions to Adèle; but he had shown them latterly with a subdued and half-distrustful air, which Adèle with her keen insight had not been slow to understand.

A TRUST FOR PHIL

Yet it was not easy for Phil, or indeed for any other, to comprehend or explain the manner of Adèle at this time. Elated she certainly was in the highest degree at the thought of meeting and welcoming her father; and there was an exuberance in her spirits when she talked of it, that seemed almost unnatural; but the coming shadow of the new mother whom she was bound to welcome dampened all. The Doctor indeed had warned her against the Romish prejudices of this newly-found relative, and had entreated her to cling by the faith in which she had been reared; but it was no fear of any such conflict that oppressed her;—creeds all vanished under the blaze of that natural affection which craved a motherly embrace and which foresaw only falsity.

What wonder if her thought ran back, in its craving, to the days long gone,—to the land where the olive grew upon the hills, and the sunshine lay upon the sea,—where an old godmother, with withered hands clasped and raised, lifted up her voice at nightfall and chanted,—

> " O sanctissima,
> O piissima,
> Dulcis virgo Maria!"

The Doctor would have been shocked had

DOCTOR JOHNS

he heard the words tripping from the tongue of Adèle; yet, for her, they had no meaning save as expressive of a deep yearning for motherly guidance and motherly affection.

Mrs. Elderkin, with her kindly instinct, had seen the perplexity of Adèle, and had said to her one day, "Ady, my dear, is the thought not grateful to you that you will meet your mother once more, and be clasped in her arms?"

"If I could, if I could!" said Adèle, with a burst of tears.

"But you will, my child, you will. The Doctor has shown us the letters of your father. Even now she must be longing to greet you."

"Why does she not come then?"—with a tone that was almost taunting.

"But, Adèle, my dear, there may be reasons of which you do not know or which you could not understand."

"I could,—I do!" said Adèle, with spirit mastering her grief. " 'T is not my mother, my true mother; she is in the grave-yard; I know it!"

"My dear child, do not decide hastily. We love you; we all love you. And whatever may happen, you shall have a home with us. I will be a mother to you, Adèle."

A TRUST FOR PHIL

The girl kissed her good hostess, and the words lingered on her ear long after nightfall. Why not her mother? What home more grateful? And should she bring dishonor to it then? Could she be less sensitive to that thought than her father had already shown himself? She perceives, indeed, that within a short time, and since the latter communications from her father, the manner of those who had looked most suspiciously upon her has changed. But they do not know the secret of that broidered kerchief—the secret of that terrible death-clasp which she never, never can forget. She will be true to her own sense of honor; she will be true, too, to her own faith, —the faith in which she has been reared,— whatever may be the persuasions of that new relative beyond the seas whom she so dreads to meet.

Indeed, it is with dreary anticipations that she forecasts now her return to that *belle France* which has so long borne olive-branches along its shores for welcome; she foresees struggle, change, hypocrisies, may be, —who can tell?—and she begins to count the weeks of her stay amid the quiet of Ashfield in the same spirit in which youngsters score off the remaining days of the long vacation.

Adèle finds herself gathering and pressing within the leaves of some cherished book, little sprays of dead bloom that shall be, in the dim and mysterious future, mementos of the walks, the frolics, the joys that have belonged to this staid New England home. From the very parsonage door she has brought away a sprig of a rampant sweet-briar that has grown there this many a year, and its delicate leaflets are among her chiefest treasures.

More eagerly than ever she listens to the kindly voices that greet her and speak cheer to her in the home of the Elderkins,—voices which she feels bitterly will soon be heard no more by her. Even the delicate and always respectful attentions of Phil have an added, though a painful charm, since they are so soon to have an end. She knows that she will remember him always, though his tenderest words can waken no hopes of a brighter future for her. She even takes him partially into her confidence, and, strolling with him down the street one day, she decoys him to the churchyard gate, where she points out to him the stone she had placed over the grave that was so sacred to her.

"Phil," said she, "you have always been full of kindness for me. When I am gone, have a

A TRUST FOR PHIL

care of that stone and grave, please, Phil. My best friend lies there."

"I don't think you know your best friends," stammered Phil.

"I know you are one," said Adèle, calmly, "and that I can trust you to do what I ask about this grave. Can I, Phil?"

"You know you can, Adèle; but I don't like this talk of your going, as if you were never to be among us again. Do you think you can be happiest yonder with strangers, Adèle?"

"It's not—where I can be happiest, Phil; I don't ask myself that question; I fear I never can;"—and her lips trembled as she said it.

"You can—you ought," burst out Phil, fired at sight of her emotion, and would have gone on bravely and gallantly, may be, with the passion that was surging in him, if a look of hers and a warning finger had not stayed him.

"We'll talk no more of this, Phil"; and her lips were as firm as iron now.

Both of them serious and silent for a while; until at length Adèle, in quite her old manner, says: "Of course, Phil, father may bring me to America again some day; and if so, I shall certainly beg for a little visit in Ashfield. It would be very ungrateful in me not to remember the pleasant times I've had here."

But Phil cannot so deftly change the color of his talk; his chattiness has all gone from him. Nor does it revive on reaching home. Good Mrs. Elderkin says, "What makes you so crusty, Phil?"

LX

Father and Child

MAVERICK arrives, as he had promised to do, some time in early July; comes up from the city without announcing himself in advance; and, leaving the old coach, which still makes its periodical trips from the river, a mile out from the town, strolls along the highway. He remembers well the old outline of the hills; and the straggling hedge-rows, the scattered granite boulders, the whistling of a quail from a near fence in the meadow,—all recall the old scenes which he knew in boyhood. At a solitary house by the wayside a flaxen-haired youngster is blowing off soap-bubbles into the air,—with obstreperous glee whenever one rises above the house-tops,—while the mother, with arms akimbo, looks admiringly from the

FATHER AND CHILD

open window. It was the home to which the feet of Adèle had latterly so often wandered.

Maverick is anxious for a word with the Doctor before his interview with Adèle even. He does not know her present home; but he is sure he can recall the old parsonage, in whose exterior, indeed, there have been no changes for years. The shade of the embowering elms is grateful as he strolls on into the main street of the town. It is early afternoon, and there are few passers-by. Here and there a blind is coyly turned, and a sly glance cast upon the stranger. A trio of school-boys look wonderingly at his foreign air and dress. A few loiterers upon the tavern steps—instructed, doubtless, by the stage-driver, who has duly delivered his portmanteau—remark upon him as he passes.

And now at last he sees the old porch,—the diamond lights in the door. Twenty and more years ago, and he had lounged there, as the pretty Rachel drove up in the parson's chaise. The same rose-brier is nodding its untrimmed boughs by the door. From the open window above he catches a glimpse of a hard, thin face, with spectacles on nose, that scans him curiously. The Doctor's hat and cane are upon the table at the foot of the stairs within. He taps with his knuckles upon the study-door,—and again the two college mates are met together. At sight of the visitor, whom he recognizes at a glance, the heart of the old man is stirred by a little of the old youthful feeling.

"Maverick!" and he greets him with open hand.

"Johns, God bless you!"

The parson was white-haired, and was feeble to a degree that shocked Maverick; while the latter was still erect and prim. His coquettings for sixty years with the world, the flesh, and the Devil had not yet reduced his *physique* to that degree of weakness which the multiplied spiritual wrestlings had entailed upon the good Doctor. The minister recognized this with a look rather of pity than of envy, and may possibly have bethought himself of that Dives who "in his lifetime received good things," but "now is tormented."

Yet he ventured upon no warning; there is, indeed, a certain assured manner about the man of the world who has passed middle age, which a country parson, however good or earnest he may be, would no more attempt to pierce than he would attempt a thrust of his pen through ice.

Their conversation, after the first greetings,

FATHER AND CHILD

naturally centres upon Adèle. Maverick is relieved to find that she knows, even now, the worst; but he is grievously pained to learn that she is still in doubt, by reason of that strange episode which had grown out of the presence and death of Madame Arles,—an episode which, even now, he is at a loss to explain.

"She will be unwilling to return with me then," said Maverick, in a troubled manner.

"No," said the Doctor, "she expects. that. You will find in her, Maverick, a beautiful respect for your authority; and, I think, a still higher respect for the truth."

So it was with disturbed and conflicting feelings that Maverick made his way to the present home of Adèle.

The windows and doors of the Elderkin mansion were all open upon that July day. Adèle had seen him, even as he entered the little gate, and, recognizing him on the instant, had rushed down to meet him in the hall.

"Papa! papa!" and she had buried her face upon his bosom.

"Adèle, darling! you are glad to welcome me then?"

"Delighted, papa."

DOCTOR JOHNS

And Maverick kissed, again and again, that fair face of which he was so proud.

We recoil from the attempt to transcribe the glowing intimacy of their first talk.

After a time, Maverick says, "You will be glad to return with me,—glad to embrace again your mother?"

"My own, true mother?" said Adèle, the blood running now swift over cheek and brow.

"Your own, Adèle,—your own! As God is true!"

Adèle grows calm,—an unwonted calmness. "Tell me how she looks, papa," said she.

"Your figure, Adèle; not so tall, perhaps, but slight like you; and her hair,—you have her hair, darling (and he kissed it). Your eye too, for color, with a slight, hardly noticeable cast in it." And as Adèle turned an enquiring glance upon him, he exclaimed: "You have that too, my darling, as you look at me now."

Adèle, still calm, says: "I know it, papa; I have seen her. Do not deceive me. She died in these arms, papa!"—and with that her calmness is gone. She can only weep upon his shoulder.

"But, Adèle, child, this cannot be; do not trust to so wild a fancy. You surely believe me, darling?"

FATHER AND CHILD

Had she argued the matter, he would have been better satisfied. She did not, however. Her old tranquillity came again.

"I will go with you, papa, cheerfully," said she.

It was only too evident to Maverick that there was a cause of distrust between them. Under all of Adèle's earnest demonstrations of affection, which were intensely grateful to him, there was still a certain apparent reserve of confidence, as if some great inward leaning of her heart found no support in him or his. This touched him to the quick. The Doctor— had he unfolded the matter to him fully— would have called it, may be, the sting of retribution. Nor was Maverick at all certain that the shadowy doubt which seemed to rest upon the mind of Adèle with respect to the identity of her mother was the sole cause of this secret reserve of confidence. It might be, he thought, that her affections were otherwise engaged, and that the change to which she assented with so little fervor would be at the cost of other ties to which he was a stranger.

On this score he consulted with the Doctor. As regarded Reuben, there could be no doubt. Whatever tie may have existed there was long since broken. With respect to Phil Elderkin the parson was not so certain. Maverick had been attracted by his fine, frank manner, and was not blind to his capital business capacities and prospects. If the happiness of Adèle were in question, he could entertain the affair. He even ventured to approach the topic—coyly as he could—in a talk with Adèle; and she, as the first glimmer of his meaning dawned upon her, says, "Don't whisper it, papa. It can never be."

And so Maverick—not a little disconcerted at the thought that he cannot now, as once, fathom all the depths of his child's sensibilities—sets himself resolutely to the work of preparation for departure. His *affaires* may keep him a month, and involve a visit to one or two of the principal cities; then, ho for *la belle France!* Adèle certainly lends seemingly a cheerful assent. He cannot doubt—with those repeated kisses on his cheek and brow—her earnest filial affection; and if her sentiment slips beyond his control, or parries all his keenness of vision, what else has a father, verging upon sixty, to expect in a daughter, tenderly affectionate as she may be? Maverick's philosophy taught him to "take the world as it is." Only one serious apprehension of disquietude oppressed him; the doubts and vagaries of Adèle would clear themselves under

FATHER AND CHILD

the embrace of Julie; but in respect to the harmony of their religious beliefs he had grave doubts. There had grown upon Adèle, since he had last seen her, a womanly dignity, which even a mother must respect; and into that dignity—into the woof and warp of it—were inwrought all her religious sympathies. Was his home yonder across the seas to become the scene of struggles about creeds? It certainly was not the sort of domestic picture he had foreshadowed to himself at twenty-five. But at sixty a man blows bubbles no longer—except that of his own conceit. The heart of Maverick was not dead in him; a kiss of Adèle wakened a thrilling, delicious sensation there, of which he had forgotten his capability. He followed her graceful step and figure with an eye that looked beyond and haunted the past —vainly, vainly! Her "Papa!"—sweetly uttered—stirred sensibilities in him that amazed himself, and seemed like the phantoms of dreams he dreamed long ago.

But in the midst of Maverick's preparations for departure a letter came to hand from Mrs. Maverick, which complicated once more the situation.

LXI

The Truth at Last

THE mother has read the letter of her child,—the letter in which appeal had been made to the father in behalf of the "unworthy" one whom the daughter believed to be sleeping in her grave. The tenderness of the appeal smote the poor woman to the heart. It bound her to the child she scarce had seen by bonds into which her whole moral being was knitted anew. But we must give the letter entire, as offering explanations which can in no way be better set forth. The very language kindles the ardor of Adèle. Her own old speech again, with the French echo of her childhood in every line.

"*Mon cher Monsieur,*"—in this way she begins; for her religious severities, if not her years, have curbed any disposition to explosive tenderness,—"I have received the letter of our child, which was addressed to you. I cannot tell you the feelings with which I have read it. I long to clasp her to my heart. And she appeals to you, for me,—the dear child! Yes,

THE TRUTH AT LAST

you have well done in telling her that I was unworthy (*méchante*). It is true,—unworthy in forgetting duty,—unworthy in loving too well. O Monsieur! if I could live over again that life,—that dear young life among the olive orchards! But the good Christ (thank Him!) leads back the repentant wanderers into the fold of His Church.

'Laus tibi, Christe!'

"And the poor child believes that I am in my grave. May be that were better for her and better for me. But no, I shall clasp her to my heart once more,—she, the poor babe! But I forget myself; it is a woman's letter I have been reading. What earnestness! what maturity! what dignity! what tenderness! And will she be as tender to the living as to the erring one whom she believes dead? My heart stops when I ask myself. Yes, I know she will. The Blessed Virgin whispers me that she will, and I fly to greet her! A month, two months, three months, four months?—It is an age.

"Monsieur! I cannot wait. I must take ship—sail—wings (if I could find them), and go to meet my child. Until I do there is a tempest in my brain—heart—everywhere. You are surprised, Monsieur: but there is another reason why I should go to this land where Adèle has lived. Do you wish to know it? Listen, then, Monsieur!

"Do you know who this poor sufferer was whom our child had learned so to love, who died in her arms, who sleeps in the grave-yard there, and of whom Adèle thinks as of a mother? I have inquired, I have searched high and low, I have fathomed all. Ah, my poor, good sister Marie! Only Marie! You have never known her. In those other days at dear Arles she was too good for you to know her. Yet even then she was a guardian angel,—a guardian too late. *Mea culpa! Mea culpa!*

"I know it can be only Marie; I know it can be only she, who sleeps under the sod in Ash——(*ce nom m'échappe*).

"Listen again: in those early, bitter, charming days, when you, Monsieur, knew the hillsides and the drives about our dear old town of Arles, poor Marie was away; had she been there, I had never listened, as I did listen, to the words you whispered in my ear. Only when it was too late, she came. Poor, good Marie! how she pleaded with me! How

THE TRUTH AT LAST

her tender, good face spoke reproaches to me! If I was the pride of our household, she was the angel. She it was, who, knowing the worst, said, 'Julie, this must end!' She it was who labored day and night to set me free from the wicked web that bound me. I reproached her, the poor, good Marie, in saying that she was the plainer, that she had no beauty, that she was devoured with envy. But the Blessed Virgin was working ever by her side. Whatever doubts you may have entertained of me, Monsieur,—she created them; whatever suspicions tortured you,—she fed them, but always with the holiest of motives. And when shame came, as it did come, the poor Marie would have screened me,—would have carried the odium herself. Good Marie! the angels have her in keeping!

"Listen again, Monsieur! When that story, that false story, of the death of my poor child, came to light in the journals, who but Marie should come to me—deceived herself as I was deceived—and say, 'Julie, dear one, God has taken the child in mercy; there is no stigma can rest upon you in the eyes of the world. Live now as the Blessed Magdalen lived when Christ had befriended her.' And by her strength I was made strong; the Blessed Virgin be thanked!

"Finally, it came to her knowledge one day, —the dear Marie!—that the rumor of the death was untrue,—that the babe was living, —that the poor child had been sent over the seas to your home, Monsieur. Well, I was far away in the East. Does Marie tell me? No, the dear one! She writes me, that she is going 'over seas,'—tired of *la belle France,*—she who loved it so dearly! And she went,—to watch, to pray, to console. And I, the mother!— *Mon Dieu, Monsieur,* the words fail me. No wonder our child loved her; no wonder she seems a mother to her.

"Listen yet again, Monsieur. My poor sister died yonder, in that heretical land,—maybe without absolution. I must go, if it be only to find her grave, and to secure her burial in some consecrated spot. She waits for me,— her ghost, her spirit,—I must go; the holy water must be sprinkled; the priestly rites be said. Marie, poor Marie, I will not fail you.

"Monsieur, I must go!—not alone to greet our child, but to do justice to my sainted sister! Listen well! All that has been devotional in my poor life centres here. I must go, —I must do what I may to hallow my poor sister's grave. Adèle will not give up her welcome surely, if I am moved by such religious purpose. She, too, must join me in an *Ave Maria* over that resting-place of the departed.

"I shall send this letter by the overland and British mail, that it may come to you very swiftly. It will come to you while you are with the poor child,—our Adèle. Greet her for me as warmly as you can. Tell her I shall hope, God willing, to bring her into the bosom of his Holy Church Catholic. I shall try and love her, though she remain a heretic; but this will not be.

"If I can enough curb myself, I shall wait for your answer, Monsieur; but it is necessary that I go yonder. Look for me; kiss our child for me. And if you ever prayed, Monsieur, I should say, pray for

"Votre amie,
"JULIE."

The letter is of the nature of a revelation to Adèle; her doubts respecting Madame Arles vanish on the instant. The truth, as set forth in her mother's language, blazes upon her mind like a flame. She loves the grave none the less, but the mother by far the more. She, too, wishes to greet her amid the scenes which she has known so long. Nor is Maverick himself averse to this new disposition of affairs, if indeed he possessed any power (which he somewhat doubts) of readjusting it.

Adèle, after her first period of exultation over the recent news is passed, relapses—perhaps by reason of its excess—into something of her old vague doubt and apprehension of coming evil. The truth—if it be truth—is so strange!—so mysteriously strange that she shall indeed clasp her mother to her heart; the grave yonder is so real! and that fearful embrace in death so present to her! Or it may be an anticipation of the fearful spiritual estrangement that must ensue, and of which she seems to find confirmation in the earnest talk and gloomy forebodings of the Doctor.

Maverick effects a diversion by proposing a jaunt of travel, in which Rose shall be their companion. Adèle accepts the scheme with delight,—a delight, after all, which lies as much in the thought of watching the eager enjoyment of Rose as in any pleasant distractions of her own. The pleasure of Maverick is by no means so great as in that trip of a few years back. Then he had for companion an enthusiastic girl, to whom life was fresh, and all the clouds that seemed to rest upon it so shadowy,

THE TRUTH AT LAST

that each morning sun lifting among the mountains dispersed them utterly.

Now, Adèle showed the thoughtfulness of a woman,—her enthusiasms held in check by a more calm estimate of the life that opened before her,—her sportiveness overborne by a soberness, which, if it gave dignity, gave also a womanly gravity. Yet she did not lack filial devotion; she admired still that easy world-manner of his which had once called out her enthusiastic regard, but now queried in her secret heart if its acquisition had not involved cost of purity of conscience. She loved him too,—yes, she loved him; and her evening and morning kiss and embrace were reminders to him of a joy he might have won, but had not,—of a home peace that might have been his, but whose image now only lifted above his horizon like some splendid mirage crowded with floating fairy shapes, and like the mirage melted presently into idle vapor.

It was a novel experience for Maverick to find himself (as he did time and again upon this summer trip in New England) sandwiched, of a Sunday, between his two blooming companions and some sober-sided deacon, in the pew of a country meeting-house. How his friend Papiol would have stared! And the suggestion, coming to him with the buzz of a summer fly through the open windows, did not add to his devotional sentiment. Yet Maverick would follow gravely the scramble of the singers through the appointed hymn with a sober self-denial, counting the self-denial a virtue. We all make memoranda of the small religious virtues when the large ones are missing.

Upon the return to Ashfield there is found a new letter from Madame Maverick. She can restrain herself no longer. Under the advice of her brother, she will, with her maid, take the first safe ship leaving Marseilles for New York. She longs to bring Adèle with herself, by special consecration, under the guardianship of the Holy Virgin.

The Doctor is greatly grieved in view of the speedy departure of Adèle, and tenfold grieved when Maverick lays before him the letter of the mother, and he sees the fiery zeal which the poor child must confront.

Over and over in those last interviews he seeks to fortify her faith; he warns her against the delusions, the falsities, the idolatries of Rome; he warns her to distrust a religion of creeds, of human authority, of traditions.

Christ, the Bible,—these are the true monitors; and "Mind, Adaly," says he, "hold fast always to the Doctrine of the Westminster Divines. That is sound,—that is sound!"

LXII

Reuben at Rome

REUBEN went with a light heart upon his voyage. The tender memories of Ashfield were mostly lived down. (Had the letter of Adèle ever reached him, it might have been far different.) Rose, Phil, the Tourtelots, the Tew partners (still worrying through a green old age), the meeting-house, even the Doctor himself and Adèle, seemed to belong to a sphere whose interests were widely separate from his own, and in which he should appear henceforth only as a casual spectator. The fascinations of his brilliant business successes had a firm grip upon him. He indulges himself, indeed, from time to time, with the fancy that some day, far off now, he will return to the scenes of his boyhood, and astonish some of the old landholders by buying them out at a fabulous price, and by erecting a "castle" of his own, to be enlivened by the fairy graces of some sylph not yet fairly determined upon. Surely not Rose, who would hardly be equal to the grandeur of his proposed establishment, if she were not already engrossed by that "noodle" (his thought expressing itself thus wrathfully) of an assistant minister. Adèle, —and the name has something in it that electrifies, in spite of himself,—Adèle, if she ever overcomes her qualms of conscience, will yield to the tender persuasions of Phil. "Good luck to him!"—and he says this, too, with a kind of wrathful glee.

Still, he builds his cloud castles; some one must needs inhabit them. Some paragon of refinement and of beauty will one day appear, for whose tripping feet his wealth will lay down a path of pearls and gold. The lonely, star-lit nights at sea encourage such phantasms; and the break of the waves upon the bow, with their myriad of phosphorescent sparkles, cheats and illumines the fancy. We will not follow him throughout his voyage. On a balmy morning of July he wakes with the great cliff of Gibraltar frowning on him. After this come light, baffling winds, and for a week he looks southward upon the myste-

REUBEN AT ROME

rious, violet lift of the Barbary shores, and pushes slowly eastward into the blue expanse of the Mediterranean. In the Sicilian ports he is abundantly successful. He has ample time to cross over to Naples, to ascend Vesuvius, and to explore Herculaneum and Pompeii. But he does not forget the other side of the beautiful bay, Baiæ and Pozzuoli. He takes, indeed, a healthful pleasure in writing to the Doctor a description of this latter, and of his walk in the vicinity of the great seaport where St. Paul must have landed from his ship of the *Castor and Pollux,* on his way from Syracuse. But he does not tell the Doctor that, on the same evening, he attended an opera at the San Carlo in Naples, of which the ballet, if nothing else, would have called down the good man's anathema.

An American of twenty-five, placed for the first time upon the sunny pavements of Naples, takes a new lease of life,—at least of its imaginative part. The beautiful blue stretch of sea, the lava streets, the buried towns and cities, the baths and ruins of Baiæ, the burning mountain, piling its smoke and fire into the serene sky, the memories of Tiberius, of Cicero, of Virgil,—all these enchant him. And beside these are the things of to-day,—the luscious melons, the oranges, the figs, the war-ships lying on the bay, the bloody miracle of St. Januarius, the Lazzaroni upon the church steps, the processions of friars, and always the window of his chamber, looking one way upon blue Capri, and the other upon smouldering Vesuvius.

At Naples Reuben hears from the captain of the *Meteor*—in which good ship he has made his voyage, and counts upon making his return—that the vessel can take up half her cargo at a better freight by touching at Marseilles. Whereupon Reuben orders him to go thither, promising to join him at that port in a fortnight. A fortnight only for Rome, for Florence, for Pisa, for the City of Palaces, and then the marvellous Cornice road along the shores of the sea. Terracina brought back to him the story of Mr. Alderman Popkins and the Principessa, and the bandits; after this came the heights of Albano and Soracte, and there, at last, the Tiber, the pyramid tomb, the great church dome, the stone pines of the Janiculan hill,—Rome itself. Reuben was not strong or curious in his classics; the galleries and the churches took a deeper hold upon him than the Forum and the ruins. He wandered for hours together under the arches of St.

Peter's. He wished he might have led the Doctor along its pavement into the very presence of the mysteries of the Scarlet Woman of Babylon. He wished Miss Almira, with her saffron ribbons, might be there, sniffing at her little phial of salts, and may be singing treble. The very meeting-house upon the green, that was so held in reverence, with its belfry and spire atop, would hardly make a scaffolding from which to brush the cobwebs from the frieze below the vaulting of this grandest of temples. Oddly enough, he fancies Deacon Tourtelot, in his snuff-colored surtout, pacing down the nave with him, and saying,—as he would be like to say,—"Must ha' been a smart man that built it; but I guess they don't have better preachin,' as a gineral thing, than the old Doctor gives us on Fast-Days or in 'protracted' meetin's."

Such queer humors and droll comparisons flash into the mind of Reuben, even under all his sense of awe,—a swift, disorderly mingling of the themes and offices which kindled his first sense of religious awe under a home atmosphere with the wondrous forms and splendor which kindle a new awe now. The great dome enwalling with glittering mosaics a heaven of its own, and blazing with figured saints, and the golden distich, "Thou art Peter,—to thee will I give the keys of the kingdom of heaven,"—all this seems too grand to be untrue. Are not the keys verily here? Can falsehood build up so august a lie? A couple of friars shuffle past him, and go to their prayers at some near altar; he does not even smile at their shaven pates and their dowdy, coarse gowns of serge. Low music from some far-away chapel comes floating under the panelled vaultings, and loses itself under the great dome, with a sound so gentle, so full of entreaty, that it seems to him the dove on the high altar might have made it with a cooing and a flutter of her white wings. A mother and two daughters, in black, glide past him, and drop upon their knees before some saintly shrine, and murmur their thanksgivings, or their entreaty. And he, with no aim of worship, yet somehow shocked out of his unbelief by the very material influences around him.

Reuben's old wranglings and struggles with doubt had ended—where so many are apt to end, when the world is sunny and success weaves its silken meshes for the disport of self—in a quiet disbelief that angered him no longer, because he had given over all fight with

REUBEN AT ROME

it. But the great dome, flaming with its letters, *Ædificabo meam Ecclesiam,* shining there for ages, kindled the fight anew. And strange as it may seem, and perplexing as it was to the Doctor (when he received Reuben's story of it), he came out from his first visit to the great Romish temple with his religious nature more deeply stirred than it had been for years.

Ædificabo meam Ecclesiam. He had uttered it. There was then something to build, —something that had been built, at whose shrine millions worshipped trustingly.

Under the sombre vaultings of the great Florentine Cathedral, the impression was not weakened. The austere gloom of it chimed more nearly with his state of unrest. Then there are the galleries, the painted ceilings,— angels, saints, martyrs, holy families,—can art have been leashed through so many ages with a pleasant fiction? Is there not somewhere at bottom an earnest, vital truth, which men must needs cling by if they be healthful and earnest themselves? Even the meretricious adornments of the churches of Genoa afford new evidence of the way in which the heart of a people has lavished itself upon belief; and if belief, why, then, hope.

Upon the Cornice road, with Italy behind

him and home before (such home as he knows), he thinks once more of those he has left. Not that he has forgotten them altogether; he has purchased a rich coral necklace in Naples, which will be the very thing for his old friend Rose; and, in Rome, the richest cameos to be found in the Via Condotti he has secured for Adèle; even for Aunt Eliza he has brought away from Florence a bit of the *pietra dura,* a few olive-leaves upon a black ground. Nor has he forgotten a rich piece of the Genoese velvet for Mrs. Brindlock; and, for his father, an old missal, which, he trusts, dates back far enough to save it from the odium he attaches to the present Church, and to give it an early Christian sanctity. He has counted upon seeing Mr. Maverick at Marseilles, but learns, with surprise, upon his arrival there, that this gentleman had sailed for America some months previously. The ship is making a capital freight, and the captain informs him that application has been made for the only vacant state-room in their little cabin by a lady attended by her maid. Reuben assents cheerfully to this accession of companionship; and, running off for a sight of the ruins at Nismes and Arles, returns only in time to catch the ship upon the day of its departure. As they pass out of harbor, the lady passenger, in deep black, (the face seems half familiar to him,) watches wistfully the receding shores, and as they run abreast the chapel of Nôtre Dame de la Garde, she devoutly crosses herself and tells her beads.

Reuben is to make the voyage with the mother of Adèle. Both bound to the same quiet township of New England; he, to reach Ashfield once more, there to undergo swiftly a new experience,—an experience that can come to no man but once; she, to be clasped in the arms of Adèle,—a cold embrace and the last!

LXIII

The Voyage

Reuben had heard latterly very little of domestic affairs at Ashfield. He knew scarce more of the family relations of Adèle than was covered by that confidential announcement of the parson's which had so set on fire his generous zeal. The spinster, indeed, in one of her later letters had hinted, in a roundabout manner, that Adèle's family misfortunes were not looking so badly as they once did,—that the poor girl (she believed) felt tenderly still toward her old playmate,—and that Mr. Maverick was, beyond all question, a gentleman of very easy fortune. But Reuben was not in a mood to be caught by any chaff administered by his most respectable aunt. If, indeed, he had known all,—if that hearty burst of Adèle's gratitude had come to him,—if he could once have met her with the old freedom of manner, —ah! then—then—

But no; he thinks of her now as one under social blight, which he would have lifted or borne with her had not her religious squeamishness forbidden. He tries to forget what was most charming in her, and has succeeded passably well.

"I suppose she is still modelling her heroes on the Catechism," he thought, "and Phil will very likely pass muster."

The name of Madame Maverick as attaching to their fellow-passenger—which came to his ear for the first time on the second day out from port—considerably startled him. Madame Maverick is, he learns, on her way to join her husband and child in America. But he is by no means disposed to entertain a very ex-

THE VOYAGE

alted respect for any claimant of such name and title. He finds, indeed, the prejudices of his education (so he calls them) asserting themselves with a fiery heat; and most of all he is astounded by the artfully arranged religious drapery with which this poor woman—as it appears to him—seeks to cover her shortcomings. He had brought away from the atmosphere of the old cathedrals a certain quickened religious sentiment, by the aid of which he had grown into a respect, not only for the Romish faith, but for Christian faith of whatever degree. And now he encountered what seemed to him its gross prostitution. The old Doctor then was right: this Popish form of heathenism was but a device of Satan,—a scarlet covering of iniquity. It was easy for him to match the present hypocrisy with hypocrisies that he had seen of old.

Meantime, the good ship *Meteor* was skirting the shores of Spain, and had made a good hundred leagues of her voyage before Reuben had ventured to make himself known as the old schoolmate and friend of the child whom Madame Maverick was on her way to greet after so many years of separation. The truth was, that Reuben, his first disgust being overcome, could not shake off the influence of something attractive and winning in the manner of Madame Maverick. In her step and in her lithe figure he saw the step and figure of Adèle. All her orisons and *aves,* which she failed not to murmur each morning and evening, were reminders of the earnest faith of her poor child. It is impossible to treat her with disrespect. Nay, it is impossible,—as Reuben begins to associate more intimately the figure and the voice of this quiet lady with his memories of another and a younger one,—quite impossible, that he should not feel his whole chivalrous nature stirred in him, and become prodigal of attentions. If there were hypocrisy, it somehow cheated him into reverence.

The lady is, of course, astounded at Reuben's disclosure to her. *"Mon Dieu!* you, then, are the son of that good priest of whom I have heard so much! And you are Puritan? I would not have thought that. They love the vanities of the world then,"—and her eye flashed over the well-appointed dress of Reuben, who felt half an inclination to hide, if it had been possible, the cluster of garish charms which hung at his watchchain. "You have shown great kindness to my child, Monsieur. I thank you with my whole heart."

THE VOYAGE

"She is very charming, Madame," said Reuben, in an easy, *dégagé* manner, which, to tell the truth, he put on to cover a little embarrassing revival of his old sentiment.

Madame Maverick looked at him keenly. "Describe her to me, if you will be so good, Monsieur."

Whereupon Reuben ran on,—jauntily, at first, as if it had been a ballet-girl of San Carlo whose picture he was making out; but his old hearty warmth declared itself by degrees; and his admiration and his tenderness gave such warm color to his language as it might have shown if her little gloved hand had been shivering even then in his own passionate clasp. And as he closed, with a great glow upon his face, Madame Maverick burst forth,—

"Mon Dieu, how I love her! Yet is it not a thing astonishing that I should ask you, a stranger, Monsieur, how my own child is looking? *Culpa mea! Culpa mea!"* and she clutched at her rosary, and mumbled an *ave,* with her eyes lifted and streaming tears.

Reuben looked upon her in wonder, amazed at the depth of her emotion.

"Tenez!" said she, recovering herself, and reading, as it were, his doubts. "You count

these" (lifting her rosary) "baubles yonder, and our prayers pagan prayers; my husband has told me, and that she, Adèle, is taught thus, and that the *Bon Dieu* has forsaken our Holy Church,—that He comes near now only to your—what shall I call them?—meeting-houses? Tell me, Monsieur, does Adèle think this?"

"I think," said Reuben, "that your daughter would have charity for any religious faith which was earnest."

"Charity! *Mon Dieu!* Charity for sins, charity for failings,—yes, I ask it; but for my faith! No, Monsieur, no,—no—a thousand times, no!"

"This is real," thought Reuben.

"Tell me, Monsieur," continued she, with a heat of language that excited his admiration, "what is it you believe there? What is the horror against which your New England teachers would warn my poor Adèle? May the Blessed Virgin be near her!"

Whereupon, Reuben undertook to lay down the grounds of distrust in which he had been educated; not, surely, with the fervor or the logical sequence which the old Doctor would have given to the same, but yet inveighing in good set terms against the vain ceremonials,

THE VOYAGE

the idolatries, the mummeries, the confessional, the empty absolution; and summing up all with the formula (may be he had heard the Doctor use the same language) that the piety of the Romanist was not so much a deep religious conviction of the truth, as a sentiment.

"Sentiment!" exclaims Madame Maverick. "What else? What but love of the good God?"

But not so much by her talk as by the everyday sight of her serene unfaltering devotion is Reuben won into a deep respect for her faith.

Those are rare days and rare nights for him, as the good ship *Meteor* slips down past the shores of Spain to the Straits,—days all sunny, nights moonlit. To the right,—not discernible, but he knows they are there,—the swelling hills of Catalonia and of Andalusia, the marvellous Moorish ruins, the murmurs of the Guadalquivir; to the left, a broad sweep of burnished sea, on which, late into the night, the moon pours a stream of molten silver, that comes rocking and widening toward him, and vanishes in the shadow of the ship. The cruise has been a splendid venture for him,— twenty-five thousand at the least. And as he paces the decks,—in the view only of the silent man at the wheel and of the silent stars,—he forecasts again the palaces he will build. The feeble Doctor shall have ease and every luxury; he will be gracious in his charities; he will astonish the old people by his affluence; he will live—

Just here, he spies a female figure stealing from the companion-way, and gliding beyond the shelter of the wheel-house. Half concealed as he chances to be in the shadow of the rigging, he sees her fall upon her knees, and, with head uplifted, cross her hands upon her bosom. 'T is a short prayer, and the instant after she glides below.

"Good God! what trust!"—it is an ejaculatory prayer of Reuben's, rather than an oath. And with it, swift as the wind, comes a dreary sense of unrest. The palaces he had built vanish. The stars blink upon him kindly, and from their wondrous depths challenge his thought. The sea swashes idly against the floating ship. He too afloat,—afloat. Whither bound? Yearning still for a belief on which he may repose. And he bethinks himself,—does it lie somewhere under the harsh and dogmatic utterances of the Ashfield pulpit? At the thought, he recalls the weary iteration of cumbersome formulas, that passed through his brain like leaden plummets, and the swift lashings of rebuke, if he but reached over for a single worldly floweret, blooming beside the narrow path; and yet,—and yet, from the leaden atmosphere of that past, saintly faces beam upon him,—a mother's, Adèle's,—nay, the kindly fixed gray eyes of the old Doctor glow upon him with a fire that must have been kindled with truth.

Does it lie in the melodious *aves,* and under the robes of Rome? The sordid friars, with their shaven pates, grin at him; some Rabelais head of a priest in the confessional-stall leers at him with mockery: and yet the golden letters of the great dome gleam again with their blazing legend, and the figure of the Magdalen yonder has just now murmured, in tones that must surely have reached a gracious ear,—

"Tibi, Christe, redemptori,
Nostro vero salvatori!"

Is the truth between? Is it in both? Is it real? And if real, why may not the same lips declare it under the cathedral or the meeting-house roof?

LXIV

A Wreck

THE *Meteor* is a snug ship, well found, well manned, and, as the times go, well officered. The captain, indeed, is not over-alert or fitted for high emergencies; but what emergencies can belong to so placid a voyage? For a week after the headlands of Tarifa and Spartel have sunk under the eastern horizon, the vessel is kept every day upon her course,—her top-gallant and studding sails all distent with the wind blowing freely from over Biscay. After this come light, baffling, westerly breezes, with sometimes a clear sky, and then all is overclouded by the drifting trade-mists. Zigzagging on, quietly as ever, save the bustle and whiz and flapping canvas of the ship "in stays," the good *Meteor* pushes gradually westward.

Meantime a singular and almost tender intimacy grew up between Reuben and the lady voyager. It is always agreeable to a young man to find a listening ear in a lady whose age puts her out of the range of any flurry of sentiment, and whose sympathy gives kindly welcome to his confidence. All that early life of his he detailed to her with a particularity and a warmth (himself unconscious of the warmth) which brought the childish associations of her daughter fresh to the mind of poor Madame Maverick. No wonder that she gave a willing ear! No wonder that the glow of his language kindled her sympathy! Nor with such a listener does he stop with the boyish life of Ashfield. He unfolds his city career, and the bright promises that are before him,— promises of business success, which (he would make it appear) are all that fill his heart now. In the pride of his twenty-five years he loves to represent himself as *blasé* in sentiment.

Madame Maverick has been taught, in these latter years, a large amount of self-control; so she can listen with a grave, nay, even a kindly face, to Reuben's sweeping declarations. And if, at a hint from her,—which he shrewdly counts Jesuitical,—his thought is turned in the direction of his religious experiences, he has his axioms, his common-sense formulas, his irreproachable coolness, and, at times, a noisy show of distrust, under which it is easy to see an eager groping after the ends of that great tangled skein of thought within, which is a weariness.

"If you could only have a talk with Father Ambrose!" says Madame Maverick with half a sigh.

"I should like that of all things," says Reuben, with a touch of merriment. "I suppose he's a jolly old fellow, with rosy cheeks and full of humor. By Jove! there go the beads again!" (He says this latter to himself, however, as he sees the nervous fingers of the poor lady plying her rosary, and her lips murmuring some catch of a prayer.)

Yet he cannot but respect her devotion profoundly, wondering how it can have grown up under the heathenisms of her life; wondering perhaps, too, how his own heathenism could have grown up under the roof of a parsonage. It will be an odd encounter, he thinks, for this woman, with the people of Ashfield, with the Doctor, with Adèle.

There are gales, but the good ship rides them out jauntily, with but a single reef in her topsails. Within five weeks from the date of her leaving Marseilles she is within a few days' sail of New York. A few days' sail! It may mean over-much; for there are mists and hazy weather, which forbid any observation. The

A WRECK

last was taken a hundred miles to the eastward of George's Shoal. Under an easy offshore wind the ship is beating westward. But the clouds hang low, and there is no opportunity for determining position. At last, one evening, there is a little lift, and, for a moment only, a bright light blazes over the starboard bow. The captain counts it a light upon one of the headlands of the Jersey shore; and he orders the helmsman (she is sailing in the eye of an easy westerly breeze) to give her a couple of points more "northing"; and the yards and sheets are trimmed accordingly. The ship pushes on more steadily as she opens to the wind, and the mists and coming night conceal all around them.

"What do you make of the light, Mr. Yardley?" says the captain, addressing the mate.

"Can't say, sir, with such a bit of a look. If it should be Fire Island, we're in a bad course, sir."

"That's true enough," said the captain, thoughtfully. "Put a man in the chains, Mr. Yardley, and give us the water."

"I hope we shall be in the bay by morning, Captain," said Reuben, who stood smoking leisurely near the wheel. But the captain was preoccupied, and answered nothing.

A little after, a voice from the chains came chanting full and loud, "By the mark—nine!"

"This 'll never do, Mr. Yardley," said the captain, "Jersey shore or any other. Let all hands keep by to put the ship about."

A voice forward was heard to say something of a roar that sounded like the beat of surf; at which the mate stepped to the side of the ship and listened anxiously.

"It 's true, sir," said he, coming aft. "Captain, there's something very like the beat of surf, here away to the no'th'ard."

A flutter in the canvas caught the captain's attention. "It 's the wind slacking; there 's a bare capful," said the mate, "and I 'm afeard there 's mischief brewing yonder." He pointed as he spoke a little to the south of east, where the darkness seemed to be giving way to a luminous gray cloud of mist.

"And a half—six!" shouts again the man in the chains.

The captain meets it with a swelling oath, which betrays clearly enough his anxiety. "There 's not a moment to lose, Yardley; see all ready there! Keep her a good full, my boy!" (To the man at the wheel.)

The darkness was profound. Reuben, not a little startled by the new aspect of affairs, still

A WRECK

kept his place upon the quarter-deck. He saw objects flitting across the waist of the ship, and heard distinctly the coils flung down with a clang upon the wet decks. There was something weird and ghostly in those half-seen figures, in the indistinct maze of cordage and canvas above, and the phosphorescent streaks of spray streaming away from either bow.

"Are you ready there?" says the captain.

"Ay, ay, sir," responds the mate.

"Put your helm a-lee, my man!—Hard down!"

"Hard down it is, sir!"

The ship veers up into the wind; and, as the captain shouts his order, "Mainsail haul!" the canvas shakes; the long, cumbrous yard groans upon its bearings; there is a great whizzing of the cordage through the blocks; but, in the midst of it all,—coming keenly to the captain's ear,—a voice from the fore-hatch exclaims, "By G—, she touches!"

The next moment proved it true. The good ship minded her helm no more. The fore-yards are brought round by the run and the mizzen, but the light wind—growing lighter—hardly clears the flapping canvas from the spars.

In the sunshine, with so moderate a sea,

DOCTOR JOHNS

't would seem little; in so little depth of water they might warp her off; but the darkness magnifies the danger; besides which, an ominous sighing and murmur are coming from that luminous misty mass to the southward. Through all this, Reuben has continued smoking upon the quarter-deck; a landsman under a light wind, and with a light sea, hardly estimates at their true worth such intimations as had been given of the near breaking of the surf, and of the shoaling water. Even the touch upon bottom, of which the grating evidence had come home to his own perceptions, brought up more the fate of his business venture than any sense of personal peril. We can surely warp her off in the morning, he thought; or, if the worst came, insurance was full, and it would be easy boating to the shore.

"It 's lucky there 's no wind," said he to Yardley.

"Will you obleege me, Mr. Johns? Take a good strong puff of your cigar,—here, upon the larboard rail, sir," and he took the lantern from the companionway that he might see the drift of the smoke. For a moment it lifted steadily; then, with a toss it vanished away—shoreward. The first angry puffs of the southeaster were coming.

A WRECK

The captain had seen all, and with an excited voice said, "Mr. Yardley, clew up, fore and aft,—clew up every thing; put all snug, and make ready the best bower."

"Mr. Johns," said he, approaching Reuben, "we are on a lee shore; it should be Long Island beach by the soundings; with calm weather, and a kedge, we might work her off with the lift of the tide. But the Devil and all is in that puff from the sou'east."

"Oh, well, we can anchor," says Reuben.

"Yes, we can anchor, Mr. Johns; but if that sou'easter turns out the gale it promises, the best anchor aboard won't be so good as a gridiron."

"Do you advise taking to the boats, then?" asked Reuben, a little nervously.

"I advise nothing, Mr. Johns. Do you hear the murmur of the surf yonder? It 's bad landing under such a pounding of the surf, with daylight; in the dark, where one can't catch the drift of the waves, it might be— hell!"

The word startled Reuben. His philosophy had always contemplated death at a distance, toward which easy and gradual approaches might be made: but here it was, now, at a cable's length!

And yet it was very strange; the sea was not high; no gale as yet; only an occasional grating thump of the keel was a reminder that the good *Meteor* was not still afloat. But the darkness! Yes, the darkness was complete, (hardly a sight even of the topmen who were aloft—as in the sunniest of weather—stowing the canvas,) and to the northward that groan and echo of the resounding surf; to the southward, the whirling white of waves that are lifting now, topped with phosphorescent foam.

The anchor is let go, but even this does not bring the ship's head to the wind. Those griping sands hold her keel fast.

Three hours more of watching, of waiting, of weary anxieties; then the force of the rising gale strikes her full abeam, giving her a great list to shore. It is in vain the masts are cut away, and the rigging drifts free; the hulk lifts only to settle anew in the grasping sands. Every old seaman upon her deck knows that she is a doomed ship.

From time to time, as the crashing spars or the leaden thump upon the sands have startled those below, Madame Maverick and her maid have made their appearance, in a wild flutter of anxiety, asking eager questions; (Reuben alone can understand them or answer them;)

A WRECK

but as the southeaster grows, as it does, into a fury of wind, and the poor hulk reels vainly, and is overlaid with a torrent of biting salt spray, Madame Maverick becomes calm. Instinctively, she sees the worst.

"Could I only clasp Adèle once more in these arms, I would say cheerfully, '*Nunc dimittis.*'"

Reuben regarded her calm faith with a hungry eagerness. Not, indeed, that calmness was lacking in himself. Great danger, in many instances, sublimates the faculties of keenly strung minds. But underneath his calmness there was an unrest, hungering for repose,—the repose of a fixed belief. If even then the breaking waves had whelmed him in their mad career, he would have made no wailing outcry, but would have clutched—how eagerly!—at the merest shred of that faith which, in other days and times, he had seen illuminate the calm face of the father. Something to believe,—on which to float upon such a sea!

But the waves and winds make sport of beliefs. Prayers count nothing against that angry surge. Two boats are already swept from the davits, and are gone upon the whirling waters. A third, with infinite pains, is dropped into the yeast. It is hard to tell who gives the orders. But, once afloat, there is a rush upon it, and away it goes,—overcrowded, and within eyeshot lifts, turns, and a crowd of swimmers float for a moment—one with an oar, another with a thwart that the waves have torn out,—and in the yeast of waters they vanish.

One boat only remains, and it is launched with more careful handling; three cling by the wreck; the rest—save only Madame Maverick and Reuben—are within her, as she tosses still in the lee of the vessel.

"There's room!" cries some one; "jump quick! for God's sake!"

And Reuben, with some strange, generous impulse, seizes upon Madame Maverick, and before she can rebel or resist, has dropped her over the rail. The men grapple her and drag her in; but in the next moment the little cockle of a boat is drifted yards away.

The few who are left—the boatswain among them—are toiling on the wet deck to give a last signal from the little brass howitzer on the forecastle. As the sharp crack breaks on the air,—a miniature sound in that howl of the storm,—the red flash of the gun gives Reuben, as the boat lurches toward the

A WRECK

wreck again, a last glance of Madame Maverick,—her hands clasped, her eyes lifted, and calm as ever. More than ever too her face was like the face of Adèle,—such as the face of Adèle must surely become, when years have sobered her, and her buoyant faith has ripened into calm. And from that momentary glance of the serene countenance, and that flashing associated memory of Adèle, a subtile, mystic influence is born in him, by which he seems suddenly transfused with the same trustful serenity which just now he gazed upon with wonder. If indeed the poor lady is already lost,—he thinks it for a moment,—her spirit has fanned and cheered him as it passed. Once more, as if some mysterious hand had brought them to his reach, he grapples with those lost lines of hope and trust which in that youthful year of his exuberant emotional experience he had held and lost,—once more, now, in hand,—once more he is elated with that wonderful sense of a religious poise, that, it would seem, no doubts or terrors could overbalance.

The boom of a gun is heard to the northward. It must be from shore. There are helpers at work, then. Some hope yet for this narrow tide of life, which just seemed losing itself in some infinite flow beyond. Life is, after all, so sweet! The boatswain forward labors desperately to return an answering signal; but the spray, the slanted deck, the overleaping waves, are too much for him. Darkness and storm and despair rule again.

The wind, indeed, has fallen; the force of the gale is broken; but the waves are making deeper and more desperate surges. The wreck, which had remained fixed in the fury of the wind, lifts again under the great swell of the sea, and is dashed anew and anew upon the shoal. With every lift her timbers writhe and creak, and all the remaining upper works crack and burst open with the strain.

Reuben chances to espy an old-fashioned round life-buoy lashed to the taffrail, and, cutting it loose, makes himself fast to it. He overhears the boatswain say, yonder by the forecastle, "These thumpings will break her in two in an hour. Cling to a spar, Jack."

The gray light of dawn at last breaks, and shows a dim line of shore, on which parties are moving, dragging some machine, with which they hope to cast a line over the wreck. But the swell is heavier than ever, the timbers nearer to parting. At last a flash of lurid light from the dim shore-line,—a great boom of sound, and a line goes spinning out like a spider's web up into the gray, bleak sky. Too far! too short! and the line tumbles, plashing into the water. A new and fearful lift of the sea shatters the wreck, the fore part of the ship still holding fast to the sands; but all abaft the mainmast lifts, surges, reels, topples over; with the wreck, and in the angry swirl and torment of waters, Reuben goes down.

LXV

The Saved and Lost

THAT morning,—it was the 22d of September, in the year 1842,—Mr. Brindlock came into his counting-room some two hours before noon, and says to his porter and factotum, as he enters the door, "Well, Roger, I suppose you'll be counting this puff of a southeaster the equinoctial, eh?"

"Indeed, sir, and it's an awful one. The *Meteor*'s gone ashore on Long Beach; and there's talk of young Mr. Johns being lost."

"Good heavens!" said Brindlock, "you don't tell me so!"

By half-past three he was upon the spot; a

little remaining fragment only of the *Meteor* hanging to the sands, and a great *débris* of bales, spars, shattered timbers, bodies, drifted along the shore,—Reuben's among them.

But he is not dead; at least so say the wreckers, who throng upon the beach; the life-buoy is still fast to him, though he is fearfully shattered and bruised. He is borne away under the orders of Brindlock to some near house, and presently revives enough to ask that he may be carried—"home."

As, in the opening of this story, his old grandfather, the Major, was borne away from the scene of his first battle by easy stages homeward, so now the grandson, far feebler and after more terrible encounter with death, is carried by "easy stages" to his home in Ashfield. Again the city, the boat, the river,—with its banks yellowing with harvests, and brightened with the glowing tints of autumn; again the sluggish brigs drifting down with the tide, and sailors in tasseled caps leaning over the bulwarks; again the flocks feeding leisurely on the rock-strewn hills; again the ferryman, in his broad, cumbrous scow, oaring across; again the stoppage at the wharf of the little town, from which the coach still plies over the hills to Ashfield.

THE SAVED AND LOST

On the way thither, a carriage passes them, in which are Adèle and her father. The news of disaster flies fast; they have learned of the wreck, and the names of passengers. They go to learn what they can of the mother, whom the daughter has scarce known. The passing is too hasty for recognition. Brindlock arrives at last with his helpless charge at the door of the parsonage. The Doctor is overwhelmed at once with grief and with joy. The news had come to him, and he had anticipated the worst. But "Thank God! 'Joseph, my son, is yet alive!' Still a probationer; there is yet hope that he may be brought into the fold."

He insists that he shall be placed below, upon his own bed, just out of his study. For himself, he shall need none until the crisis is past. But the crisis does not pass; it is hard to say when it will. The wounds are not so much; but a low fever has set in, (the physician says,) owing to exposure and excitement, and he can predict nothing as to the result. Even Aunt Eliza is warmed into unwonted attention as she sees that poor battered hulk of humanity lying there.

Days and days pass. Reuben hovering between life and death; and the old Doctor, catching chance rest upon the little cot they have placed for him in the study, looks yearningly by the dim light of the sick-lamp upon that dove which his lost Rachel had hung upon his wall above the sword of his father. He fancies that the face of Reuben, pinched with suffering, resembles more than ever the mother. Of sickness, or of the little offices of friends which cheat it of pains, the old gentleman knows nothing: sick souls only have been his care. And it is pitiful to see his blundering, eager efforts to do something, as he totters round the sick-chamber, where Reuben, with very much of youthful vigor left in him, makes fight against the arch-enemy who one day conquers us all. For many days after his arrival there is no consciousness,—only wild words (at times words that sound to the ears of the good Doctor strangely wicked, and that make him groan in spirit),—tender words, too, of dalliance, and eager, loving glances,—murmurs of boyish things, of sunny, school-day noonings,—hearing which, the Doctor thinks that, if this light must go out, it had better have gone out in those days of comparative innocence.

Over and over the father appeals to the village physician to know what the chances may

THE SAVED AND LOST

be,—to which that old gentleman, fumbling his watch-key, and looking grave, makes very doubtful response. He hints at a possible undermining of the constitution in these later years of city life.

God only knows what habits the young man may have formed in these last years; surely the Doctor does not; and he tells the physician as much, with a groan of anguish.

Meantime, Maverick and Adèle have gone upon their melancholy search; and, as they course over the island to the southern beach, the sands, the plains, the houses, the pines, drift by the eye of Adèle as in a dream. At last she sees a great reach of water,—piling up, as it rolls lazily in from seaward, into high walls of waves that are no sooner lifted than they break and send sparkling floods of foam over the sands. Bits of wreck, dark clots of weed, are strewed here and there,—stragglers scanning every noticeable heap, every floating thing that comes in.

Is she dead? is she living? They have heard only on the way that many bodies are lying in the near houses,—many bruised and suffering ones; while some have come safe to land, and gone to their homes. They make their way from that dismal surf-beaten shore to the nearest house. There are loiterers about the door; and within,—within, Adèle finds her mother at last, clasps her to her heart, kisses the poor dumb lips that will never more open,—never say to her rapt ears, "My child! my darling!"

Maverick is touched as he has never been touched before; the age of early sentiment comes drifting back to his world-haunted mind; nay, tears come to those eyes that have not known them for years. The grief, the passionate, vain tenderness of Adèle, somehow seems to sanctify the memory of the dead one who lies before him, her great wealth of hair streaming dank and fetterless over the floor.

Not more tenderly, scarce more tearfully, could he have ministered to one who had been his life-long companion. Where shall the poor lady be buried? Adèle answers that, with eyes flashing through her tears,—nowhere but in Ashfield, nowhere except beside the sister, Marie.

It is a dismal journey for the father and the daughter; it is almost a silent journey. Does she love him less? No, a thousand times, no. Does he love her less? No, a thousand

THE SAVED AND LOST

times, no. In such presence love is awed into silence. As the mournful *cortége* enters the town of Ashfield, it passes the home of that fatherless boy, Arthur, for whom Adèle had shown such sympathy. The youngster is there swinging upon the gate, his cap gayly set off with feathers, and he looking wonderingly upon the bier. He sees, too, the sad face of Adèle, and, by some strange rush of memory, recalls, as he looks on her, the letter which she had given him long ago, and which till then, had been forgotten. He runs to his mother: it is in his pocket,—it is in that of some summer jacket. At last it is found; and the poor woman herself, that very morning, with numberless apologies, delivers it at the door of the parsonage.

Phil is the first to meet this exceptional funeral company, and is the first to tell Adèle how Reuben lies stricken almost to death at the parsonage. She thanks him: she thanks him again for the tender care which he shows in all relating to the approaching burial. We never forget such offices.

Of course, the arrival of this strange freight in Ashfield gives rise to a world of gossip. We cannot follow it; we cannot rehearse it. The poor woman is buried, as Adèle had wished, beside her sister. No *De Profundis* except the murmur of the winds through the crimson and the scarlet leaves of later September.

The Tourtelots have been eager with their gossip. The dame has queried if there should not be some town demonstration against the burial of the Papist. But the little Deacon has been milder; and we give our last glimpse of him—altogether characteristic—in a suggestion which he makes in a friendly way to Squire Elderkin, who is the host of the French strangers.

"Square, have they ordered a moniment yit for Miss Maverick?"

"Not that I 'm aware of, Deacon."

"Waäl, my nevvy 's got a good slab of Varmont marble, which he ordered for his fust wife; but the old folks did n't like it, and it 's in his barn on the heater-piece. 'T ain't engraved, nor nothin'. If it should *suit* the Mavericks, I dare say they could git it tol'able low."

LAST SCENES

LXVI

Last Scenes

REUBEN is still floating between death and life. There is doubt whether the master of the long course or of the short course will win. However that may be, his consciousness has returned; and it has been with a great glow of gratitude that the poor Doctor has welcomed that look of recognition in his eye,—the eye of Rachel!

He is calm,—he knows all. That calmness which had flashed into his soul when last he saw the serene face of his fellow-voyager upon that mad sea is *his* still.

The poor father had been moved unwontedly by that unconsciousness which was blind to all his efforts at spiritual consolation; but he is not less moved when he sees reason stirring again,—a light of eager inquiry in those eyes fearfully sunken, but from their cavernous depths seeing farther and more keenly than ever.

"Adèle's mother,—was she lost?" He whispers it to the Doctor; and Miss Eliza, who is

DOCTOR JOHNS

sewing yonder, is quickened into eager listening.

"Lost! my son, lost! Lost, I apprehend, in the other world as well as this. I fear the true light never dawned upon her."

A faint smile—as of one who sees things others do not see—broke over the face of Reuben. " 'T is a broad light, father; it reaches beyond our blind reckoning."

There was a trustfulness in his manner that delighted the Doctor. "And you see it, my son?—Repentance, Justification by Faith, Adoption, Sanctification?"

"Those words are a weariness to me, father; they suggest methods, dogmas, perplexities. Christian hope, pure and simple, I love better."

The Doctor is disturbed; he cannot rightly understand how one who seems inspired by so calm a trust—the son of his own loins too—should find the authoritative declarations of the divines a weariness.

Of course the letter of Adèle, which had been so long upon its way, Miss Eliza had handed to Reuben after such time as her caution suggested, and she had explained to him its long delay.

Reading is no easy matter for him; but he races through those delicately penned lines

LAST SCENES

with quite a new strength. The spinster sees the color come and go upon his wan cheek, and with what a trembling eagerness he folds the letter at the end, and, making a painful effort, tries to thrust it under his pillow. The good woman has to aid him in this. He thanks her, but says nothing more. His fingers are toying nervously at a bit of torn fringe upon the coverlet. It seems a relief to him to make the rent wider and wider. A little glimpse of the world has come back to him, which disturbs the repose with which but now he would have quitted it forever.

Adèle has been into the sick-chamber from time to time,—once led away weeping by the good Doctor, when the son had fallen upon his wild talk of school-days; once, too, since consciousness has come to him again, but before her letter had been read. He had met her with scarce more than a touch of those fevered fingers, and a hard, uncertain quiver of a smile, which had both shocked and disappointed the poor girl. She thought he would have spoken some friendly consoling word of her mother; but his heart, more than his strength, failed him. Her mournful, pitying eyes were a reproach to him; they had haunted him through the wakeful hours of two succeeding nights, and now, under the light of that laggard letter, they blaze with a new and an appealing tenderness. His fingers still puzzle wearily with that tangle of the fringe. The noon passes. The aunt advises a little broth. But no, his strength is feeding itself on other aliment. The Doctor comes in with a curiously awkward attempt at gentleness and noiselessness of tread, and, seeing his excited condition, repeats to him some texts which he believes must be consoling. Reuben utters no open dissent; but through and back of all he sees the tender eyes of Adèle, which, for the moment, outshine the promises, or at the least illuminate them with a new meaning.

"I must see Adèle," he says to the Doctor; and the message is carried,—she herself presently bringing answer, with a rich glow upon her cheek.

"Reuben has sent for me,"—she murmurs it to herself with pride and joy.

She is in full black now; but never has she looked more radiantly beautiful than when she stepped to the side of the sick-bed, and took the hand of Reuben with an eager clasp—that was met, and met again. The Doctor is in his study, (the open door between,) and the spin-

LAST SCENES

ster is fortunately just now busy at some of her household duties.

Reuben fumbles under his pillow nervously for that cherished bit of paper, (Adèle knows already its history,) and when he has found it and shown it (his thin fingers crumpling it nervously) he says, "Thank you for this, Adèle!"

She answers only by clasping his hand with a sudden mad pressure of content, while the blood mounted into either cheek with a rosy exuberance that magnified her beauty tenfold.

He saw it,—he felt it all; and through her beaming eyes, so full of tenderness and love, saw the world to which he had bidden adieu shining before him more beguilingly than ever. Yesterday it was a dim and weary world that he could leave without a pang; to-day it is a brilliant world, where hopes, promises, joys pile in splendid proportions.

He tells her this. "Yesterday I would have died with scarce a regret; to-day, Adèle, I would live."

"You will, you will, Reuben!" and she grappled more and more passionately those shrunken fingers. "'T is not hopeless!" (sobbing).

DOCTOR JOHNS

"No, no, Adèle, darling, not hopeless. The cloud is lifted,—not hopeless!"

"Thank God, thank God!" said she, dropping upon her knees beside him, and with a smile of ecstasy he gathered that fair head to his bosom.

The Doctor, hearing her sobs, came softly in. The son's smile, as he met his father's inquiring look, was more than ever like the smile of Rachel. He has been telling the poor girl of her mother's death, thinks the old gentleman; yet the Doctor wonders that he could have kept so radiant a face with such a story.

Of these things, however, Reuben goes on presently to speak: of his first sight of the mother of Adèle, and of her devotional attitude as they floated down past the little chapel of Nôtre Dame to enter upon the fateful voyage; he recounts their talks upon the tranquil moonlit nights of ocean; he tells of the mother's eager listening to his description of her child.

"I did not tell her the half, Adèle; yet she loved me for what I told her."

And Adèle smiles through her tears.

At last he comes to those dismal scenes of the wreck, relating all with a strange vividness; living over again, as it were, that fear-

LAST SCENES

ful episode, till his brain whirled, his self-possession was lost, and he broke out into a torrent of delirious raving.

He sleeps brokenly that night, and the next day is feebler than ever. The physician warns against any causes of excitement. He is calm only at intervals. The old school-days seem present to him again; he talks of his fight with Phil Elderkin as if it happened yesterday.

"Yet I like Phil," he says (to himself), "and Rose is like Amanda, the divine Amanda. No—not she. I've forgotten: it's the French girl. She's a—— Pah! who cares? She's as pure as heaven; she's an angel. Adèle! Adèle! Not good enough! I'm not good enough. Very well, very well, now I'll be bad enough! Clouds, wrangles, doubts! Is it my fault? *Meam Ecclesiam!* How they kneel! Puppets! mummers! No, not mummers; they see a Christ. What if they see it in a picture? You see him in words. Both in earnest. Belief—belief! That is best. Adèle, Adèle, I believe!"

The Doctor is a pained listener of this incoherent talk of his son. "I am afraid,— I am afraid," he murmurs to himself, "that he has no clear views of the great scheme of the Atonement."

DOCTOR JOHNS

The next day Reuben is himself once more, but feeble, to a degree that startles the household. It is a charming morning of later September; the window is wide open, and the sick one looks out over a stretch of orchard (he knew its every tree), and upon wooded hills beyond (he knew every coppice and thicket), and upon a background of sky over which a few dappled white clouds floated at rest.

"It is most beautiful!" said Reuben.

"All things that He has made are beautiful," said the Doctor; and thereupon he seeks to explore his way into the secrets of Reuben's religious experience,—employing, as he was wont to do, all the Westminster formulas by which his own belief stood fast.

"Father, father, the words are stumbling-blocks to me," says the son.

"I would to God, Reuben, that I could make my language always clear."

"No, father, no man can, in measuring the Divine mysteries. We must carry this draggled earth-dress with us always,—always in some sort fashionists, even in our soberest opinions. The robes of light are worn only Beyond. Thought, at the best, is hampered by this clog of language, that tempts, obscures, misleads."

LAST SCENES

"And do you see any light, my son?"

"I hope and tremble. A great light is before me; it shines back upon outlines of doctrines and creeds where I have floundered for many a year."

"But some are clear,—some are clear, Reuben!"

"Before, all seems clear; but behind"—

"And yet, Reuben," (the Doctor cannot forbear the discussion,) "there is the cross,— Election, Adoption, Sanctification"—

"Stop, father; the cross, indeed, with a blaze of glory, I see; but the teachers of this or that special form of doctrine I see catching only radiations of the light. The men who teach, and argue, and exorcise, are using human weapons; the great light only strikes here and there upon some sword-point which is nearest to the cross."

"He wanders," says the Doctor to Adèle, who has slipped in and stands beside the sick-bed.

"No wandering, father; on the brink where I stand, I cannot."

"And what do you see, Reuben, my boy?" (tenderly).

Is it the presence of Adèle that gives a new fervor, a kind of crazy inspiration to his talk?

DOCTOR JOHNS

"I see the light-hearted clashing cymbals; and those who love art, kneeling under blazing temples and shrines; but the great light touches the gold no more effulgently than the steeple of your meeting-house, father, but no less. I see eyes of chanting girls streaming with joy in the light; and haggard men with ponderous foreheads working out contrivances to bridge the gap between the finite and the infinite. Father, they are no nearer to a passage than the radiant girls who chant and tell their beads. Angels in all shapes of beauty flit over and amid the throngs I see,—in shape of fleecy clouds that fan them,—in shape of brooks that murmur praise,—in shape of leafy shadows that tremble and flicker,—in shape of birds that make a concert of song." The birds even then were singing, the clouds floating in his eye, the leafy shadows trailing on the chamber floor, and from the valley, the murmur of the brook came to his sensitive ear.

"He wanders,—he wanders!" said the poor Doctor.

Reuben turns to Adèle. "Adèle, kiss me!" A rosy tint ran over her face as she stooped and kissed him with a freedom a mother might have shown,—leaving one hand toying caressingly with his hair. "The cloud is passing, Adèle,—passing! God is Justice; Christ is Mercy. In Him I trust."

"Reuben, darling," says Adèle, "come back to us!"

"Darling,—darling!" he repeated with a strange, eager, satisfied smile,—so sweet a sound it was.

The chamber was filled with the delightful perfume of a violet bed beneath the window. Suddenly there came from the Doctor, whose old eyes caught sooner than any the change, a passionate outcry. "Great God! Thy will be done!"

With that one loud, clear utterance, his firmness gave way,—for the first time in sixty years broke utterly; and big tears streamed down his face as he gazed yearningly upon the dead body of his first-born.

LXVII

The End

In the autumn of 1845, three years after the incidents related in our last chapter, Mr. Philip Elderkin, being at that time president of a railroad company, which was establishing an important connection of travel that was to pass within a few miles of the quiet town of Ashfield, was a passenger on the steamer *Caledonia* for Europe. He sailed, partly in the interest of the company,—to place certain bonds,—and partly in his own interest, as an intelligent man, eager to add to his knowledge of the world.

At Paris, where he passed some time, it chanced that he was one evening invited to the house of a resident American, where, he was gayly assured, he would meet with a very attractive American heiress, the only daughter of a merchant of large fortune.

Philip Elderkin—brave, straightforward fellow that he was—had never forgotten his early sentiment. He had cared for those French graves in Ashfield with an almost religious attention. In all the churchyard there was not such scrupulously shorn turf, or such orderly array of bloom. He counted—in a fever of doubt—upon a visit to Marseilles before his sail for home.

But at the *soirée* we have mentioned he was amazed and delighted to meet, in the person of the heiress, Adèle Maverick,—not changed essentially since the time he had

THE END

known her. That life at Marseilles—even in the well-appointed home of her father—has none of that domesticity which she had learned to love; and this first winter in Paris for her does not supply the lack. That she has a great company of admirers it is easy to understand; but yet she gives a most cordial greeting to Phil Elderkin,—a greeting that by its manner makes the pretenders doubtful. Philip finds it possible to reconcile the demands of his business with a week's visit to Marseilles. To the general traveller it is not a charming region. The dust abounds; the winds are terrible; the sun is scalding. But Mr. Philip Elderkin found it delightful. And, indeed, the country-house of Mr. Maverick had attractions of its own; attractions so great that his week runs over into two,—into three. There are excursions to the Pont du Gard, to the Arène of Arles. And, before he leaves, he has an engagement there (which he has enforced by very peremptory proposals) for the next spring.

On his return to Ashfield, he reports a very successful trip. To his sister Rose (now Mrs. Catesby, with a blooming little infant, called Grace Catesby) he is specially communicative. And she thinks it was a glorious trip, and

DOCTOR JOHNS

longs for the time when he will make the next. He, furthermore, to the astonishment of Dame Tourtelot (whose husband sleeps now under the sod), has commenced the establishment of a fine home, upon a charming site, overlooking all Ashfield. The Squire, still stalwart, cannot resist giving a hint of what is expected to the old Doctor, who still wearily goes his rounds, and prays for the welfare of his flock.

He is delighted at the thought of meeting again with Adèle, though he thinks with a sigh of his lost boy. Yet he says in his old manner, " 'T is the hand of Providence: she first bloomed into grace under the roof of our church; she comes back to adorn it with her faith and her works."

At a date three years later we take one more glimpse at that quiet village of Ashfield, where we began our story. The near railway has brought it into more intimate connection with the shore towns and the great cities. But there is no noisy clatter of the cars to break the quietude, On still days, indeed, the shriek of the steam-whistle or the roar of a distant train is heard bursting over the hills, and dying in strange echoes up and down the valley.

THE END

The stage-driver's horn is heard no longer; no longer the coach whirls into the village and delivers its leathern pouch of letters. The Tew partners we once met are now partners in the grave. Deacon Tourtelot (as we have already hinted) has gone to his long home; and the dame has planted over him the slab of "Varmont" marble, which she has bought at a bargain from his "nevvy."

The Boody tavern-keeper has long since disappeared; no teams wheel up with the old dash at the doors of the Eagle Tavern. The creaking sign-board even is gone from the overhanging sycamore.

Miss Almira is still among the living. She sings treble, however, no longer; she wears spectacles; she writes no more over mystical asterisks for the "Hartford Courant." Age has brought to her at least this much of wisdom.

The mill groans, as of old, in the valley. A new race of boys pelt the hanging nests of the orioles; a new race of school-girls hang swinging on the village gates at the noonings.

As for Miss Johns, she lives still,—scarce older to appearance than twenty years before, —prim, wiry, active,—proof against all ailments, it would seem. It is hard to conceive of her as yielding to the great conqueror. If the tongue and an inflexibility of temper were the weapons, she would whip Death from her chamber at the last. It seems like amiability almost to hear such a one as she talk of her approaching, inevitable dissolution,—so kindly in her to yield that point!

And she does; she declares it over and over; there are far feebler ones who do not declare it half so often. If she is to be conquered and the Johns banner go down, she will accept the defeat so courageously and so long in advance that the defeat shall become a victorious confirmation of the Johns prophecy.

She is still earnest in all her duties; she gives castaway clothing to the poor, and good advice with it. She is rigorous in the observance of every propriety; no storm keeps her from church. If the children of a new generation climb unduly upon the pew-backs, or shake their curly heads too wantonly, she lifts a prim forefinger at them, which has lost none of its authoritative meaning. She is the impersonation of all good severities. A strange character! Let us hope that, as it sloughs off its earthly cerements, it may in the Divine presence scintillate charities and draw toward it the love of others. A good kind, bad gen-

THE END

tlewoman,—unwearied in performance of duties. We wonder as we think of her! So steadfast, we cannot sneer at her,—so true to her line of faith, we cannot condemn her,—so utterly forbidding, we cannot love her! May God give rest to her good stubborn soul!

Upon Sundays of August and September there may be occasionally seen in the pew of Elderkin Junior a gray-haired old gentleman, dressed with scrupulous care, and still carrying an erect figure, though somewhat gouty in his step. This should be Mr. Maverick, a retired merchant, who is on a visit to his daughter. He makes wonderful gifts to a certain little boy who bears a Puritan name, and gives occasionally ponderous sums to the parish. In winter, his head-quarters are at the Union Club.

And Doctor Johns? Yes, he is living still,—making his way wearily each morning along the street with his cane. Going oftenest, perhaps, to the home of Adèle, who is now a matron,—a tender, and most womanly and joyful matron,—and with her little boy —Reuben Elderkin by name—he wanders often to the graves where sleep his best beloved,—Rachel, so early lost,—the son, in respect to whom he feels at last a "reasonable assurance" that the youth has entered upon a glorious inheritance in those courts where one day he will join him, and the sainted Rachel too, and clasp again in his arms (if it be God's will) the babe that was his but for an hour on earth.

THE END.